REINVENTING
JUVENILE JUSTICE

REINVENTING JUVENILE JUSTICE

Barry Krisberg
James F. Austin

SAGE Publications
International Educational and Professional Publisher
Newbury Park   London   New Delhi

For information address:

 SAGE Publications, Inc.
2455 Teller Road
Newbury Park, California 91320

SAGE Publications Ltd.
6 Bonhill Street
London EC2A 4PU
United Kingdom

SAGE Publications India Pvt. Ltd.
M-32 Market
Greater Kailash I
New Delhi 110 048 India

Printed in the United States of America

Library of Congress Cataloging-in-Publication Data

Krisberg, Barry.
    Reinventing juvenile justice / Barry Krisberg, James F. Austin.
        p.   cm.
    Includes bibliographical references (pp. 188-196) and index.
    ISBN 0-8039-4828-X (cl).—ISBN 0-8039-4829-8 (pb)
    1. Juvenile Justice, Administration of—United States.
    2. Juvenile justice, Administration of—United States—History.
    I. Austin, James, 1948-   . II. Title.
    HV9104.K75   1993
    364.3'6—dc20   93-46

94 95 96 10 9 8 7 6 5 4 3

Sage Production Editor: Diane S. Foster

Contents

Preface

The most recent crime data released by the Federal Bureau of Investigation (FBI) show a dramatic increase in the numbers of juveniles arrested for violent crimes. For example, the number of 15-year-olds arrested for murder increased by 217% from 1985 to 1991. Arrests of juveniles for violent offenses have increased steadily since 1985. These dire statistics are harbingers for bad times.

Our society is changing. The "baby boom" generation is "graying." Early in the 21st century the largest proportion of our population will be approaching retirement age. There will also be a rise in the young adult population as the children of the baby boomers mature through their adolescent years. The United States is becoming a more diverse society in terms of ethnicity and race. The economy is undergoing enormous and global transformations.

The rise in youth violence is intimately tied to the social forces described above. Life experiences for both the young and the old are changing. The economic environment is more difficult and competitive. Three decades ago, the most likely poor person was a senior citizen; today it is a child. The traditional socializing institutions of the community—the family, the schools, the churches—have been weakened.

Adding to this explosive societal mix has been the easy availability of dangerous drugs and guns. The popular culture, as reflected in television, movies, pop music, and newspapers, is saturated with violent messages. Indeed, a visitor from outer space who viewed the mass culture might reasonably conclude that our civilization is the most violent in the Earth's history.

A central question raised in this book is whether the juvenile court can or should survive in the years ahead. Could it be that the celebrated "children's court" has outlived its usefulness? Can juvenile justice be reformed to meet these challenges? Answers to these questions are inextricably tied to the social forces impacting children and their families.

Current observers of the juvenile court include critics who are both liberals and conservatives. The court lacks a core constituency in the political arena. Legal victories that were achieved on behalf of children in the 1960s and 1970s have been eroded due to budgetary constraints and a less sympathetic judiciary. The political debate on youth crime has been dominated by the advocates of "get tough" laws. Terms such as *delinquency prevention* are hardly ever heard anymore. The upsurge in violent juvenile crime will only increase the pressure to handle more children in adult courts and correctional facilities. This book is intended for students and professionals who seek an honest, albeit somewhat painful, view of the current status of justice for young people. It is a work dedicated to assisting those seeking change in our methods of caring for troubled and troublesome youngsters.

Assembling materials for this manuscript provided an opportunity for us to update our prior work on the history and current functioning of the juvenile justice system. Earlier versions of chapters 2 and 3 appeared in the text *The Children of Ishmael: Critical Perspectives on Juvenile Justice*, published by Mayfield Press in 1978. We also were able to bring together a number of research studies conducted under the auspices of the National Council on Crime and Delinquency (NCCD). Although some of these materials have appeared as NCCD pamphlets, they have never been available to the general reader.

Going from concept to reality required the support of Sage Publications editors Mitch Allen, Diane Foster, and C. Terry Hendrix. Frances Terry and Sonya Rudestine were invaluable as research assistants, helping prepare the final manuscript. We especially thank Laura Chin, who performed all word processing tasks with great accuracy and speed.

We lovingly acknowledge our companions and life partners, Indy den Daas Austin and Karen McKie, for their strength and wise judgments. In no small measure, this book is dedicated to Moshe and Zaid McKie-Krisberg, members of that generation of young people on which the world's future so urgently depends.

Reinventing Juvenile Justice

Goals for the Juvenile Justice System

The concept of a separate "children's court" evolved in the latter half of the 19th century, culminating in the Illinois Juvenile Court Law of 1899. However, as the United States moves through the last decade of the 20th century the future of juvenile justice is very much in doubt. Some have argued that the juvenile court should be abolished (Wolfgang, 1982). Others have argued that the juvenile court should abandon its traditional emphasis on rehabilitation (Feld, 1988c). There are also those who contend that the juvenile court can reclaim its historical mission of "pursuing the best interests of the child" and become an important part of a total adolescent care system (Krisberg, 1988). To reach any of these proposed objectives, the juvenile court system must be reinvented. This book offers a careful diagnosis of some of the major problems confronting our current juvenile justice system and suggests pathways to significant reform.

The juvenile court presents us with a curious mixture of uplifting ideology and harsh daily realities. Its rhetoric is steeped in concepts such as "compassionate care" and "individualized treatment." Yet, too often the reality is assembly-line justice in which large numbers of youngsters and their families are quickly "disposed of" through a limited set of options that rarely are adequately funded. Conservatives consistently have attacked the juvenile court for its leniency, but liberals likewise have criticized the court for its excessive use of detention and jailing for minor offenders.

The sense that the juvenile court is at odds with itself is reflected in the multiplicity of objectives and purposes one finds in the various state laws establishing the juvenile court. Typically, the juvenile court is asked both to protect the public and to be a guardian of wayward children. The court is urged to preserve families, whenever possible, as well as to provide necessary care and guidance. Juvenile courts also must hold youths accountable for their behavior; however, this accountability must be tempered by the unique circumstances of the child. The court must be fair and uniform in its dispositions, and yet judicial officers are directed to individualize their dispositions to meet the special needs of their clients.

Public opinion polls suggest that the average citizen holds conflicting and sometimes confused views about the goals of the juvenile court. In 1982, the National Council on Crime and Delinquency (NCCD), the Field Institute, and the Hubert Humphrey Institute of Public Affairs commissioned a national opinion poll conducted by the Opinion Research Corporation (ORC) (Haugen, Costello, Schwartz, Krisberg, & Litsky, 1982). The poll found that 87% of those surveyed believed juvenile crime was rising at an alarming rate. Approximately 78% felt the juvenile court was too lenient with juveniles convicted of serious crimes. Despite these responses reflecting fear and concern, the poll also showed that most Americans (73%) favored a juvenile court whose primary mission was treatment and rehabilitation, rather than punishment. When asked about the most effective strategies to reduce youth crime rates, the largest group (89%) favored expanded employment opportunities. At the same time, a majority of the public (57%) felt that incarcerating young offenders served as an effective deterrent to other adolescents.

The public showed a strong preference for preventive services and most (61%) felt that juvenile status offenders (truants, runaways, and youths in chronic conflict with their parents) should be handled by community agencies and not by the juvenile court. A clear majority of respondents (61%) felt not enough money was being spent to prevent delinquency.

Another survey conducted by NCCD and the Field Institute examined the attitudes of Californians toward youth crime (Steinhart, 1988b). The results supported and, in some instances, amplified the results of the ORC national data. The California data also are significant in that the state has what many regard as the toughest juvenile sentencing policies in the nation (Demuro, Demuro, & Lerner, 1988).

Similar to the respondents in the national ORC poll, Californians are convinced that juvenile crime is rising rapidly and that juvenile courts are too lenient with juvenile offenders. Yet, Californians strongly endorse rehabilitation as the prime objective of the juvenile court (71%). By a wide margin (84%) Californians reject the practice of housing juveniles with adult offenders. They also favor shorter sentences for juveniles (62%).

On virtually every question asked, the California respondents showed their overwhelming support for treatment, rehabilitation, and employment strategies. A remarkable 92% believe incarcerated youths should have access to job training, education, and counseling before they return to the community. As in the national ORC survey, the California poll suggests strong public support for funding prevention programs. The California results are especially significant in that the survey was conducted during a presidential campaign that made crime a major issue. Southern Californians who have been plagued by high levels of gang violence and drug crimes responded similarly to citizens in other parts of the state.

Other polls conducted by the Center for the Study of Youth Policy (CSYP) at the University of Michigan echo the California findings (Schwartz, Guo, & Kerbs, 1992). The CSYP conducted in-depth surveys of Michigan residents as well as a national opinion poll. Both surveys reported grave public concern about rising rates of youth violence. But the CSYP research continued to record high levels of public support for the juvenile court's traditional treatment philosophy. For example, the Michigan state survey reported that the majority of the public wanted juveniles tried in adult courts for crimes of violence (76%), serious property crimes (57%), and dealing large quantities of drugs (72%). However, the Michigan residents did not favor placing juvenile offenders in adult prisons. The Michigan survey also revealed strong support for community-based programs for juveniles in lieu of placement in juvenile correctional facilities.

Interestingly, the vast majority of respondents (87%) supported expansion to juveniles of the same due process legal protection now enjoyed by adults. The CSYP studies suggest that the public is disenchanted with the operation of the juvenile court, but does not necessarily seek harsher penalties for young offenders. These public perceptions reflect the public's lack of knowledge about how the juvenile court operates. Often the court's proceedings are shrouded in closed hearings that contribute to public misinformation.

All of these measurements of public attitudes seem at odds with the political rhetoric that has dominated debate on juvenile justice policy for the last decade. If one only listened to the political dia-logue, one would conclude that citizens are fed up with the "out-dated liberal philosophy" of the juvenile court. For example, a recent report issued by the United States attorney (Barr, 1992) suggests that "Excessive leniency, on the other hand, is a misguided attempt at kindness that all too often will simply result in additional crime and hardened criminals" (p. 26).

Public opinion is not identical to political rhetoric or governmental practice. There is hardly agreement on goals among those who work in the juvenile justice system. However, the poll data indicate strong support for juvenile justice reforms that respond to public safety concerns and simultaneously advance improved treatment for juve-nile offenders.

The Juvenile Court in Search of the Child

Almost by definition, the juvenile justice system should be guided by a developmental perspective. The central premise of the juvenile court is that children should be treated differently from adults. The court's jurisprudence assumes that adolescents possess somewhat less responsibility for their actions and need protection. Many cases are handled on the basis of the "least restrictive alternative" with a strong preference for informal versus formal dispositions of minor offenses. Criminologist Franklin Zimring (1977) compares the juve-nile court to a "learner's permit," in that society expects young people to make mistakes and wants them to learn from these indis-cretions without exacting full adult criminal penalties. This assump-tion is supported by research on delinquency suggesting that most youths mature out of illegal behaviors (Wolfgang, Figlio, & Sellin, 1972).

In practice, the juvenile justice system incorporates rudimentary notions of child development. Younger offenders are more likely to be diverted to social service agencies by police and courts. Younger adolescents (usually below age 13) are less likely to be detained or placed out of their homes than their older counterparts (Snyder, et al., 1990). A significant exception to this rule occurs for those youths arrested for juvenile status offenses (these are offenses only if com-mitted by a juvenile, such as truancy, drinking alcohol, or running away). Younger status offenders are slightly more likely to be incar-cerated than older youths—presumably because they are in greater need of societal protection. The court is less inclined to intervene in parent-child conflicts as the youngster approaches the legal age of majority.

Another example of how the juvenile justice system incorporates a generalized developmental perspective is the removal of children from adult jails and lockups. Federal juvenile justice legislation enacted in 1974 required states to separate juveniles from adults in correctional facilities as a condition of receiving grant funds. In 1980, Congress strengthened this policy direction, mandating the complete removal of juveniles from adult facilities. Federal courts have interpreted this federal jail removal mandate as creating a private cause of action under federal civil rights laws for juveniles held in adult jails (Soler, 1988). However, the federal requirements allow states to utilize their own legal definitions of who is a juvenile. Further, children who are transferred to adult criminal courts are not covered under the federal rules. Although many states have made significant progress in removing juveniles from adult facilities, as many as 20 states have as yet failed to meet the federal mandate (Steinhart, 1988a).

The most typical cases in which the juvenile court's vague understanding about adolescent development is severely tested is when youngsters commit violent crimes. Neither political nor judicial agreement exists on exactly where to draw the appropriate boundaries between adult responsibility versus the mitigated accountability of young people.

The process of deciding which youngsters should be tried as adults illustrates the extreme difficulty for the juvenile court in implementing a truly developmental perspective. To begin with, states have widely different definitions of the age boundary separating children from adults. Whereas most states give the juvenile court original jurisdiction for youngsters through age 17, New York, North Carolina, and Connecticut set that limit as low as age 14. Further, for specific crimes there are automatic and discretionary procedures for transferring juveniles to adult courts (Hamparian, 1982). Jurisdictions also differ on how they handle youths who fall between these two worlds. For example, an adolescent transferred to adult court in Illinois is held in a juvenile facility. In California this adolescent would be held in an adult jail and in New York City the young person would be held in a special adolescent facility operated by the Department of Corrections. Once sentenced as an adult, a youth in Illinois is housed separately from adults until the age of 18, whereas in Texas this child would be confined with adult offenders.

Not surprisingly, these diverse rules lead to a wide disparity in outcomes (Fagan, Forst, & Vivona, 1987). Research suggests that these transfers often are made according to arbitrary and capricious criteria (Bortner, 1986; Eigen, 1981). Moreover, the question of transferring juveniles to adult courts remains an ongoing "hot button" issue, especially after notorious crimes committed by very young persons. After a particularly brutal and well-publicized juvenile crime in New York City, a New Hampshire congressman introduced a bill requiring all states receiving federal funds to automatically transfer all violent offenders over age 15 to adult courts. Ironically, this bill is patterned after current law in New York, which obviously was not a deterrent to the notorious crime in question.

The policy question of judicial transfers does not reflect a consensus of juvenile justice professionals. This means that a consistent developmental perspective is not utilized in routine decision making. Rather than clinical judgments or diagnostic assessments, questions of child development are determined largely by political and adversarial considerations. In the main, it is lawyers, not trained child psychologists, who make these decisions.

In sum, the juvenile justice system lacks a coherent and consistent perspective on how to define those children who should be handled in special juvenile courts and those who require adult court referrals. The handling of specific cases based on maturity levels or age is determined by laws and by localized and informal court cultures. Juvenile justice practitioners are largely unaware of the research and theory about adolescent development. Further, few juvenile courts possess trained personnel who could authentically respond to the developmental needs of their diverse clientele. For example, a recent research effort (Grisso, 1980) suggests that adolescents under age 15 do not even comprehend the meaning of their current legal rights in the juvenile court. Grisso recommends that very young juveniles should not be permitted to waive these rights voluntarily. Yet, it is routine in most juvenile courts for youngsters and their families to volunteer to drop their rights to legal representation and other evidentiary protections (Grisso, 1980).

Reinventing Juvenile Justice

The noted U.S. legal philosopher Roscoe Pound wrote that the juvenile court was a magnificent step forward in Anglo-American jurisprudence. However, Pound (1957) also worried that the virtually unrestrained powers of the juvenile court could make it into a "star chamber." This ambivalence over the juvenile court's potential for helping or harming adolescents is shared by contemporary child advocates (Schwartz, 1989).

The juvenile court is beset by major societal forces and does not lack for critics. If the juvenile court is to survive at all, our system for dealing with troubled and troublesome young people will need major reforms. This book is about the possible shape of that reform effort. Our first goal is to provide a critical perspective on the evolution of the current juvenile justice system. We first try to provide a social and political perspective on the historical legacy that continues to dominate contemporary thinking about juvenile justice. Next, we provide an overview on how the current juvenile justice system operates, focusing on empirical studies of the various components of that system. We have chosen to pay particular attention to issues of racial and gender bias in juvenile justice. The reality of discriminatory handling of youngsters is a central challenge to the juvenile court's claims for moral legitimacy.

More than court procedures, the juvenile justice system contains a diversity of programs and services designed to treat and rehabilitate wayward youngsters. Although there is an enormous research literature that attempts to evaluate these efforts, we have chosen to focus attention on the dramatic juvenile corrections reforms led by Jerome Miller in Massachusetts in the early 1970s. For more than a century, the large-scale, congregate training school was the central paradigm for treating delinquents. Jerome Miller exposed the hidden brutality and corruption of the Massachusetts training schools and demonstrated that a genuinely community-based system of care could be established. Miller's experiment remains at the core of today's debate on the future of juvenile justice. We report on extensive research on the Massachusetts Division of Youth Services. We also provide information about other states that attempted to follow the principles of the Massachusetts reforms.

In the final chapter, we offer a profile of innovative programs and ideas on how the concept of a separate children's juvenile system can be reinvented to meet the challenges of its second century. We also discuss the opportunities for and barriers to positive change.

2

History of the Control and Prevention of Juvenile Delinquency in the United States

The first institution for the control of juvenile delinquency in the United States was the New York House of Refuge, founded in 1825. But specialized treatment of wayward youth has a much longer history—one tied to change in the social structure of medieval Europe. These same changes prompted the colonization of the New World and led to attempts to control and exploit the labor of African, European, and Native American children.

Virtually all aspects of life were in a state of flux for the people of Europe in the later Middle Ages (16th and 17th centuries). The economy was being transformed from a feudal system based on sustenance agriculture to a capitalistic, trade-oriented system focusing on cash crops and the consolidation of large tracts of land. In religious matters, the turmoil could be amply witnessed in the intense struggles of the Reformation. Politically, power was increasingly concentrated in the hands of a few monarchs, who were fashioning strong centralized states. The growth of trade and exploration exposed Europeans to a variety of world cultures and peoples.

For the lower classes of European society, these were "the worst of times." The rising population density as well as primitive methods of agricultural production led to a virtual exhaustion of the land.

Increasing urban populations created new demands for cheap grain, and landlords responded by increasing the fees paid by peasants who worked the land. Large numbers of peasants were displaced from the land to permit the growth of a capitalist pasturage system. The standard of living of the European peasantry dropped sharply and this new, displaced class streamed into the cities and towns in search of means of survival. The workers and artisans of the cities were deeply threatened by the prospect that this pauper class would drive down the general wage level. Most European towns experienced sharp rises in crime, rioting, and public disorder.

To control and defuse the threat of this new "dangerous class," the leaders of the towns enacted laws and other restrictions to discourage immigration and contain the movement of the impoverished peasantry. "Poor laws" were passed, preventing the new migrants from obtaining citizenship, restricting their membership in guilds, and often closing the city gates to them. Vagrancy laws were instituted to control and punish those who seemed a threat to the social order. Certain legislation, such as the Elizabethan Statute of Artificers (1562), restricted access into certain trades, forcing the rural young to remain in the countryside.

Urban migration continued despite most attempts to curtail it. The collective units of urban life, the guild and the family, began to weaken under the pressure of social change. Children often were abandoned or released from traditional community restraints. Countless observers from the period tell of bands of youths roaming the cities at night, engaging in thievery, begging, and other forms of misbehavior (Sanders, 1970).

At this time family control of children was the dominant model for disciplining wayward youth. The model of family government, with the father in the role of sovereign, was extended to those without families through a system of *binding out* the young to other families. Poor children or those beyond parental control were apprenticed to householders for a specified period of time. Unlike the apprenticeship system for the privileged classes, the binding out system did not oblige the master to teach his ward a trade. Boys generally were assigned to farming tasks and girls were brought into domestic service.

As the problem of urban poverty increased, the traditional modes of dealing with delinquent or destitute children became strained. Some localities constructed institutions to control wayward youth. The Bridewell (1555) in London is generally considered the first institution specifically designed to control youthful beggars and vagrants. In 1576 the English Parliament passed a law establishing a similar institution in every English county. The most celebrated of these early institutions was the Amsterdam House of Corrections (1595), which was viewed as an innovative solution to the crime problem of the day.[1] The houses of correction combined the principles of the poorhouse, the workhouse, and the penal institution. The youthful inmates were forced to work within the institution, and thus develop habits of industriousness. Upon release they were expected to enter the labor force, so house of correction inmates often were hired out to private contractors. Males rasped hardwoods used in the dyeing industry, and when textile manufacturing was introduced to the houses of correction, this became the special task of young woman inmates.

The early houses of correction, or so-called *Bridewells*, accepted all types of children including the destitute, the infirm, and the needy. In some cases, parents placed their children in these institutions because they believed the regimen of work would have a reformative effect. Although it is debatable whether the houses of correction were economically efficient, the founders of such institutions clearly hoped to provide a cheap source of labor to local industries. The French institutions, called *hospitaux generaux*, experimented with technological improvements and different labor arrangements. This often brought charges of unfair competition from guilds, who feared the demise of their monopoly on labor, and businessmen, who felt threatened by price competition at the marketplace. Some authors stress the economic motive of these early penal institutions (Rusche & Kirchheimer, 1968): "The institution of the houses of correction in such a society was not the result of brotherly love or of an official sense of obligation to the distressed. It was part of the development of capitalism" (p. 50).

The enormous social, political, and economic dislocations taking place in Europe provided a major push toward colonization of the Americas. People emigrated for many reasons—some to get rich, some to escape political or religious oppression, and some because they simply had nothing to lose. Settlement patterns and the resulting forms of community life varied considerably. In the Massachusetts Bay Colony, for example, the Puritans attempted to establish a deeply religious community to serve God's will in the New World. The Puritans brought families with them, and from the outset made provisions for the care and control of youths.

In contrast, the settlement of Virginia was more directly tied to economic considerations. There were persistent labor shortages, and the need for labor prompted orders for young people to be sent over from Europe. Some youths were sent over by *Spirits*, who were agents of merchants or shipowners. The Spirits attempted to persuade young people to emigrate to America. They often promised that the New World would bring tremendous wealth and happiness to the youthful immigrants. The children typically agreed to work a specific term (usually 4 years) in compensation for passage across the Atlantic and for services rendered during the trip. These agreements of service were then sold to inhabitants of the new colonies, particularly in the South. One can imagine that this labor source must have been quite profitable for the plantations of the New World. Spirits were often accused of kidnapping, contractual fraud, and deception of a generally illiterate, destitute, and young clientele.

Other children coming to the New World were even more clearly coerced. For example, it became an integral part of penal practice in the early part of the 18th century to transport prisoners to colonial areas. Children held in the overcrowded Bridewells and poorhouses of England were brought to the Americas as indentured servants. After working a specified number of years as servants or laborers, the children were able to win their freedom. In 1619 the colony of Virginia regularized an agreement for the shipment of orphans and destitute children from England.

That same year, Africans, another group of coerced immigrants, made their first appearance in the Virginia Colony. The importation of African slaves eventually displaced reliance on the labor of youthful poor because of greater economic feasibility. The black chattels were physically able to perform strenuous labor under extreme weather conditions without adequate nutrition. These abilities would finally be used to describe them as beasts. Also, the high death rates experienced under these conditions did not have to be accounted for. The bondage of Africans was soon converted into lifetime enslavement, which passed on through generations. The southern plantation system, dependent on the labor of African slaves, produced tremendous wealth, further entrenching this inhuman system (Stamp, 1956; Yetman, 1970). Racism, deeply lodged in the English psyche, provided the rationale and excuse for daily atrocities and cruelties.[2]

Studies of slavery often overlook the fact that most slaves were children. Slave traders thought children would bring higher prices. Accounts of the slave trade emphasize the economic utility of small children, who could be jammed into the limited cargo space available. Children were always a high proportion of the total slave population because slave owners encouraged the birth of children to increase their capital. Little regard was paid by slave owners to keeping families together. African babies were a commodity to be exploited just as one might exploit the land or the natural resources of a plantation, and young slave women often were used strictly for breeding. A complete understanding of the social control of children must include an examination of the institution of slavery, comparing this to the conditions faced by children in other sections of the country.[3]

Another group of children who often are ignored in discussions of the history of treatment of youth in North America are Native Americans. In 1609 officials of the Virginia Company were authorized to kidnap Native American children and raise them as Christians. The stolen youths were to be trained in the religion of the colonists, as well as in their language and customs. The early European colonists spread the word of the Gospel to help rationalize their conquests of lands and peoples. But an equally important motivation was their interest in recruiting a group of friendly natives to assist in trade negotiations and pacification programs among the native peoples. The early Indian schools resembled penal institutions, with heavy emphasis on useful work, Bible study, and religious worship. Although a substantial amount of effort and money was invested in Indian schools, the results were considerably less than had been originally hoped (Bremner, Barnard, Hareven, Mennel, 1970):

> Missionaries could rarely bridge the chasm of mistrust and hostility that resulted from wars, massacres and broken promises. With so many colonists regarding the Indian as the chief threat to their security and the Indians looking upon the colonists as hypocrites, it is little wonder that attempts to win converts and to educate should fail. (p. 72)

Unlike attempts to enslave children of African descent, early efforts with Native Americans were not successful. Relations between European colonists and Native Americans during this period centered around trading and the securing of land rights. These contrasting economic relationships resulted in divergent practices in areas such as education. Although there was general support for bringing "the blessings of Christian education" to the Native American children, there was intense disagreement about the merits of educating African slaves. Whereas some groups, such as the Society for the Propagation of the Gospel, argued that all heathens should be educated and converted, others feared that slaves who were baptized would claim the status of freemen. There was concern among whites that education of slaves would lead to insurrection and revolt. As a result, South Carolina and several other colonies proclaimed that conversion to Christianity would not affect the status of slaves (Bremner et al., 1970, p. 97). Many southern colonies made it a crime to teach reading and writing to slaves. A middle-ground position evolved, calling for religious indoctrination without the more dangerous education in literacy (Bremner et al., 1970, pp. 316-339; Gossett, 1965).

In the early years of colonization, the family was the fundamental mode of juvenile social control, as well as the central unit of economic production. Even in situations where children were apprenticed or indentured, the family still served as the model for discipline and order. Several of the early colonies passed laws requiring single persons to live with families. The dominant form of poor relief at this time was placing the needy with other families in the community (Rothman, 1971, pp. 3-56). A tradition of family government evolved in which the father was empowered with absolute authority over all affairs of the family. Wives and children were expected to give complete and utter obedience to the father's wishes. This model complemented practices in political life, where absolute authority was thought crucial to the preservation of civilization.

Colonial laws supported and defended the primacy of family government. The earliest laws concerning youthful misbehavior prescribed the death penalty for children who disobeyed their parents. For example, part of the 1641 Massachusetts *Body of Liberties* reads as follows (Hawes, 1971):

> If any child, or children, above sixteen years of age, and of sufficient understanding, shall CURSE or SMITE their natural FATHER or MOTHER, he or they shall be putt to death, unless it can be sufficiently testified that the Parents have been very unchristianly negligent in the education of such children: so provoked them by extreme and cruel correction, that they have been forced thereunto, to preserve themselves from death or maiming: *Exod* 21:17, *Lev* 20:9, *Exod* 21:15. (p. 13)

Although there is little evidence that children were actually put to death for disobeying their parents, this same legal principle was used to justify the punishment of rebellious slave children in the southern colonies. Family discipline typically was maintained by corporal punishment. Not only were parents held legally responsible for providing moral education for their children, but also a Massachusetts law of 1642 mandated that parents should teach their children reading and writing. Later, in 1670, public officials called tithingmen were assigned to assist the selectmen (town councilmen) and constables in supervising family government. The tithingmen visited families who allegedly were ignoring the education and socialization of their children. Although there are records of parents brought to trial due to their neglect of parental duties, this manner of supervising family government was not very successful.

The family was the central economic unit of colonial North America. Home-based industry, in which labor took place on the family farm or in a home workshop, continued until the end of the 18th century. Children were an important component of family production, and their labor was considered valuable and desirable. A major determinant of a child's future during this time was the father's choice of apprenticeship for his child. Ideally the apprenticeship system was to be the stepping stone into a skilled craft, but this happy result was certain only for children of the privileged classes. As a consequence, children of poor families might actually be *bound out* as indentured servants. The term of apprenticeship was generally 7 years and the child was expected to regard his master with the same obedience due natural parents. The master was responsible for the education and training of the young apprentice and he acted *in loco parentis,* assuming complete responsibility for the child's material and spiritual welfare. Although apprenticeships were voluntary for the wealthier citizens, for the wayward or destitute child they were unavoidable. The use of compulsory apprenticeships was an important form of social control exercised by town and religious officials upon youths perceived as troublesome (Bremner et al., 1970, pp. 572-583).

The industrial revolution in North America, beginning at the end of the 18th century, brought about the gradual transformation of the labor system of youth. The family-based productive unit gave way to an early factory system. Child labor in industrial settings supplanted the apprenticeship system. As early as the 1760s there were signs that the cotton industry in New England would transform the system of production, and by 1791 all stages in the manufacture of raw cotton into cloth were performed by factory machinery. The Samuel Slater factory in Providence, Rhode Island, employed 100 children aged 4 to 10 years in cotton manufacture. Here is a description of the workplace environment (Bremner et al., 1970):

> They worked in one room where all the machinery was concentrated under the supervision of a foreman, spreading the cleaned cotton on the carding machine to be combed and passing it though the roving machine, which turned the cotton into loose rolls ready to be spun. Some

of the children tended the spindles, removing and attaching bobbins. Small, quick fingers were admirably suited for picking up and knotting broken threads. To the delight of Tench Coxe, a champion of American industry, the children became "the little fingers . . . of the gigantic automatons of labor-saving machinery." (p. 146)

During the next 2 decades, the use of children in New England industrial factories increased, and children comprised 47% to 55% of the labor force in the cotton mills. The proliferation of the factory system transformed the lives of many Americans. On one hand, enormous wealth began to accumulate in the hands of a few individuals. At the same time, the switch from a family-based economy to a factory system where workers sold their labor meant that many families were displaced from the land. A large class of permanently impoverished Americans evolved. The use of child labor permitted early industrialists to depress the general wage level. Moreover, companies provided temporary housing and supplies to workers at high prices, so that workers often incurred substantial debts rather than financial rewards.

Increased child labor also contributed to the weakening of family ties, because work days were long and often competed with family chores. Children were now responsible to two masters—their fathers and their factory supervisors. Work instruction became distinct from general education and spiritual guidance as the family ceased to be an independent economic unit. Conditions of poverty continued to spread, and the social control system predicated upon strong family government began to deteriorate. During the first decades of the 19th century one could begin to observe a flow of Americans from rural areas to the urban centers. As increasing economic misery combined with a decline in traditional forms of social control, an ominous stage was being set. Some Americans began to fear deeply the growth of a "dangerous class" and attempted to develop new measures to control the wayward youth who epitomized this threat to social stability.

The Houses of Refuge (1825-1860)[4]

Severe economic downturns in the first 2 decades of the 19th century forced many Americans out of work. At the same time, increasing numbers of Irish immigrants arrived in the United States. These changes in the social structure, combined with the growth of the factory system, contributed to the founding of specialized institutions for the control and prevention of juvenile delinquency in the United States (Hawes, 1971, pp. 27-60; Mennel, 1973, pp. 3-31; Pickett, 1969).

As early as 1817, the more privileged Americans became concerned about the apparent connection between increased pauperism and the rise of delinquency. The Society for the Prevention of Pauperism was an early attempt to evaluate contemporary methods of dealing with the poor and suggest policy changes. This group also led campaigns against taverns and theaters, which they felt contributed to the problem of poverty. The efforts of several members of this group in New York City led to the founding of the first House of Refuge in 1825. The group conducted investigations, drew up plans and legislation, and lobbied actively to gain acceptance of their ideas. In other northeastern cities, such as Boston and Philadelphia, similar efforts were under way.

A number of historians have described these early 19th-century philanthropists as *Conservative Reformers* (Coben & Ratner, 1970; Mennel, 1973). These men were primarily from the wealthy, established families and often were prosperous merchants or professionals. Ideologically, they were close to the thinking of the colonial elite and, later, to the Federalists. Popular democracy was anathema to them because they viewed themselves as God's elect and felt bound to accomplish His charitable objectives in the secular world. Leaders of the movement to establish the houses of refuge, such as John Griscom, Thomas Eddy, and John Pintard, viewed themselves as responsible for the moral health of the community, and they intended to regulate community morality through the example of their own proper behavior as well as through benevolent activities. The poor and the deviant were the objects of their concern and their moral stewardship.

Although early 19th-century philanthropists relied on religion to justify their good works, they primary motivation was protection of their class privileges. Fear of social unrest and chaos dominated their thinking (Mennel, 1973, pp. 6-9). The rapid growth of a visible impoverished class, coupled with apparent increases in crime, disease, and immorality, worried those in power. The bitter class struggles of the French Revolution and periodic riots in urban areas of the United States signaled danger to the status quo. The philanthropy of this group was aimed at reestablishing social order, while preserving the existing property and status relationships. They were responsible for founding such organizations as the American Sunday School Union, the American Bible Society, the African Free School Society, and the Society for Alleviating the Miseries of Public Prisons. They often were appointed to positions on boards of managers for lunatic asylums, public hospitals, workhouses for the poor, and prisons.

The idea for houses of refuge was part of a series of reform concepts designed to reduce juvenile delinquency. Members of the Society for the Prevention of Pauperism were dissatisfied with the prevailing practice of placing children in adult jails and workhouses. Some reformers felt exposing children to more seasoned offenders would increase the chances of such children becoming adult criminals. Another issue was the terrible condition of local jails. Others worried that due to the abominable conditions of local jails, judges and juries would lean toward acquittal of youthful criminals to avoid sending them to such places. Reformers also objected that the punitive character of available penal institutions would not solve the basic problem of pauperism. The reformers envisioned an institution with educational facilities, set in the context of a prison. John Griscom called for "the erection of new prisons for juvenile offenders." A report of the Society for the Prevention of Pauperism (Mennel, 1973) suggested the following principles for such new prisons:

> These prisons should be rather schools for instruction, than places of punishment, like our present state prisons where the young and the old are confined indiscriminately. The youth confined there should be placed under a course of discipline, severe and unchanging, but alike calculated to subdue and conciliate. A system should be adopted that would provide a mental and moral regimen. (p. 11)

By 1824 the society had adopted a state charter in New York under the name of the Society for the Reformation of Juvenile Delinquents, and had begun a search for a location for the house of refuge.

On New Year's Day, 1825, the New York House of Refuge opened with solemn pomp and circumstance. A year later the Boston House of Reformation was started, and in 1828 the Philadelphia House of Refuge began to admit wayward youth. These new institutions accepted both children convicted of crimes and destitute children. Because they were founded as preventive institutions, the early houses of refuge could accept children who "live an idle or dissolute life, whose parents are dead or if living, from drunkenness, or other vices, neglect to provide any suitable employment or exercise any salutary control over said children" (Bremner et al., 1970, p. 681). Thus, from the outset, the first special institutions for juveniles housed together delinquent, dependent, and neglected children—a practice still observed in most juvenile detention facilities today.[5]

The development of this new institution of social control necessitated changes in legal doctrines in order to justify the exercise of power by refuge officials. In *Commonwealth v. M'Keagy* (1831), the Pennsylvania courts had to rule on the legality of a proceeding whereby a child was committed to the Philadelphia House of Refuge on the weight of his father's evidence that the child was "an idle and disorderly person." The court affirmed the right of the state to take a child away from a parent in cases of vagrancy or crime. But because this child was not a vagrant, nor was the father poor, the court ruled that the child should not be committed. Judicial officials did not wish to confuse protection of children with punishment, because this might engender constitutional questions as to whether children committed to houses of refuge had received the protection of due process of law.

The related question of whether parental rights were violated by involuntary refuge commitments was put to a legal test in *Ex parte Crouse* (1838). The father of a child committed to the Philadelphia House of Refuge attempted to obtain her release through a writ of habeas corpus. The state supreme court denied the motion, holding that the right of parental control is a natural but not inalienable right (*Ex parte Crouse*, 1838):

> The object of the charity is reformation, by training the inmates to industry; by imbuing their minds with principles of morality and religion; by furnishing them with means to earn a living; and, above all, by separating them from the corrupting influence of improper associates. To this end, may not the natural parents, when unequal to the task of education, or unworthy of it, be superseded by the *parens patriae*, or common guardian of the community? . . . The infant has been snatched from a course which must have ended in confirmed depravity; and, not only is the restraint of her person lawful, but it would have been an act of extreme cruelty to release her from it.

The elaboration of the doctrine of *parens patriae* in the Crouse case was an important legal principle, used to support the expanded legal powers of the juvenile court. It is important to recognize the significance of both social class and hostility toward Irish immigrants in the legal determination of the Crouse case.[6] Because Irish immigrants were viewed at this time as corrupt and unsuitable as parents, it is easy to see how anti-immigrant feelings could color judgments about the suitability of parental control. As a result, children of immigrants made up the majority of inmates of the houses of refuge.

The early houses of refuge either excluded blacks or housed them in segregated facilities. In 1849 the city of Philadelphia opened the

House of Refuge for Colored Juvenile Delinquents. Racially segregated refuges were maintained in New York City and Boston only through the limited funds donated by antislavery societies. Because refuge managers viewed all young woman delinquents as sexually promiscuous with little hope for eventual reform, young women also received discriminatory treatment.[7]

The managers of houses of refuge concentrated on perfecting institutional regimens that would result in reformation of juveniles. Descriptions of daily activities stress regimentation, absolute subordination to authority, and monotonous repetition (Bremner et al., 1970):

> At sunrise, the children are warned, by the ringing of a bell, to rise from their beds. Each child makes his own bed, and steps forth, on a signal, into the Hall. They then proceed, in perfect order, to the Wash Room. Thence they are marched to parade in the yard, and undergo an examination as to their dress and cleanliness; after which they attend morning prayer. The morning school then commences, where they are occupied in summer, until 7 o'clock. A short intermission is allowed, when the bell rings for breakfast; after which, they proceed to their respective workshops, where they labor until 12 o'clock, when they are called from work, and one hour allowed them for washing and eating their dinner. At one, they again commence work, and continue at it until five in the afternoon, when the labors of the day terminate. Half an hour is allowed for washing and eating their supper, and at half-past five, they are conducted to the school room, where they continue at their studies until 8 o'clock. Evening Prayer is performed by the Superintendent; after which, the children are conducted to their dormitories, which they enter, and are locked up for the night, when perfect silence reigns throughout the establishment. The foregoing is the history of a single day, and will answer for every day in the year, except Sundays, with slight variations during stormy weather, and the short days in winter. (p. 688)[8]

Routines were enforced by corporal punishment as well as other forms of control. Houses of refuge experimented with primitive systems of classification based on the behavior of inmates. The Boston House of Reformation experimented with inmate self-government as a control technique. But despite public declarations to the contrary, there is ample evidence of the use of solitary confinement, whipping, and other physical punishments.

Inmates of the houses of refuge labored in large workshops manufacturing shoes, producing brass nails, or caning chairs. Young woman delinquents often were put to work spinning cotton and doing laundry. It is estimated that income generated from labor sold to outside contractors supplied up to 40% of the operating expenses of the houses of refuge. The chief problem for refuge managers was that economic depressions could dry up the demand for labor, and there was not always sufficient work to keep the inmates occupied. Not only were there complaints that contractors improperly abused children, but also such employment prepared youngsters for only the most menial work.

Youths were committed to the houses of refuge for indeterminate periods of time until the legal age of majority. Release was generally obtained through an apprenticeship by the youths to some form of service. The system was akin to the binding out practices of earlier times. Males typically were apprenticed on farms, on whaling boats, or in the merchant marine. Young women usually were placed into domestic service. Only rarely was a house-of-refuge child placed in a skilled trade. Apprenticeship decisions often were made to ensure that the child would not be reunited with his or her family, because this was presumed to be the root cause of the child's problems. As a result, there are many accounts of siblings and parents vainly attempting to locate their lost relatives.

The founders of the houses of refuge were quick to declare their own efforts successful. Prominent visitors to the institutions, such as Alexis de Tocqueville and Dorothea Dix, echoed the praise of the founders. Managers of the refuges produced glowing reports attesting to the positive results of the houses. Sharp disagreements over the severity of discipline required led to the replacement of directors who were perceived as too permissive. Elijah Devoe (1848), a house of refuge assistant superintendent, wrote poignantly of the cruelties and injustices in these institutions. There are accounts of violence within the institutions as well. Robert Mennel (1973) estimates that approximately 40% of the children escaped either from the institutions or from their apprenticeship placements. The problems that plagued the houses of refuge did not dampen the enthusiasm of the philanthropists, who assumed that the reformation process was a difficult and tenuous business at best.

Public relations efforts proclaiming the success of the houses of refuge helped lead to a rapid proliferation of similar institutions (Rothman, 1971). While special institutions for delinquent and destitute youth increased in numbers, the public perceived that delinquency was continuing to rise and become more serious. The founders of the houses of refuge argued that the solution to the delinquency problem lay in the perfection of better methods to deal with incarcerated children. Most of the literature of this period assumes the necessity of institutionalized treatment for children. The debates centered around whether to implement changes in architecture or in the institutional routines. Advocates of institutionalized care of delinquent and dependent youths continued to play the dominant role in formulating social policy for the next century.

The Growth of Institutionalization and the Child Savers (1850-1890)

In the second half of the 19th century, a group of reformers known as the Child Savers instituted new measures to prevent juvenile delinquency (Hawes, 1971, pp. 87-111; Mennel, 1973, pp. 32-77; Platt, 1968). Reformers including Lewis Pease, Samuel Gridley Howe, and Charles Loring Brace founded societies to save children from depraved and criminal lives. They created the Five Points Mission (1850), the Children's Aid Society (1853), and the New York Juvenile Asylum (1851). The ideology of this group of reformers differed from that of the founders of the houses of refuge only in that this group was more optimistic about the possibilities of reforming youths. Centers were established in urban areas to distribute food and clothing, provide temporary shelter for homeless youth, and introduce contract systems of shirt manufacture to destitute youth.

The Child Savers criticized the established churches for not doing more about the urban poor. They favored an activist clergy that would attempt to reach the children of the streets. Although this view was somewhat unorthodox, they viewed the urban masses as a potentially dangerous class that could rise up if misery and impoverishment were not alleviated. Charles Loring Brace observed (quoted in Mennel, 1973): "Talk of heathen! All the pagans of Golconda would not hold a light to the ragged, cunning, forsaken, godless, keen devilish boys of Leonard Street and the Five Points. . . . Our future voters, and President-makers, and citizens! Good Lord deliver us, and help them!" (p. 34). Brace and his associates knew from firsthand experience in the city missions that the problems of poverty were widespread and growing more serious. Their chief objection to the houses of refuge was that long-term institutionalized care did not reach enough children. Moreover, the Child Savers held the traditional view that family life is superior to institutional routines for generating moral reform.

Brace and his Children's Aid Society believed that delinquency could be solved if vagrant and poor children were gathered up and *placed out* with farm families on the western frontier. Placing out as a delinquency prevention practice was based on the idealized notion of the U.S. farm family. Such families were supposed to be centers of warmth, compassion, and morality; they were "God's reformatories" for wayward youth. Members of the Children's Aid Society provided food, clothing, and sometimes shelter to street waifs, and preached to them about the opportunities awaiting them if they migrated westward. Agents of the Children's Aid Society vigorously urged poor urban youngsters to allow themselves to be placed out with farm families. Many believed that western families provided both a practical and economical resource for reducing juvenile delinquency. The following passage from a Michigan newspaper gives a vivid picture of the placing out process (Mennel, 1973):

> Our village has been astir for a few days. Saturday afternoon, Mr. C. C. Tracy arrived with a party of children from the Children's Aid Society in New York. . . .
>
> Sabath day Mr. Tracy spoke day and evening, three times, in different church edifices to crowded and interested audiences. In the evening, the children were present in a body, and sang their "Westward Ho" song. Notice was given that applicants would find unappropriated children at the store of Carder and Ryder, at nine o'clock Monday morning. Before the hour arrived a great crowd assembled, and in two hours *every child was disposed of,* and more were wanted.
>
> We *Wolverines* will never forget Mr. Tracy's visit. It cost us some tears of sympathy, some dollars, and some smiles. We wish him a safe return to Gotham, a speedy one to us with the new company of destitute children, for whom good homes are even now prepared. (p. 39)

Contrary to the benevolent image projected by this news story, there is ample evidence that the children were obliged to work hard for their keep, and were rarely accepted as members of the family. The Boston Children's Aid Society purchased a home in 1864, which was used to help adjust street youth to their new life in the West. The children were introduced to farming skills and taught manners that might be expected of them in their new homes.

Another prevention experiment during the middle part of the 19th century was the result of the work of a Boston shoemaker, John Augustus. In 1841, Augustus began to put up bail for men charged with drunkenness, although he had no official connection with the court. Soon after, he extended his services to young people. Augustus supervised the youngsters while they were out on bail, provided clothing and shelter, was sometimes able to find them jobs, and often paid court costs to keep them out of jail. This early probation system was later instituted by local child-saving groups, who would find placements for the children. By 1869 Massachusetts had a system by which agents of the Board of State Charities took charge of delinquents before they appeared in court. The youths often were released on probation, subject to good behavior in the future.

These noninstitutional prevention methods were challenged by those who felt an initial period of confinement was important before children were placed out. Critics also argued that the Children's Aid Societies neither followed up on their clients nor administered more stringent discipline to those who needed it. One critic phrased it this way (Mennel, 1973):

> The "vagabond boy" is like a blade of corn, coming up side by side with a thistle. You may transplant both together in fertile soil, but you will have the thistle still. . . . I would have you pluck out the vagabond first, and then let the boy be thus provided with "a home," and not before. (p. 46)

Many midwesterners were unsettled by the stream of "criminal children" flowing into their midst. Brace and his colleagues were accused of poisoning the West with the dregs of urban life. To combat charges that urban youths were responsible for the rising crime in the West, Brace conducted a survey of western prisons and almshouses to show that few of his children had gotten into further trouble in the West.

Resistance continued to grow against the efforts of the Children's Aid Societies. Brace, holding that asylum interests were behind the opposition, maintained that the longer a child remains in an asylum, the less likely he will reform. (The debate over the advantages and disadvantages of institutionalized care of delinquent youth continues to the present day.) Brace continued to be an active proponent of the placing out system. He appeared before early conventions of reform school managers to present his views and debate the opposition. As the struggle continued over an idealogy to guide prevention efforts, the problem of delinquency continued to grow. During the 19th century, poverty, industrialization, and immigration, as well as the Civil War, helped to swell the ranks of the "dangerous classes."[9]

Midway through the 19th century, state and municipal governments began taking over the administration of institutions for juvenile delinquents. Early efforts had been supported by private philanthropic groups with some state support. But the growing fear of class strife, coupled with increasing delinquency, demanded a more centralized administration. Many of the newer institutions were termed *reform schools* to imply a strong emphasis on formal school-ing. In 1876, of the 51 refuges or reform schools in the United States, nearly three quarters were operated by state or local governments. By 1890, almost every state outside the South had a reform school, and many jurisdictions had separate facilities for male and female delinquents. These institutions varied considerably in their admis-sions criteria, their sources of referral, and the character of their inmates. Most of the children were sentenced to remain in reform schools until they reached the age of majority (18 years for girls and 21 for boys), or until they were reformed. The length of confinement, as well as the decision to transfer unmanageable youths to adult penitentiaries, was left to the discretion of reform school officials.

Partially in response to attacks by Brace and his followers, many institutions implemented a cottage or family system between 1857 and 1860. The cottage system involved dividing the youths into units of 40 or fewer, each with its own cottage and schedule. Although work was sometimes performed within the cottages, the use of large congregate workshops continued. The model for the system was derived from the practice of European correctional officials. There is evidence from this period of the development of a self-conscious attempt to refine techniques to mold, reshape, and reform wayward youth (Hawes, 1971, pp. 78-86).

During this period, a movement was initiated to locate institutions in rural areas, because it was felt that agricultural labor would facilitate reformative efforts. As a result, several urban houses of refuge were relocated in rural settings. Many rural institutions used the cottage system, as it was well suited to agricultural production. In addition, the cottage system gave managers the opportunity to segregate children according to age, sex, race, school achievement, or "hardness." Critics of the institutions, such as Mary Carpenter, pointed out that most of the presumed benefits of rural settings were artificial and that the vast majority of youths who spent time in these reform schools ultimately returned to crowded urban areas.

The Civil War deeply affected institutions for delinquent youth. Whereas prisons and county jails witnessed declines in population, the war brought even more youths into reform schools. Institutions were strained well beyond their capacities. Some historians believe that the participation of youths in the draft riots in northern cities produced an increase in incarcerated youths. Reform schools often released older youngsters to military service, in order to make room for additional children. Due to the high inflation rates of the war, the amount of state funds available for institutional upkeep steadily declined. Many institutions were forced to resort to the contract labor system to increase reform school revenues in order to meet operating expenses during the war and in the postwar period.

Voices were raised in protest over the expansion of contract labor in juvenile institutions. Some charged that harnessing the labor of inmates, rather than the reformation of youthful delinquents, had become the raison d'être of these institutions. There were growing rumors of cruel and vicious exploitation of youth by work supervisors. An 1871 New York Commission on Prison Labor, headed by Enoch Wines, found that refuge boys were paid 30 cents per day for labor that would receive $4 a day on the outside. In the Philadelphia House of Refuge, boys were paid 25 cents a day, and were sent elsewhere if they failed to meet production quotas. Economic depressions throughout the 1870s increased pressure to end the contract system. Workingmen's associations protested against the contract system, because prison and reform school laborers created unfair competition. Organized workers claimed that refuge managers were making huge profits from the labor of their wards (Mennel, 1973):

> From the institutional point of view, protests of workingmen had the more serious result of demythologizing the workshop routine. No longer was it believable for reform school officials to portray the ritual as primarily a beneficial aid in inculcating industrious habits or shaping youth for "usefulness." The violence and exploitation characteristic of reform school workshops gave the lie to this allegation. The havoc may have been no greater than that which occasionally wracked the early houses of refuge, but the association of conflict and the contract system in the minds of victims and outside labor interests made it now seem intolerable. (p. 61)

The public became aware of stabbings, fighting, arson, and attacks upon staff of these institutions.

All signs pointed toward a decline of authority within the institutions. The economic troubles of the reform schools continued to worsen. Additional controversy was generated by organized Catholic groups, who objected to Protestant control of juvenile institutions housing a majority of Catholics. This crisis in the juvenile institutions led to a series of investigations into reform school operations.[10] The authors of these reports proposed reforms to maximize efficiency of operation and increase government control over the functioning of institutions in their jurisdictions. One major result of these investigative efforts was the formation of Boards of State Charity. Members of these boards were appointed to inspect reform schools and make recommendations for improvements, but were to avoid the evils of the patronage system. Board members, who were described as "gentlemen of public spirit and sufficient leisure," uncovered horrid institutional conditions, and made efforts to transfer youngsters to more decent facilities. Men such as Frederick Wines, Franklin Sanborn, Hastings Hart, and William Pryor Letchworth were among the pioneers of this reform effort.

Although it was hoped that the newly formed boards would find ways to reduce the proliferation of juvenile institutions, such facilities continued to grow, as did the number of wayward youths. These late 19th-century reformers looked toward the emerging scientific disciplines for solutions to the problems of delinquency and poverty. They also developed a system to discriminate among delinquents, so that "hardened offenders" would be sent to special institutions such as the Elmira Reformatory. It was generally recognized that new methods would have to be developed to restore order within the reform schools, and to make some impact upon delinquency.

Juvenile institutions in the South and the far West developed much later than those in the North or the East, but essentially along the same lines. One reason for this was that delinquency was primarily a city problem, and the South and far West were less urbanized. In the South, black youths received radically different treatment from whites. Whereas there was toleration for the misdeeds of white youth, black children were controlled under the disciplinary systems of slavery. Even after Emancipation, the racism of southern whites prevented them from treating black children as fully human and worth reforming. The Civil War destroyed the prison system of the South. After the war, southern whites used the notorious Black Codes, and often trumped up criminal charges to arrest thousands of impoverished former slaves, placing them into a legally justified forced labor system. Blacks were leased out on contract to railroad companies, mining interests, and manufacturers. Although many of these convicts were children, no special provisions were made because of age. Conditions under the southern convict lease system were miserable, and rivalled the worst cruelties of slavery. Little in the way of specialized care for delinquent youth was accomplished in the South until well into the 20th century. The convict lease system eventually was replaced by county road gangs and prison farms, characterized by grossly inhumane conditions of confinement. These were systems of vicious exploitation of labor and savage racism (McKelvey, 1972, pp. 172-189).

Juvenile Delinquency and the Progressive Era

The period from 1880 to 1920, often referred to by historians as the Progressive Era, was a time of major social structural change in the United States. The nation was in the process of becoming increasingly urbanized, and unprecedented numbers of European immigrants were migrating to cities in the Northeast. The United States was becoming an imperialist power, and was establishing worldwide military and economic relationships. Wealth was becoming concentrated in the hands of a few individuals, who sought to dominate U.S. economic life. Labor violence was on the rise, and the country was in the grip of a racial hysteria affecting all peoples of color. The tremendous technological development that was occurring reduced the need for labor (Weinstein, 1968; Williams, 1973, pp. 343-412).

During the Progressive Era, those in positions of economic power feared that the urban masses would destroy the world they had built. Internal struggles developing among the wealthy heightened the tension. From all sectors came demands that new action be taken to preserve social order, and to protect private property and racial privilege (Gossett, 1965, pp. 54-369). Up to this time, those in positions of authority had assumed a laissez-faire stance, fearing that government intervention might extend to economic matters. Although there was general agreement of the need for law enforcement to maintain social order, there was profound skepticism about attempts to alleviate miserable social conditions or reform deviant individuals. Some suggested that if society consisted of a natural selection process in which the fittest would survive, then efforts to extend the life chances of the poor or "racially inferior" ran counter to the logic of nature.

Others during this era doubted the wisdom of a laissez-faire policy, and stressed that the threat of revolution and social disorder demanded scientific and rational methods to restore social order. The times demanded reform, and before the Progressive Era ended, much of the modern welfare state and the criminal justice system were constructed. Out of the turmoil of this age came such innovations as widespread use of the indeterminate sentence, the public defender movement, the beginning of efforts to professionalize the police, extensive use of parole, the rise of mental and I.Q. testing, scientific study of crime, and ultimately the juvenile court.

Within correctional institutions at this time, there was optimism that more effective methods would be found to rehabilitate offenders.

One innovation was to institute physical exercise training, along with special massage and nutritional regimens. Some believed that neglect of the body had a connection with delinquency and crime. Those who emphasized the importance of discipline in reform efforts pressed for the introduction of military drill within reform schools. There is no evidence that either of these treatment efforts had a reformative effect upon inmate. But it also is easy to understand why programs designed to keep inmates busy and under strict discipline would be popular at a time of violence and disorder within prisons and reform schools. As institutions faced continual financial difficulties, the contract labor system came under increasing attack. Criticism of reform schools resulted in laws in some states to exclude children under 12 years old from admission to reform schools. Several states abolished the contract labor system, and efforts were made to guarantee freedom of worship among inmates of institutions. Once again, pleas were made for community efforts to reduce delinquency, rather than society relying solely upon reform schools as a prevention strategy. The arguments put forth were reminiscent of those of Charles Loring Brace and the Child Savers. For example, Homer Folks (quoted in Mennel, 1973), president of the Children's Aid Society of Pennsylvania, articulated these five major problems of reform schools in 1891:

1. The temptation it offers to parents and guardians to throw off their most sacred responsibilities. . .
2. The contaminating influence of association. . .
3. The enduring stigma . . . of having been committed. . .
4. . . . renders impossible the study and treatment of each child as an individual.
5. The great dissimilarity between life in an institution and life outside. (p. 111)

One response was to promote the model of inmate self-government within the institution's walls. One such institution, the George Junior Republic, developed an elaborate system of inmate government in 1893, in which the institution became a microcosm of the outside world. Self-government was viewed as an effective control technique, because youths became enmeshed in the development and enforcement of rules, while guidelines for proper behavior continued to be set by the institutional staff. The inmates were free to construct a democracy, so long as it conformed to the wishes of the oligarchic staff (Hawes, 1971, pp. 153-157).

The populist governments of several southern states built reform schools, partly due to their opposition to the convict lease system. But these institutions too were infused with the ethos of the Jim Crow laws, which attempted to permanently legislate an inferior role for black Americans in southern society. One observer described the reform school of Arkansas as a place "where white boys might be taught some useful occupation and the negro boys compelled to work and support the institution while it is being done" (Mennel, 1973, p. 12). Black citizens, obviously displeased with discrimination within southern reform schools, proposed that separate institutions for black children should be administered by the black community. A few such institutions were established, but the majority of black children continued to be sent to jail, or were the victims of lynch mobs.

Growing doubt about the success of reform schools in reducing delinquency led some to question the wisdom of applying an unlimited *parens patriae* doctrine to youth. In legal cases, such as *The People v. Turner* (1870), *State v. Ray* (1886), and *Ex parte Becknell* (1897), judges questioned the quasi-penal character of juvenile institutions and wondered whether there ought not to be some procedural safeguards for children entering court on delinquency charges.

The state of Illinois, which eventually became the first state to establish a juvenile court law, had almost no institutions for the care of juveniles. Most early institutions in Illinois had been destroyed in fires, and those that remained were regarded as essentially prisons for children. Illinois attempted a privately financed system of institutional care, but this also failed. As a result, progressive reformers in Chicago complained of large numbers of children languishing in the county jail, and pointed out that children sometimes received undue leniency due to a lack of adequate facilities.

A new wave of Child Savers emerged, attempting to provide Chicago and the state of Illinois with a functioning system for handling wayward youth.[11] These reformers, members of the more wealthy and influential Chicago families, were spiritual heirs of Charles Loring Brace, in that they, too, feared that social unrest could destroy their authority. But through their approach, they hoped to alleviate some of the suffering of the impoverished, and ultimately win the loyalty of the poor. Reformers such as Julia Lathrop, Jane Addams, and Lucy Flower mobilized the Chicago Women's Club on behalf of juvenile justice reform. Other philanthropic groups, aligning with the powerful Chicago Bar Association, helped promote a campaign leading to the eventual drafting of the first juvenile court law in the United States. Although previous efforts had been made in Massachusetts and Pennsylvania to initiate separate trials for juveniles, the Illinois law is generally regarded as the first comprehensive child welfare legislation in this country.

The Illinois law, passed in 1899, established a children's court that would hear cases of delinquent, dependent, and neglected children. The *parens patriae* philosophy, which had imbued the reform schools, now extended to the entire court process. The definition of delinquency was broad, so that a child would be adjudged delinquent if he or she violated any state law, or any city or village ordinance. In addition, the court was given jurisdiction in cases of incorrigibility, truancy, and lack of proper parental supervision. The court had authority to institutionalize children, send them to orphanages or foster homes, or place them on probation. The law provided for unpaid probation officers, who would assist the judges and supervise youngsters. In addition, the law placed the institutions for dependent youth under the authority of the State Board of Charities, and regulated the activities of agencies sending delinquent youth from the East into Illinois.

The juvenile court idea spread so rapidly that within 10 years of the passage of the Illinois law, 10 states had established children's courts. By 1912, 22 states had juvenile court laws, and by 1925 all but 2 states had established specialized courts for children. Progressive reformers proclaimed the establishment of the juvenile court as the most significant reform of this period. The reformers celebrated what they believed to be a new age in the treatment of destitute and delinquent children. In *Commonwealth v. Fisher* (1905), the Pennsylvania Supreme Court defended the juvenile court ideal in terms reminiscent of the court opinion in the Crouse case of 1838:

> To save a child from becoming a criminal, or continuing in a career of crime, to end in maturer years in public punishment and disgrace, the legislatures surely may provide for the salvation of such a child, if its parents or guardians be unwilling or unable to do so, by bringing it into one of the courts of the state without any process at all, for the purpose of subjecting it to the state's guardianship and protection.

Critics, pointing to the large number of children who remained in jails and detention homes for long periods, expressed doubt that the court would achieve its goal. Some judges, including the famous Judge Ben Lindsey of Denver, decried the seemingly unlimited discretion of the court. With so much diversity among jurisdictions in the United States, it is difficult to describe the functioning of a typical court. As the volume of cases in the urban areas soon overwhelmed existing court resources, judges became unable to give the close personal attention to each case advocated by the reformers. As little as 10 minutes was devoted to each case as court calendars became increasingly crowded. Similarly, as caseloads soared, the quality of probationary supervision deteriorated and became perfunctory.

It is important to view the emergence of the juvenile court in the context of changes taking place in U.S. society at that time. Juvenile court drew support from a combination of optimistic social theorists, sincere social reformers, and the wealthy, who felt a need for social control. The juvenile court movement has been viewed as an attempt to stifle legal rights of children by creating a new adjudicatory process based on principles of equity law. This view misses the experimental spirit of the Progressive Era by assuming a purely conservative motivation on the part of the reformers.

Although most reformers of the period understood the relationship between poverty and delinquency, they responded with vastly different solutions. Some reformers supported large-scale experimentation with new social arrangements, such as the Cincinnati Social Unit Experiment, an early forerunner of the community organization strategy of the war on poverty of the 1960s (Shaffer, 1971, pp. 159-172). Other reformers looked to the emerging social science disciplines to provide a rational basis for managing social order. During the Progressive Era, there was growth in the profession of social work, whose members dealt directly with the poor.[12] Progressive reformers conducted social surveys to measure the amount of poverty, crime, and juvenile dependency in their communities. They supported social experiments to develop new behavior patterns among the lower classes to help them adjust to the emerging corporate economy. The development of mental testing became crucial in defining access to the channels of social mobility, and for demonstrating, to the satisfaction of the white ruling class, their own racial superiority. Moreover, biological explanations of individual and social pathology rationalized the rise in crime and social disorder, without questioning the justice or rationality of existing social arrangements.

The thrust of Progressive Era reforms was to found a more perfect control system to restore social stability while guaranteeing the continued hegemony of those with wealth and privilege. Reforms such as the juvenile court are ideologically significant because they preserved the notion that social problems (in this case delinquency, dependency, and neglect) could be dealt with on a case-by-case basis, rather than through broad-based efforts to redistribute wealth and power throughout society. The chief dilemma for advocates of the juvenile court was to develop an apparently apolitical or neutral system, while preserving differential treatment for various groups of children. The juvenile court at first lacked a core of functionaries who could supply the rationale for individualized care for wayward youth, but soon these needs were answered by the emergence of psychiatry, psychology, and criminology, as well as by the expanding profession of social work.

The Child Guidance Clinic Movement

In 1907, Illinois modified its juvenile court law to provide for paid probation officers, and the Chicago Juvenile Court moved into new facilities with expanded detention space. The Juvenile Protective League, founded by women active in establishing the first juvenile court law, was intended to stimulate the study of the conditions leading to delinquency. The members of the Juvenile Protective League were especially troubled that large numbers of wayward youth repeatedly returned to juvenile court. Jane Addams (quoted in Hawes, 1971), a major figure in U.S. philanthropy and social thought, observed, "At last it was apparent that many of the children were psychopathic cases and they and other borderline cases needed more skilled care than the most devoted probation officer could give them" (p. 244).

But the new court facilities did provide an opportunity to examine and study all children coming into the court. The Juvenile Protective League promised to oversee this study of delinquency, and Ellen Sturges Dummer donated the necessary money to support the effort. Julia Lathrop was chosen to select a qualified psychologist to head the project. After consulting with William James, she selected one of his former students, Dr. William A. Healy. Healy proposed a 4- to 5-year study to compare some 500 juvenile court clients with patients in private practice. The investigation, according to Healy (quoted in Hawes, 1971), "would have to involve all possible facts about heredity, environment, antenatal and postnatal history, etc." (p. 250).

In 1909, the Juvenile Protective League established the Juvenile Psychopathic Institute, with Healy as its first director, and Julia Lathrop, Jane Addams, and Judge Julian W. Mack on the executive committee.[13] The group, in its opening statement (Hawes, 1971), expressed its plans

> to undertake . . . an inquiry into the health of delinquent children in order to ascertain as far as possible in what degrees delinquency is caused or influenced by mental or physical defect or abnormality and with the purpose of suggesting and applying remedies in individual cases whenever practicable as a concurrent part of the inquiry. (pp. 250-251)

Jane Addams added her concern that the study investigate the conditions in which the child lives, as well as the mental and physical history of his ancestors.

Healy held an M.D. degree from the University of Chicago, and had served as a physician at the Wisconsin State Hospital. He had taught university classes in neurology, mental illness, and gynecology; had studied at the great scientific centers of Europe; and was familiar with the work of Sigmund Freud and his disciples. The major tenet of Healy's scientific credo was that the individual was the most important unit for study. Healy argued that the individualization of treatment depended upon scientific study of individual delinquents.

Healy and his associates published *The Individual Delinquent: A Textbook of Diagnosis and Prognosis for All Concerned in Understanding Offenders* in 1915. This book, based on a study of 1,000 thousand cases of repeat juvenile offenders, was intended as a practical handbook. The methodology involved a study of each offender from social, medical, and psychological viewpoints. Healy even did anthropometric measurements, suggested by Lombroso and his followers, although Healy doubted that delinquents formed a distinctive physical type.[14] But Healy never was able to locate a limited set of causes for delinquency through empirical observation. He stressed the wide range of potential causes of delinquency, including the influence of bad companions, the love of adventure, early sex experiences, and mental conflicts. At this stage Healy (quoted in Mennel, 1973) adopted an eclectic explanation of delinquency: "Our main conclusion is that every case will always need study by itself. When it comes to arraying data for the purpose of generalization about relative values of causative factors we experience difficulty" (p. 165). Despite exhaustive researches, Healy and his associates could not find distinctive mental or physical traits to delineate delinquents from nondelinquents.

Later, in 1917, Healy advanced his theory of delinquency in *Mental Conflict and Misconduct*. In this work, Healy stressed that although the individual may experience internal motivation toward misbehavior, this usually results in his merely feeling some anxiety. When mental conflict becomes more acute, the child may respond by engaging in misconduct. These ideas were heavily influenced by the work of Adolf Meyer, whose interpretation of Freud had a major influence on U.S. psychiatry. Healy (quoted in Hawes, 1973) agreed with Meyer that the family was a crucial factor in delinquency: "The basis for much prevention of mental conflict is to be found in close comfortable relations between parents and children" (p. 255). Healy's emphasis on the family was well received by those in the delinquency prevention field who had traditionally viewed the family as God's reformatory.

The significance of Healy's work cannot be overemphasized, as it provided ideological rationale to defend the juvenile court. Healy's work gave legitimacy to the flexible and discretionary operations of the court. Although some used Healy's emphasis on the individual to minimize the importance of social and economic injustice, there is evidence that Healy understood that delinquency was rooted in the nature of the social structure (Healy, Bronner, & Shimberg, 1935):

> If the roots of crime lie far back in the foundations of our social order, it may be that only a radical change can bring any large measure of cure. Less unjust social and economic conditions may be the only way out, and until a better social order exists, crime will probably continue to flourish and society continue to pay the price. (p. 211)

Healy's work also gave support to the concept of professionalism in delinquency prevention. Because juvenile delinquency was viewed as a complex problem with many possible causes, this rationale was used to explain the increased reliance on "experts." In the process, the juvenile court became insulated from critical scrutiny by its clients and the community. If actions taken by the court did not appear valid to the layman, this was because of a higher logic, known only to the experts, which explained that course of action. Moreover, the failure of a specific treatment program often was attributed to the limits of scientific knowledge, or to the failure of the court to follow scientific principles in its dispositions.

After his work in Chicago, Healy went to the Judge Harvey Baker Foundation in Boston to continue his research, where he began actual treatment of youths. Healy became a proselytizer for the child guidance clinic idea. Working with the Commonwealth Fund and the National Committee for Mental Hygiene, Healy aided the development of child guidance clinics across the nation. These efforts were so successful that by 1931, 232 such clinics were in operation.

There is even a report of a travelling child guidance clinic that visited rural communities in the West to examine children. The child guidance clinic movement became an important part of a broader campaign to provide mental hygiene services to all young people. The clinics initially were set up in connection with local juvenile courts, but later some of them became affiliated with hospitals and other community agencies.

In Sheldon and Eleanor Glueck's classic delinquency research they evaluated the success of Healy's Boston clinic. In *One Thousand Delinquents: Their Treatment by the Court and Clinic* (1934), the Gluecks found high rates of recidivism among children treated at the clinic. Healy, though deeply disappointed by the results, continued his efforts. The Gluecks continued, in a series of longitudinal studies, to search for the causes of delinquency and crime.[15] Like Healy, they maintained a focus on the individual, and they increased efforts to discover the factors behind repeated delinquency. The work of the Gluecks reflected a less optimistic attitude about the potential for treatment and rehabilitation than that found in Healy's work. They emphasized the importance of the family, often ignoring the impact of broader social and economic factors. It is ironic that the thrust of delinquency theories in the 1930s should be toward individual and family conflicts. As 20% of the American people were unemployed, the effects of the depression of the 1930s must have been apparent to the delinquents and their families, if not to the good doctors who studied them with such scientific rigor.

The Chicago Area Project

The Chicago Area Project of the early 1930s is generally considered the progenitor of large-scale, planned, community-based efforts with delinquent youth. The project differed from the dominant approaches of the time, which relied on institutional care and psychological explanations for delinquent behavior. The Chicago Area Project, conceived by University of Chicago sociologist Clifford Shaw, was an attempt to implement a sociological theory of delinquency in the delivery of preventive services. The theoretical heritage of the project is found in such works as *The Jack-Roller* (1930), *Brothers in Crime* (1936), and *Juvenile Delinquency and Urban Areas* (1969), all by Shaw and his associates. They attributed variations in delinquency rates to demographic or socioeconomic conditions in different areas of cities. This ecological approach assumed that delinquency was symptomatic of social disorganization. The adjustment problems of recent immigrants, together with other problems of urban life, strained the influence on adolescents of traditional social control agencies such as family, church, and community. Delinquency was viewed as a problem of the modern city, which was characterized by the breakdown of spontaneous or natural forces of social control. Shaw (quoted in Kobrin, 1970) contended that the rapid social change migrant rural youths are subjected to when entering the city promotes alienation from accepted modes of behavior: "When growing boys are alienated from institutions of their parents and are confronted with a vital tradition of delinquency among their peers, they engage in delinquent activity as part of their groping for a place in the only social groups available to them" (p. 579). The Chicago Area Project thus viewed delinquency as "a reversible accident of the person's social experience."

The project employed several basic operating assumptions. The first was that the delinquent is involved in a web of daily relationships. As a result, the project staff attempted to mobilize adults in the community, hoping to foster indigenous neighborhood leadership to carry out the programs with delinquent youth. The second assumption was that people participate only if they have meaningful roles; therefore the staff attempted to share decision making with neighborhood residents. To maximize community participation, staff members had to resist the urge to direct the programs themselves. The final premise of the Area Project was that within a given community there are people who, when given proper training and guidance, can organize and administer local welfare programs. A worker from within the community, with knowledge of local customs and who can communicate easily with local residents, is more effective in dealing with delinquency problems. The project staff believed that placing community residents in responsible positions would demonstrate the staff's confidence in the ability of residents to solve their own problems.

The Area Project was overseen by a board of directors, responsible for raising and distributing funds for research and community programs. In several years, 12 community committees developed Chicago as "independent, self-governing, citizens' groups, operating under their own names and charters" (Ralph Sorrento, quoted in Sechrest, 1970, p. 6). The neighborhood groups were aided by the board in obtaining grants to match local funds. Personnel from the Institute for Juvenile Research at the University of Chicago served as consultants to local groups. The various autonomous groups pursued such activities as the creation of recreation programs or of community improvement campaigns for schools, traffic safety, sanitation, and law enforcement. There were also programs aimed directly at delinquent youth, such as visitation privileges for incarcerated children, work with delinquent gangs, and volunteer assistance in parole and probation.

Most observers have concluded that the Chicago Area Project succeeded in fostering local community organizations to attack problems related to delinquency (Kobrin, 1970; Shaw & McKay, 1942). Evidence also shows that delinquency rates decreased slightly in areas affected by the project, but these results are not conclusive. Shaw (quoted in Witmer & Tufts, 1954) explained the difficulty of measuring the impact of the project as follows:

> Conclusive statistical proof to sustain any conclusion regarding the effectiveness of this work in reducing the volume of delinquency is difficult to secure for many reasons. Trends in rates for delinquents for small areas are affected by variations in the definition of what constitutes delinquent behavior, changes in the composition of the population, and changes in the administrative procedures of law enforcement agencies. (p. 16)

The Illinois State Division of Youth Services took over all 35 staff positions of the Area Project in 1957. It appears that this vibrant and successful program was quickly transformed into "a rather staid, bureaucratic organization seeking to accommodate itself to the larger social structure, that is, to work on behalf of agencies who came into the community rather than for itself or for community residents" (Sechrest, 1970, p. 15).

The Chicago Area Project, with its grounding in sociological theory and its focus on citizen involvement, contrasts sharply with other delinquency prevention efforts of the 1930s. Its focus on prevention in the community raised questions about the continued expansion of institutions for delinquent youth. Although some attributed support of the project to the personal dynamism of Clifford Shaw, this ignores the basic material and ideological motivation behind it. It would be equally shortsighted to conclude that child saving would not have occurred without Charles Loring Brace, or that the child guidance clinic movement resulted solely from the labors of William Healy. Certainly Shaw was an important advocate of the Chicago Area Project approach, and his books influenced professionals in the field, but the growth of the project also was a product of the times.

Because no detailed history exists of the founding and operation of the project, we can only speculate about the forces that shaped its development. We do know that Chicago at that time was caught in the most serious economic depression in the nation's history. Tens of thousands of people were unemployed, especially immigrants and blacks. During this period, a growing radicalization among impoverished groups resulted in urban riots (Cloward & Piven, 1971). The primary response by those in positions of power was to expand and centralize charity and welfare systems. In addition, there was considerable experimentation with new methods of delivering relief services to the needy. No doubt, Chicago's wealthy looked favorably upon programs such as the Area Project, which promised to alleviate some of the problems of the poor without requiring a redistribution of wealth or power. Both the prestige of the University of Chicago and the close supervision promised by Shaw and his associates helped assuage the wealthy and the powerful. Shaw and his associates did not advocate fundamental social change, and project personnel were advised to avoid leading communities toward changes perceived as too radical (Alinsky, 1946). Communities were encouraged to work within the system, and to organize around issues at a neighborhood level. Project participants rarely questioned the relationship of urban conditions to the political and economic superstructure of the city.

Later interpreters of the Chicago Area Project did not seem to recognize the potentially radical strategy of community organization within poor neighborhoods. Its immediate legacy was twofold: the use of detached workers, who dealt with gangs outside the agency office, and the idea of using indigenous workers in social control efforts. Although detached workers became a significant part of the delinquency prevention strategy of the next 3 decades, the use of indigenous personnel received little more than lip service, because welfare and juvenile justice agencies hired few urban poor.

The success of the Area Project depended upon relatively stable and well-organized neighborhoods with committed local leaders. Changes in the urban structure that developed over the next 2 decades did not fit the Chicago Area Project model. The collapse of southern agriculture and mass migration by rural blacks into the cities of the North and West produced major social structural changes. This movement to the North and West began in the 1920s, decreased somewhat during the depression years, and later accelerated due to the attraction provided by the war industry jobs. During this same period large numbers of Puerto Ricans settled in New York City and other eastern cities. Although economic opportunity attracted new migrants to the urban centers, there was little satisfaction for their collective dreams. Blacks, who left the South to escape the Jim Crow laws, soon were confronted by de facto segregation in schools, in the workplace, and in housing. Job prospects were slim for blacks and Puerto Ricans, and both groups were most vulnerable to being fired at the whims of employers. In many respects, racism in the North rivalled that of the South. The new migrants had the added difficulty of adapting their primarily rural experiences to life in large urban centers (Coles, 1967; Handlin, 1959).

Racial ghettos became places of poverty, disease, and crime. For the more privileged classes, the situation paralleled that of 16th-century European city dwellers who feared the displaced peasantry, or that of Americans at the beginning of the 19th century who feared the Irish immigrants. During this period, riots erupted in East St. Louis, Detroit, Harlem, and Los Angeles. To upper-class observers, these new communities of poor black and brown peoples were disorganized collections of criminals and deviants. Racism prevented white observers from recognizing the vital community traditions or the family stability that persisted despite desperate economic conditions. Moreover, the label "disorganized communities" could be used ideologically to mask the involvement of wealthy whites in the creation of racial ghettos (Ryan, 1971). A liberal social theory was developing that, though benign on the surface, actually blamed the victims for the conditions in which they were caught. Attention was focused upon deviant aspects of community life, ascribing a culture of poverty and violence to inner-city residents, and advocating remedial work with individuals and groups to solve so-called problems of adjustment. The following quote from the National Commission on the Causes and Prevention of Violence (1969) is illustrative of this posture:

> The cultural experience which Negroes brought with them from segregation and discrimination in the rural South was of less utility in the process of adaption to urban life than was the cultural experience of many European immigrants. The net effect of these differences is that urban slums have tended to become ghetto slums from which escape has been increasingly difficult. (p. 30)

Delinquency theorists suggested that lower-class communities were becoming more disorganized, because they were not characterized by the stronger ties of older ethnic communities (Cloward & Piven, 1971):

> Slum neighborhoods appear to us to be undergoing progressive disintegration. The old structures, which provided social control and avenues

of social ascent, are breaking down. Legitimate but functional substi-
tutes for these traditional structures must be developed if we are to stem
the trend towards violence and retreatism among adolescents in urban
slums. (p. 211)

Irving Spergel, leading authority on juvenile gangs, suggests that social
work agencies made little use of indigenous workers after World War
II because delinquency had become more aggressive and violent. Welfare and criminal justice officials argued that only agencies with sound
funding and strong leadership could mobilize the necessary resources
to deal with the increased incidence and severity of youth crime.

The movement toward more agency involvement brought with it a
distinctly privileged-class orientation toward delinquency prevention.
Social service agencies were preeminently the instruments of those with
sufficient wealth and power to enforce their beliefs. The agencies were
equipped to redirect, rehabilitate, and, in some cases, control those who
seemed most threatening to the status quo. Workers for these agencies
helped to perpetuate a conception of proper behavior for the poor,
consistent with their expected social role. For example, the poor are told
to defer gratification and save for the future, but the rich often are
"conspicuous consumers." Whereas poor women are expected to stay
at home and raise their families, the same conduct is not uniformly
applied to wealthy women. The well-to-do provide substantial funding
for private social service agencies, and often become members of the
boards that define policies for agencies in inner-city neighborhoods.
The criteria for staffing these agencies during the 2 decades following
World War II included academic degrees and special training that were
not made available to the poor or people of color.

Social agencies, ideologically rooted and controlled outside poor
urban neighborhoods, often were pressured to respond to "serious"
delinquency problems. During this period, the fighting gang, which
symbolized organized urban violence, received the major share of
delinquency prevention efforts. Most agencies, emphasizing psycho-
analytic or group dynamic approaches to delinquency, located the
origin of social disruption in the psychopathology of individuals and
small groups. The consequence of this orientation was that special
youth workers were assigned to troublesome gangs in an attempt to
redirect the members toward more conventional conduct. Little effort was made to develop local leadership, or to confront the issues
of racism and poverty.

Detached worker programs emphasized treatment by individual
workers, freed from the agency office base, operating in neighbor-

hood settings. These programs, with several variations, followed a basic therapeutic model. Workers initially entered gang territories, taking pains to make their entrance as inconspicuous as possible. The first contacts were made at natural meeting places in the community such as pool rooms, candy stores, or street corners (Klein, 1969):

> Accordingly, the popular image of the detached worker is a young man in informal clothing, standing on a street corner near a food stand, chatting with a half dozen rough, ill-groomed, slouching teenagers. His posture is relaxed, his countenance earnest, and he is listening to the boys through a haze of cigarette smoke. (p. 143)

The worker gradually introduced himself to the gang members. He made attempts to get jobs for them, or arranged recreational activities, while at the same time persuading the members to give up their illegal activities. Manuals for detached workers explained that the approach would work because gang members had never before encountered sympathetic, nonpunitive adults, who were not trying to manipulate them for dishonest purposes. A typical report (Crawford, Malamud, & Dumpson, 1970) states, "Their world (as they saw it) did not contain any giving, accepting people—only authorities, suckers and hoodlums like themselves" (p. 630). This particular account even suggests that some boys were willing to accept the worker as an *idealized father.* The worker was expected to influence the overall direction of the gang, but if that effort failed, he was to foment trouble among members and incite disputes over leadership. Information that the workers gathered under promises of confidentiality was often shared with police gang-control officers. Thus, despite their surface benevolence, these workers were little more than undercover agents whose ultimate charge was to break up or disrupt groups that were feared by the establishment. These techniques, which focused on black and brown youth gangs in the 1950s, were similar to those later used with civil rights groups and organizations protesting the Vietnam War.

There were many critics of the detached worker programs. Some argued that the workers actually lent status to fighting gangs, and thus created more violence. Other critics claimed that the workers often developed emotional attachments to youthful gang members, and were manipulated by them (Mattick & Caplan, 1967). Community residents often objected to the presence of detached workers, because it was feared they would provide information to downtown social welfare agencies. Although studies of the detached worker

programs did not yield positive results, virtually all major delinquency programs from the late 1940s to the 1960s used detached
workers in an attempt to "reach the fighting gang."

The Mobilization for Youth

During the late 1950s economic and social conditions were becoming more acute in the urban centers of the United States. The economy was becoming sluggish, and unemployment began to rise. Black
teenagers experienced especially high unemployment rates, and the
discrepancy between white and black income and material conditions grew each year. Technological changes in the economy contin-
ually drove more unskilled laborers out of the labor force. Social
scientists such as Daniel Moynihan (1969) and Sidney Wilhelm (1970)
view this period as the time in which a substantial number of blacks
became permanently unemployed. Social control specialists for the
privileged class surveyed the problem, and sought ways to defuse
the social danger of a surplus labor population.

The Ford Foundation was influential during this period in stimu-
lating conservative local officials to adopt more enlightened strategies in dealing with the poor (Marris & Rein, 1967, pp. 7-32; Moynihan,
1969, pp. 21-37). Once again an ideological clash occurred between
those favoring scientific and rational government programs and
those who feared the growth of the state, demanded balanced government budgets, and opposed liberal programs to improve the
quality of life of the poor. The Ford Foundation, through its Grey
Areas projects, spent large amounts of money in several U.S. cities
to foster research and planning of new programs to deal with delinquency and poverty.

The most significant program to develop out of the Grey Area
projects was the Mobilization for Youth, which began in New York
City in 1962 after 5 years of planning. It aimed to service a population
of 107,000 (approximately one-third black and Puerto Rican), living
in 67 blocks of New York City's Lower East Side. The unemployment
rate of the area was twice that of the city overall, and the delinquency
rate also was high.

The theoretical perspective of the project was drawn from the work
of Richard Cloward and Lloyd Ohlin (described in Weissman, 1969):

"a unifying principle of expanding opportunities has worked out as the
direct basis for action." This principle was drawn from the concepts

outlined by the sociologists Richard Cloward and Lloyd Ohlin in their book *Delinquency and Opportunity*. Drs. Cloward and Ohlin regarded delinquency as the result of the disparity perceived by low-income youths between their legitimate aspirations and the opportunities—social, economic, political, education—made available to them by society. If the gap between opportunity and aspiration could be bridged, they believed delinquency could be reduced; that would be the agency's goal. (p. 19)

The Mobilization for Youth project involved five areas: work training, education, group work and community organization, services to individuals and families, and training and personnel. But the core of the mobilization was to organize area residents to realize "the power resources of the community by creating channels through which consumers of social welfare services can define their problems and goals and negotiate on their own behalf" (Brager & Purcell, 1967, p. 247). Local public and private bureaucracies became the targets of mass protests by agency workers and residents. The strategy of the Mobilization for Youth (MFY) assumed that social conflict was necessary in the alleviation of the causes of delinquency. Shortly after the MFY became directly involved with struggles over the redistribution of power and resources, New York City officials charged that the organization was "riot-producing, Communist-oriented, left-wing and corrupt" (Weissman, 1969, pp. 25-28). In the ensuing months, the director resigned, funds were limited, and virtually all programs were stopped until after the 1964 presidential election. After January 1965, the MFY moved away from issues and protests toward more traditional approaches to social programming, such as detached-gang work, job training, and counseling.

Another project, Haryou-Act (Harlem Youth Opportunities Unlimited), which was developed in the black community of Harlem in New York City, experienced a similar pattern of development and struggle. The Harlem program was supported by the theory and prestige of psychologist Kenneth Clark, who suggested in *Dark Ghetto* (1965) that delinquency is rooted in feelings of alienation and powerlessness among ghetto residents. The solution, according to Clark, was to engage in community organizing to gain power for the poor. Haryou-Act met sharp resistance from city officials, who labelled the staff as corrupt and infiltrated by Communists.

Both the MFY and Haryou-Act received massive operating funds. The Mobilization for Youth received approximately $2 million a year, Haryou-Act received about $1 million a year, and 14 similar projects received over $7 million from the federal Office of Juvenile Delinquency.[16] It was significant that for the first time the federal government was pumping large amounts of money in the delinquency prevention effort. Despite intense resistance to these efforts in most cities because local public officials felt threatened, the basic model of the Mobilization for Youth was incorporated into the community action component of the War on Poverty.

In 1967, when social scientists and practitioners developed theories of delinquency prevention for President Lyndon Johnson's Crime Commission, the MFY still was basic to their thinking (President's Commission on Law Enforcement and the Administration of Justice, 1967). Their problem was to retain a focus upon delivery of remedial services in education, welfare, and job training to the urban poor without creating the intense political conflict engendered by the community action approach. The issue was complicated because leaders such as Malcolm X and Cesar Chavez, and groups such as the Black Muslims and the Black Panther Party, articulated positions of self-determination and community control. These proponents of ethnic pride and "power to the people" argued that welfare efforts controlled from outside were subtle forms of domestic colonialism. The riots of the mid-1960s dramatized the growing gap between people of color in the United States and their more affluent "benefactors."

It is against this backdrop of urban violence, a growing distrust of outsiders, and increased community-generated self-help efforts that delinquency prevention efforts of the late 1960s and early 1970s developed. A number of projects during this period attempted to reach the urban poor, who had been actively involved in ghetto riots during the 1960s. In Philadelphia, members of a teenage gang were given funds to make a film and start their own businesses. Chicago youth gangs such as Black P. Stone Nation and the Vice Lords were subsidized by federal funding, the YMCA, and the Sears Foundation. In New York City, a Puerto Rican youth group, the Young Lords, received funds to engage in self-help activities. In communities across the nation there was a rapid development of summer projects in recreation, employment, and sanitation to help carry an anxious white America through each potentially long, hot summer. Youth patrols were even organized by police departments to employ ghetto youths to "cool out" trouble that might lead to riots. Few of the programs produced the desired results and often resulted in accusations of improperly used funds by the communities. Often financial audits and investigations were made to discredit community organizers, and accuse them of encouraging political conflicts with local officials.

One proposed solution that offered more possibility of controlled social action to benefit the young was the Youth Service Bureau (Norman, 1972). The first Youth Service Bureaus (YSBs) were composed of people from the communities and representatives of public agencies who would hire professionals to deliver a broad range of services to young people. The central idea was to promote cooperation between justice and welfare agencies and the local communities. Agency representatives were expected to contribute partial operating expenses for the programs and, together with neighborhood representatives, decide on program content. Proponents of the YSB approach stressed the need for diverting youthful offenders from the criminal justice system, and for delivering necessary social services to deserving children and their families. Ideally the YSBs were designed to increase public awareness of the need for more youth services.

The Youth Service Bureaus generally met with poor results. Intense conflict often arose between community residents and agency personnel over the nature of program goals, and YSBs were criticized for not being attuned to community needs (Duxbury, 1972; U.S. Department of Health, Education, and Welfare, 1973). Funds for these efforts were severely limited in relation to the social problems they sought to rectify. In some jurisdictions YSBs were controlled by police or probation departments, with no direct community input. These agency-run programs temporarily diverted youths from entering the criminal justice process by focusing on services, such as counseling.

The most important aspect of the YSBs was their attempt to operationalize the diversion of youth from the juvenile justice process, although the effort's success seems highly questionable. Some argue that diversion programs violate the legal rights of youths, as they imply a guilty plea. Others warn that diversion programs expand the welfare bureaucracy, because youths who once simply would have been admonished and sent home by police now are channelled into therapeutic programs. Still others believe that diversion without social services does not prevent delinquency. In any case, a major shift has occurred from the community participation focus of the Mobilization for Youth to a system in which community inputs are limited and carefully controlled. This change in operational philosophy often is justified by the need to secure continued funding, as well as by claims of increasing violence by delinquents. But it is important to remember that these same rationales were used to justify a move away from the community organizing model of the

Chicago Area Projects of the 1930s. Whenever residents become involved in decision making, there are inevitably increased demands for control of social institutions affecting the community. Such demands for local autonomy question the existing distributions of money and power, and thus challenge the authority of social control agencies.

Institutional Change and Community-Based Corrections

Correctional institutions for juvenile delinquents were subject to many of the same social structural pressures as community prevention efforts. For instance, there was a disproportionate increase in the number of youths in correctional facilities as blacks migrated to the North and the West. In addition, criticism of the use of juvenile inmate labor, especially by organized labor, disrupted institutional routines. But throughout the late 1930s and the 1940s increasing numbers of youths were committed to institutions. Later on, the emergence of ethnic pride and calls for black and brown power would cause dissension within the institutions.

The creation of the California Youth Authority (CYA) just prior to the Second World War centralized the previously disjointed Californian correctional institutions.[17] During the 1940s and 1950s, California, Wisconsin, and Minnesota developed separate versions of the Youth Authority concept. Under the Youth Authority model, criminal courts committed youthful offenders from 16 to 21 years old to an administrative authority, which determined the proper correctional disposition.[18] The CYA was responsible for all juvenile correctional facilities, including the determination of placements, and parole. Rather than reducing the powers of the juvenile court judge, the Youth Authority streamlined the dispositional process in order to add administrative flexibility. The Youth Authority was introduced into California at a time when detention facilities were overcrowded, institutional commitment rates were rising, and the correctional system was fragmented and compartmentalized.

The Youth Authority model was developed by the American Law Institute, which drew up model legislation, and lobbied for its adoption in state legislatures. The American Law Institute is a nonprofit organization, seeking to influence the development of law and criminal justice. The institution is oriented toward efficiency, rationality, and effectiveness in legal administration.

The treatment philosophy of the first Youth Authorities was similar to the approach of William Healy and the child guidance clinic.

John Ellingston, formerly chief legislative lobbyist for the American Law Institute in California, related a debate between Healy and Clifford Shaw over the theoretical direction the new Youth Authority should follow. The legislators, persuaded by Healy's focus on diagnosis of individual delinquents, ensured that the clinic model became the dominant approach in California institutions.

Sociologist Edwin Lemert attributed the emergence of the California Youth Authority to the growth of an "administrative state" in the United States. In support of this assertion Lemert noted the trend toward more centralized delivery of welfare services and increased government regulation of the economy, together with the "militarization" of U.S. society produced by war. Lemert, however, did not discuss whether the purpose of this "administrative state" was to preserve the existing structure of privilege. The first stated purpose of the California Youth Authority was "to protect society by substituting training and treatment for retributive punishment of young persons found guilty of public offenses" (Lemert, 1948, pp. 49-50).

The centralization of youth correction agencies enabled them to claim the scarce state delinquency prevention funds. In-house research units publicized the latest treatment approaches. In the 1950s and the 1960s psychologically oriented treatment approaches, including guided-group interaction and group therapy, were introduced in juvenile institutions. In this period of optimism and discovery many new diagnostic and treatment approaches were evaluated. Correctional administrators and social scientists hoped for a significant breakthrough in treatment, but it never came. Although some questionable evaluation studies claimed successes, there is no evidence that the new therapies had a major impact on recidivism. In fact, some people began to question the concept of enforced therapy, and argued that treatment-oriented prisons might be more oppressive than more traditional institutional routines (Mathieson, 1965). Intense objections have been raised particularly against drug therapies and behavior modification programs. Takagi views this as the period when brainwashing techniques were first used on juvenile and adult offenders.[19]

Another major innovation of the 1960s was the introduction of community-based correctional facilities. The central idea was that rehabilitation could be accomplished more effectively outside conventional correctional facilities. This led to a series of treatment measures such as group homes, partial release programs, halfway houses, and attempts to decrease commitment rates to juvenile institutions. California was particularly active in developing community-based correctional programming. The Community Treatment Project, designed by Marguerite Warren in California, was an attempt to replace institutional treatment with intensive parole supervision and psychologically oriented therapy. Probation subsidy involved a bold campaign by CYA staff to convince the state legislature to give cash subsidies to local counties to encourage them to treat juvenile offenders in local programs. Probation subsidy programs were especially oriented toward strengthening the capacity of county probation departments to supervise youthful offenders.[20]

Proponents of the various community-based programs argued that correctional costs could be reduced and rehabilitation results improved in a community context. Reducing state expenditures became more attractive as state governments experienced the fiscal crunch of the late 1960s and the 1970s.[21] It also was thought that reducing institutional populations would alleviate tension and violence within the institutions. But it appears that these community alternatives have created a situation in which youngsters who are sent to institutions are perceived as more dangerous and, as a result, are kept in custody for longer periods of time.

The ultimate logic of the community-based corrections model was followed by the Department of Youth Services in Massachusetts, which closed all of its training schools for delinquents. Youngsters were transferred to group-home facilities, and services were offered to individual children on a community basis (Bakal, 1973). The Massachusetts strategy met intense public criticism by juvenile court judges, correctional administrators, and police officials. Some recent attempts have been made to discredit this policy, and to justify continued operation of correction facilities. But the Massachusetts strategy has influenced a move to de-institutionalize children convicted of status offenses—those considered crimes only if committed by children, such as truancy, running away, or incorrigibility. In 1975, the federal government made $15 million available to local governments that developed plans to de-institutionalize juvenile status offenders.

At the moment, the forces opposing institutionalized care are making ideological headway, due to past failures of institutional methods in controlling delinquency. But previous experience suggests that the pendulum is likely to swing back in favor of the institutional approaches. Already there is increased talk about the "violent" delinquent and the alleged increases in violent youth crime; these words have always signalled the beginning of an ideological campaign to promote more stringent control measures and extended incarceration or detention. It is also significant that most states are not firmly committed to community-based treatment. Most jurisdictions still rely on placement in institutions, with conditions reminiscent of reform schools 100 years ago. Children continue to be warehoused in large correctional facilities, receiving little care or attention. Eventually they are returned to substandard social conditions to survive as best they can.

Changes in Juvenile Court Law

In the late 1960s, the growing awareness of the limitations of the juvenile justice system resulted in a series of court decisions that altered the character of the juvenile court. In *Kent v. United States* (1966) the Supreme Court warned juvenile courts against "procedural arbitrariness," and in *In re Gault* (1967) the Court recognized the rights of juveniles in such matters as notification of charges, protection against self-incrimination, the right to confront witnesses, and the right to have a written transcript of the proceedings. Justice Abe Fortas wrote, "Under our Constitution the condition of being a boy does not justify a kangaroo court" (*In re Gault*, 1967). The newly established rights of juveniles were not welcomed by most juvenile court personnel, who claimed that the informal humanitarian court process would be replaced by a junior criminal court. Communities struggled with methods of providing legal counsel to indigent youth, and with restructuring court procedures to conform to constitutional requirements.

The principles set forth in Kent and later in the Gault decision offer only limited procedural safeguards to delinquent youth (Kittrie, 1971, pp. 113-153). Many judicial officers believe the remedy to juvenile court problems is not more formality in proceedings, but more treatment resources. In *McKiever v. Pennsylvania* (1971), the Supreme Court denied that jury trials were a constitutional requirement for the juvenile court. Many legal scholars believe the current Supreme Court has a solid majority opposing extension of procedural rights to alleged delinquents. The dominant view is close to the opinion expressed by Chief Justice Warren Burger in the Winship case (*In re Winship*, 1970):

> What the juvenile court systems need is less not more of the trappings of legal procedure and judicial formalism; the juvenile court system requires breathing room and flexibility in order to survive the repeated

assaults on this court. The real problem was not the deprivation of
constitutional rights but inadequate juvenile court staffs and facilities.

The Supreme Court's decision in *Schall v. Martin* (1984) signalled
a much more conservative judicial response to children's rights.
Plaintiffs in *Schall v. Martin* challenged the constitutionality of New
York's Family Court Act as it pertained to the preventive detention
of juveniles. It was alleged that the law was too vague and that
juveniles were denied due process. A federal district court struck
down the statute and its decision was affirmed by the U.S. Court of
Appeals. However, the U.S. Supreme Court reversed the lower courts,
holding that the preventive detention of juveniles to protect against
future crimes was a legitimate state action.

The Emergence of a Conservative Agenda
for Juvenile Justice

From the late 1970s and into the 1980s a conservative reform
agenda dominated the national debates over juvenile justice. This
new perspective emphasized deterrence and punishment as the major
goals of the juvenile court. Conservatives called for the vigorous
prosecution of serious and violent youthful offenders. They alleged
that the juvenile court was overly lenient with dangerous juveniles.
Conservatives also questioned the wisdom of diverting status
offenders from secure custody. The Reagan administration introduced new programs in the areas of "missing children" and child
pornography, which were problems allegedly created by the liberal
response to status offenders. Substantial amounts of federal funds
were spent on police intelligence programs and enhanced prosecution of juvenile offenders.
Changes in federal policy also were reflected in the actions of
many state legislatures. Beginning in 1976, over half the states made
it easier to transfer youth to adult courts. Other states stiffened
penalties for juvenile offenders via mandatory minimum sentencing
guidelines.
The most obvious impact of the conservative reform movement
was a significant increase in the number of youth in juvenile correctional facilities. In addition, from 1979 to 1984 the number of juveniles sent to adult prisons rose by 48%. By 1985 the Bureau of Justice
Statistics reported that two thirds of the nation's training schools
were chronically overcrowded.

Another ominous sign was the growing proportion of minority youth in public correctional facilities. In 1982 more than half of those in public facilities were minority youth, whereas two thirds of those in private juvenile facilities were white. Between 1979 and 1982, when the number of incarcerated youth grew by 6,178, minority youth accounted for 93% of the increase. The sharp rise in incarceration occurred even though the number of arrests of minority youth declined.

Summary

We have traced the history of the juvenile justice system in the United States in relation to significant population migrations, rapid urbanization, race conflicts, and transformation in the economy. These factors continue to influence the treatment of children. The juvenile justice system traditionally has focused on the alleged pathological nature of delinquents, ignoring how the problems of youths relate to larger political and economic issues. Both institutional and community-based efforts to rehabilitate delinquents have been largely unsuccessful. Those with authority for reforming the juvenile justice system have traditionally supported and defended the values and interests of the well-to-do. Not surprisingly, juvenile justice reforms have inexorably increased state control over the lives of the poor and their children. The central implication of this historical analysis is that the future of delinquency prevention and control will be determined largely by ways in which the social structure evolves.[22] It is possible that this future belongs to those who wish to advance social justice on behalf of young people rather than to accommodate the class interests that have dominated this history (Krisberg, 1975a; Liazos, 1974). But one must be cautious about drawing direct inferences for specific social reforms from this historical summary. William Appleman Williams (1973) reminds us, "History offers no answers per se, it only offers a way of encouraging people to use their own minds to make their own history" (p. 480).

Notes

1. Thorsten Sellin, *Pioneering in Penology*, provides an excellent description of the Amsterdam House of Corrections.
2. This issue is well treated by Winthrop Jordan in *The White Man's Burden*.

3. Sources of primary material are N. R. Yetman, *Voices From Slavery,* and Gerda Lerner, *Black Women in White America.* Another fascinating source of data is Margaret Walker's historical novel, *Jubilee.*

4. Historical data on the 19th century relies on the scholarship of Robert Mennel, *Thorns and Thistles;* Anthony Platt, *The Child Savers: The Invention of Delinquency;* Joseph Hawes, *Children in Urban Society: Juvenile Delinquency in Nineteenth Century America;* and the document collection of Robert Bremner et al. in *Children and Youth in America: A Documentary History.*

5. *Delinquent children* are those in violation of criminal codes, statutes, and ordinances. *Dependent children* are those in need of proper and effective parental care or control but having no parent or guardian to provide such care. *Neglected children* are destitute, are unable to secure the basic necessities of life, or have unfit homes due to neglect or cruelty.

6. A good description of anti-Irish feeling during this time is provided by John Higham, *Strangers in the Land.*

7. The preoccupation with the sexuality of female delinquents continues today. See Meda Chesney-Lind, "Juvenile Delinquency: The Sexualization of Female Crime."

8. This routine is reminiscent of the style of 18th-century American Indian schools. It represents an attempt to re-create the ideal of colonial family life, which was being replaced by living patterns accommodated to industrial growth and development.

9. The term *dangerous classes* was coined by Charles Loring Brace in his widely read *The Dangerous Classes of New York and Twenty Years Among Them.*

10. The classic of these studies is that of E. C. Wines, *The State of Prisons and Child-Saving Institutions in the Civilized World,* first printed in 1880.

11. Platt, *The Child Savers: The Invention of Delinquency,* pp. 101-136; and Hawes, *Children in Urban Society: Juvenile Delinquency in Nineteenth Century America,* pp. 158-190, provide the most thorough discussions of the origins of the first juvenile court law.

12. Roy Lubove, *The Professional Altruist,* is a good discussion of the rise of social work as a career.

13. A few earlier clinics specialized in care of juveniles, but these had mostly dealt with feebleminded youngsters.

14. Anthropometric measurements assess human body measurements on a comparative basis. A popular theory of the day was that criminals have distinctive physical traits that can be scientifically measured.

15. Longitudinal studies analyze a group of subjects over time.

16. By comparison, the Chicago Area Project operated on about $283,000 a year.

17. John Ellingston, *Protecting Our Children From Criminal Careers,* provides an extensive discussion of the development of the California Youth Authority.

18. California originally set the maximum jurisdictional age at 23 years, but later reduced it to 21. Some states used an age limit of 18 years, so that they dealt strictly with juveniles. In California, both juveniles and adults were included in the Youth Authority model.

19. Paul Takagi, in "The Correctional System," cites Edgar Schein, "Man Against Man: Brainwashing," and James McConnell, "Criminals Can Be Brainwashed—Now," for candid discussions of this direction in correctional policy.

20. Paul Lerman, *Community Corrections and Social Control,* is a provocative evaluation of the Community Treatment Project and Probation Subsidy.

21. See James O'Connor, *The Fiscal Crisis of the State,* for a discussion of the causes of this fiscal crunch.

22. This perspective is similar to that of Rusche and Kirchheimer in their criminological classic, *Punishment and Social Structure.*

3

The Contemporary Juvenile Justice System

Its Structure and Operation

Introduction

As indicated in Chapter 2, the founders of the juvenile court intended to create a *flexible and individualized* system of dealing with wayward youth. The early juvenile court made virtually no distinctions in its handling of delinquents, status offenders, and non-offenders (generally this last category includes abused, dependent, and neglected children). But not until the late 1960s did the legislative and judicial branches of government begin to formalize the procedures of courts and require greater differentiation in the handling of various types of youths.

For example, at the national level, the pioneering Federal Juvenile Justice and Delinquency Prevention Act of 1974 (JJDPA) offered the first clear signal to states and localities to remove status offenders from secure detention and correctional facilities and to separate juvenile from adult offenders. Most states now have revamped their relevant statutes to comply with the JJDPA requirements. However, despite sweeping reforms, the juvenile justice system continues to rely on fundamental premises favoring informal and highly discretionary processes.

The juvenile justice system receives referrals from a range of institutions and agencies including law enforcement, school, social service, community based, and parental. Similarly, the juvenile court employs a much broader range of dispositional options than the adult criminal justice system. Juvenile corrections encompass a diverse array of facilities of varying sizes, security levels, and purposes (Krisberg, 1975a; Quinney, 1969).[1] These facilities are operated by all levels of government as well as by private not-for-profit and for-profit agencies. For example, it is not uncommon to find youths being held in detention centers, after adjudication as wards of the court, who are awaiting transfers to group homes or foster placements operated under the auspices of private agencies (under contract with a state or county welfare department).

Another important aspect of the juvenile justice system is the enormous range in age among the states for court jurisdiction. In most states the age at which criminal court jurisdiction attaches is 18 years. Many states have established both upper and lower limits for juvenile court jurisdiction. However, a mélange of statutory provisions permit transfers or waivers of youths from juvenile to adult court. In summary, the 51 distinct juvenile justice systems operating today enjoy a great deal of unbridled discretion in terms of how they intervene in the lives of troubled youth.

In this chapter, we analyze how the current juvenile justice system is structured and its influence on today's youth. We begin by describing the flow of youth from the point of arrest through adjudication. The remainder of the chapter is spent describing the diverse and often contradictory purposes of the juvenile justice system that today attempts to control children who are officially perceived as troublesome or dangerous. A review is made of the juvenile codes that individual jurisdictions have constructed for their own juvenile justice systems. Issues such as definitions of delinquency, the structure and jurisdiction of the court, and the adjudicatory processes are examined in detail (Krisberg, 1975; Quinney, 1969).

Second, we analyze those agencies that uphold juvenile laws: law enforcement, prosecutors, public defenders, probation departments, and judges. In particular, we review the considerable and growing body of research that shows the impact of organizational factors and biases that negatively influence the court's ability to administer justice in an even-handed manner.

TABLE 3.1   Juvenile Arrests by Crime Type, 1990

Crime Type	N	Percentage
Index violent	91,317	5.2
Criminal homicide	2,555	0.1
Forcible rape	4,628	0.3
Robbery	32,967	1.9
Aggravated assault	51,167	2.9
Index property	564,060	32.1
Burglary	112,437	6.4
Larceny theft	372,133	21.2
Motor vehicle theft	72,930	4.2
Arson	6,560	0.4
Nonindex	1,099,165	62.6
Simple assault	119,058	6.8
Stolen property	NA	NA
Vandalism	103,754	5.9
Weapons	31,991	1.8
Other sex crimes	13,507	0.8
Drug law violations	64,740	3.7
Liquor law violations	122,047	7.0
Disorderly conduct	95,999	5.5
Other delinquent acts	480,406	27.4
Curfew and loitering	3,095	0.2
Runaways	64,568	3.7
Total Arrests	1,754,542	100.0

SOURCE: *Crime in the United States, 1990,* Uniform Crime Reports, U.S. Department of Justice, Federal Bureau of Investigation, August 11, 1991.

The Numbers of Youth Arrested and Referred to the Juvenile Court

The scope of the juvenile justice system in terms of its intrusion in the lives of our nation's youth is startling. In 1990 more than 1.7 million arrests were made of children under the age of 18, as shown in Table 3.1. The vast majority (88%) of these arrests were for non-violent crimes. Almost 4% of juvenile arrests were for "noncriminal" or status offenses such as truancy, curfew violations, or running away from home.

Because the vast majority of these youth are only between the ages of 10 and 17 it is possible to calculate the chances that a child will be arrested by police and referred to the juvenile court for further processing and sentencing. Approximately 6 out of every 100 children between the ages of 10 and 17 are arrested each year (Center for the Study of Youth Policy, 1990, p. 9). For males, who represent almost 80% of all arrests, the rate is nearly 8 per 100 male youth as opposed to the female rate of more than 2 per 100 young women of the same age group. Wolfgang, Figlio, and Sellin (1972) estimate that one third of the children in an urban birth cohort will have some contact with police by the time they reach age 18, and most of this group will come from lower-class and minority communities.

Most of these arrests triggered a referral to the juvenile justice system. The most recent national juvenile justice data show that, in 1988, nearly 1.2 million juvenile cases (or approximately 86% of all arrests) were referred to the juvenile courts (see Table 3.2). As with arrests, the vast majority of these referrals were for nonviolent crimes (84%, including simple assault). Approximately 1 out of every 20 referrals was a status offense and an additional 18% were for crimes against the "public order."

If one uses referral rates per 100 youth age 10-17, approximately 6 out of every 100 children were referred to the juvenile court in 1998 for delinquency and status offenses (Office of Juvenile Justice and Delinquency Prevention, 1991, pp. 61, 103). For males the referral rate was nearly 1 out of 10. A study of juvenile court referrals in the state of Utah and in Phoenix, Arizona (Snyder, 1988), found that one third of all youth born between 1962 and 1965 were referred to the court at least once before their 18th birthday. In that study the chance of a male being referred was one out of two.

Once a youth is referred to the court a number of decisions must be made that will determine the fate of the youth. Table 3.3 shows how the 1.2 million court delinquency and status offense referrals were processed by the juvenile justice system in 1988. The rest of this chapter discusses in greater detail the basis for these decision points. However, it is important to note the following major trends:

1. Only about half (52%) of the referrals result in a petition being filed against the youth. The petition is analogous to a complaint being filed by the prosecutor.
2. Less than one third (30%) of the referrals are formally adjudicated by the courts.
3. Less than 1% of all referrals are waived to the adult courts for trial as an adult.
4. For those cases that are not waived, the most frequent dispositions are either dismissal of charges or placement on probation (37% each, or a total of 74%).

TABLE 3.2 Juvenile Court Referrals by Crime Type, 1988

Crime Type	N	Percentage
Index violent	68,400	5.4
Criminal homicide	1,700	0.1
Forcible rape	4,000	0.3
Robbery	21,300	1.7
Aggravated assault	41,400	3.3
Index property	503,000	40.5
Burglary	130,500	10.5
Larceny theft	311,100	25.1
Motor vehicle theft	54,700	4.4
Arson	6,700	0.5
Nonindex	584,500	47.2
Simple assault	102,300	8.3
Stolen property	30,000	2.4
Trespassing	48,100	3.9
Vandalism	82,300	6.6
Weapons	22,000	1.8
Other sex crimes	17,000	1.4
Drug law violations	80,200	6.5
Obstruction of justice	78,500	6.3
Liquor law violations	14,000	1.1
Disorderly conduct	46,300	3.7
Other delinquent acts	63,800	5.2
Status offenses	82,000	6.7
Runaway	13,000	1.1
Truancy	22,000	1.8
Ungovernable	14,000	1.1
Liquor	26,000	2.1
Other	7,000	0.6
Total Referrals	1,237,900	100.0

SOURCE: *Juvenile Court Statistics, 1988*, U.S. Department of Justice, Office of Juvenile Justice and Delinquency Prevention, May 1991.

5. Less than 10% of all referrals result in a placement in some type of public or privately operated facility ranging from group homes to state-operated training schools.

Figures 3.1 and 3.2 present these same data in a more graphic manner and illustrate how status offense and delinquency cases are disposed for petitioned and adjudicated cases. These data are referred to as we proceed with our analysis of the factors that contribute to these court outcomes.

TABLE 3.3   1988 Juvenile Court Referral Outcomes

	Referrals					
	Delinquency		*Status Offense*		*Total*	
Outcomes	N	%	N	%	N	%
Total referrals	1,156,000	100	82,000	100	1,238,000	100
Cases petitioned	559,000	53	82,000	100	641,000	52
Cases adjudicated	324,000	31	50,000	61	374,000	30
Waived to adult court	12,000	1	0	0	12,000	1
Dismissed	440,000	38	23,000	28	463,000	37
Probation	425,000	37	36,000	44	461,000	37

SOURCE: Juvenile Court Statistics, 1988.

Juvenile Justice Laws and Court Procedures

The historical perspective of Chapter 2 demonstrated how the *parens patriae* philosophy was used to justify funneling large numbers of wayward children through a specially constructed court system, characterized by individualized and supposedly benevolent treatment. Obviously, the large volume of numbers has continued, but one continuously questions the appropriateness of the court's intervention in the lives of these youth. Youth who have not committed any criminal acts can be legally institutionalized until they reach the age of majority without their cases ever being reviewed by the sentencing court, while receiving treatment identical to those who have committed more serious crimes. Conversely, youths with long records of felony-type crimes, including murder, may receive less severe punishment. Such anomalies highlight the lack of uniformity that characterizes the juvenile system's processes and procedures. Indeed, many have concluded that the system is in reality little more than a collective of separate control agencies, all sanctioned under a broad legal framework, but each with its social climate and ethos (Younghusband, 1959).

To understand how such anomalies can occur, one must understand the respective legal codes of the 50 states that are the foundation of the juvenile justice system. Although these codes attempt to standardize the processing of delinquent youth, they also seek to retain an atmosphere of individualized treatment and informality that is assumed to be essential to the success of the juvenile court. The result of this basic contradiction is a set of legal codes that afford only a quasi-legal framework to define state intervention.

(text continued on page 61)

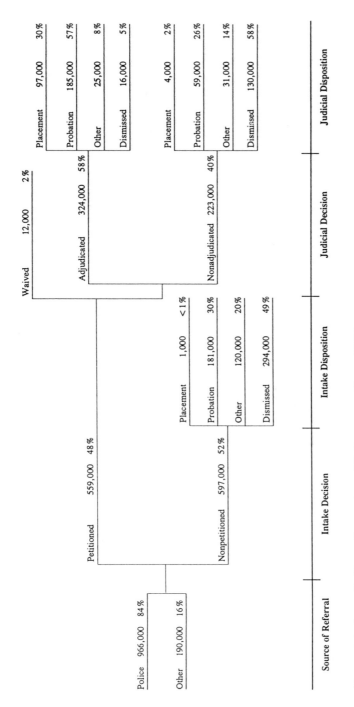

Figure 3.1. Juvenile Court Processing of Delinquency Cases, 1988

SOURCE: Juvenile Court Statistics, 1988.
NOTE: All percentages based on total number of 1988 court referrals.

59

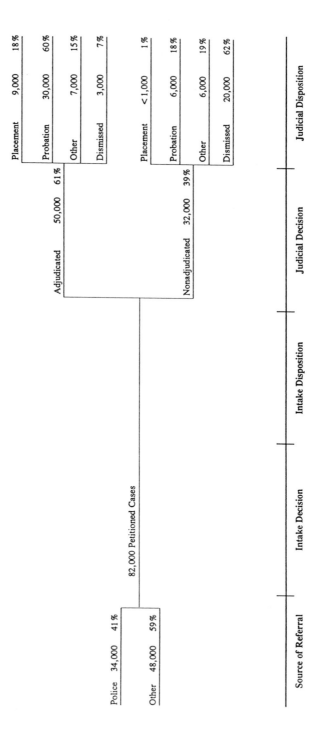

Figure 3.2. Juvenile Court Processing of Status Offense Cases, 1988

SOURCE: Juvenile Court Statistics, 1988.
NOTE: All percentages based on total number of 1988 court referrals.

By 1932, all but two states had instituted juvenile codes patterned after the Illinois model adopted in 1899. Alluding to the doctrines of *parens patriae* and benevolence, the architects of these codes universally adopted models based on the adult criminal court system, while eliminating most of the procedural safeguards protecting the constitutional rights of the accused. Many observers view this lack of procedural safeguards as the major proximal cause of inequitable and unjust treatment of children. Lemert (1970) claims that overreliance on the adult court model coupled with the absence of a true adversary system within the adjudication process has limited the system's ability to develop a viable approach to handling delinquent youths.

Lemert notes that the persistence of these contradictions can be partially attributed to the powerlessness of the clients to make articulate demands on the court. We would argue that, on the contrary, these contradictions persist because they continue to serve an important function. Unclear and contradictory codes appear to depoliticize the operations of any social control system while at the same time enabling that system to selectively concentrate and maintain its power without serious challenge from other interest groups.

The pages that follow review the current status of juvenile laws, especially those relating to jurisdiction, detention, procedural rights, adjudication, and court structure.[2] On reviewing these laws, it will become apparent to the reader that most of what Lemert terms the "anomalies" that characterized juvenile justice in the United States in the 19th century remain with us to the present day. Apart from the limited reforms embodied in the landmark Supreme Court decisions in the Kent, Gault, and Winship cases, little significant change has occurred in the legal framework that governs and determines the quality of justice for delinquent youth.

The Legal Context of the Juvenile Justice System

Traditional theories on the nature of law in a democratic society have been grounded in the concept of pluralistic consensus. This view suggests that laws—especially criminal laws—represent a negotiated consensus of the majority of the people. Society is viewed as a relatively harmonious system in which various components act in concert and are to some degree mutually dependent.[3]

Perhaps the best known proponent of this consensus view of law is Roscoe Pound (1922; 1928; 1942; 1943; 1965), who argues that in a civilized society law reflects the cumulative consciousness of the people. In such a society, Pound reasons, many individual interests can be peacefully accommodated; any conflicts that arise can be resolved through the existing legal system. This state of order is possible because a legal system controlled by the will of the people is assumed to forge fair and equitable laws.

Basic to the consensus perspective is the assumption that laws are created in the interest of society as a whole, not in the interest of the favored few. The interests of highest priority are those that seek to maintain the stability of society and perpetuate its ideals. Change is expected only through the established legal framework, and then only if change benefits the social system and accords with the popular will (Pound, 1943):

> Looked at functionally, the law is an attempt to satisfy, to reconcile, to harmonize, to adjust these overlapping and often conflicting claims and demands, either through securing them directly and immediately, or through securing certain individual interests, or through delimitations or compromises of individual interests, so as to give effect to the greatest total of interests or to the interests that weigh most in our civilization, *with the least sacrifice of the scheme of interests as a whole* (p. 39, emphasis added)

The idealized view of law and society set forth by Pound can be construed as an ideological defense of the status quo. It fails to acknowledge that the order constructed by the legal profession in fact mirrors the perceptions, values, and interests of a privileged segment of society. Access to positions in the legal profession—to serve as lawyers, judges, and, increasingly, legislators—simply is not readily available to all segments of society. It (the legal profession) is a heavily regulated enterprise in which only a few are able to participate.

An alternative view might portray society as a congeries of conflicting special interest groups, constantly competing with one another for benefits within the distributive order. Each group is armed with a measure (albeit unequal) of power, status, and resources, which enables it to withstand antagonists and to pursue its own ends.[4] Such interest groups arise in all segments of society, but owing to an imbalance in power, status, and resources, only a few are capable of consistently winning their struggles.

One means by which a segment of society develops and maintains dominance over others is by creating laws that serve the narrow interests it pursues. The formulation of criminal laws plays a particularly crucial role in this regard because criminal offenses are considered offenses against the community at large (adult criminal actions, for example, name the state as plaintiff). Such actions are potentially punishable by the most severe societal sanctions. The origins of criminal laws against vagrancy and the sale and use of drugs and alcohol have been well documented (Duster, 1987). Our analysis, in Chapter 2, of class bias in the history of delinquency prevention and control in the United States gains further dimension when we examine the groups most actively involved in the formulation of delinquency statutes.

Lemert (1970), in his analysis of changes in California juvenile court law, provides a good illustration of this phenomenon. The key actors in the reformulation of the California juvenile laws were representatives of such agencies as the California Juvenile Officers' Association; the California Probation, Parole, and Correctional Officers' Association; the California Youth Authority; and the Governor's Special Study Commission on Juvenile Justice. Although these representatives were by no means unified in all their recommendations, their disagreements arose almost exclusively over methods of control.

Our point is that laws do not always represent the will of the people or serve the best interests of all groups. Juvenile codes in particular reflect the intent of those in positions of power to maintain control over youth and their families who are disproportionately poor and disadvantaged. Although we have been led to believe that the juvenile codes and the juvenile court were created to benevolently protect the young, the opposite result frequently has occurred.

Juvenile Court Jurisdiction: The Right to Intervene

One of the critical functions of the juvenile codes is to specify and delineate the conditions under which the state may legitimately intervene in a juvenile's life (i.e., jurisdiction). State juvenile codes were adopted to eliminate the arbitrary character of juvenile justice within each jurisdiction. It was hoped that the juvenile codes would enlarge the procedural safeguards for juveniles beyond those rights already afforded juveniles by the federal Constitution. Because youths were not yet fully responsible for their actions, they should not be dealt with as harshly as their adult counterparts in the adult court. The logic of this argument is frequently cited in the 1955 case *In re Poff* (1955):

[The] original Juvenile Court Act enacted in the District of Columbia . . . was devised to afford the juvenile protections in addition to those
he already possessed under the Federal Constitution. Before this legislative enactment, the juvenile was subject to the same punishment for
an offense as an adult. It follows logically that in the absence of such
legislation the juvenile would be entitled to the same constitutional
guarantees and safeguards as an adult. If this is true, then the only
possible reason for the Juvenile Court Act was to afford the juvenile
safeguards in addition to those he already possessed. The legislative
intent was to enlarge and not diminish those protections.

Narrowly defined, *jurisdiction* refers to the areas in which juvenile
court has authority over an individual, based on geographic location, age, and behavior. In theory, the codes specify the types of
behavior that are indicative of juvenile delinquency and thus warrant state intervention into a child's life. But defining behavior that
points toward future delinquency is problematic indeed. The goal of
prevention is realized by early detection of behavior that suggests
tendencies toward more serious delinquent or criminal behavior.
The role of the court is to discover youths exhibiting such patterns,
and to treat them so their delinquent tendencies disappear. This
legitimates the court's intervention in the lives of youth who may
not have committed any crimes, but whose conduct may not reflect
the expected behavior, norms, and values as defined by the more
privileged segments of society. As Kittrie (1971) notes, there has been
an almost unlimited range of juvenile court jurisdiction over children due to the rationalized need to intervene in the early stages of
a delinquent career:

> What power should society exercise over juveniles who drop out of
> school, leave home, form undesirable associations, and appear to prog-
> ress towards crime, yet are short of it? When may society take preventive
> measures, and to what extent should social intervention depend on the
> availability of adequate treatment facilities? (pp. 114-115)

Current juvenile codes include three major categories of juvenile
behavior in which the court has jurisdiction over the youth. First, the
court may intervene in those instances where the youth has been
accused of committing an act that would be defined as criminal for an
adult, including misdemeanors and felony-type crimes. These acts are
typically referred to as *delinquent* offenses. Little controversy exists over
the right of the court to intervene in such instances, owing to the
seriousness of such behavior and the usual presence of a complainant.

Second, there are *status offenses*, which currently are the center of controversy among criminal justice practitioners and liberal reformers. Status offenses refer to acts that would not be defined as criminal if committed by an adult, including truancy, curfew violations, and running away. They are described in such phrases as "incorrigibility," "in need of supervision," "idleness," "waywardness," "beyond parental control," or "unruly behavior." As shown previously, there were 82,000 court referrals for these "offenses" in 1988.

The third behavioral category of court intervention for delinquency involves *dependency and neglect.* In such instances the child is viewed by the court as being deprived of needed support and supervision from parental figures, and the family is judged incapable of resolving its insufficiencies. The rationale used for court intervention in dependency and neglect cases is that children need to be removed from the home for their own protection and well-being.

Over the past 30 years, defenders of the juvenile justice system, recognizing some of the problems inherent in current definitions of court jurisdiction, have proposed narrower jurisdictional limitations on the juvenile court. In 1959, the National Council on Crime and Delinquency (NCCD) adopted the Standard Juvenile Court Act, which was intended to serve as a model for states in standardizing their jurisdiction criteria (Standard Juvenile Court Act, 1949):

> The court shall have exclusive original jurisdiction in proceedings: (1) Concerning any child who is alleged to have violated any federal, state, or local law or municipal ordinance, regardless of where the violation occurred . . . (2) Concerning any child . . . (b) whose environment is injurious to his welfare, or whose behavior is injurious to his own or others' welfare; or (c) who is beyond the control of his parent or other custodian. (p. 8)

The broad and vague terms of this model and well-intentioned legislation probably would be held unconstitutional if used as a basis for formulating adult criminal codes.

The International Association of Chiefs of Police, noting the problem of defining juvenile jurisdictions, in 1973 proposed that the following standards be used by states in developing model legislation (Kobetz & Bosarge, 1973):

> (i) It is recommended that the term "juvenile delinquent" be applied only to a child who has committed a criminal offense and who is in need of supervision, treatment or rehabilitation.

(ii) It is recommended that the terminology "unruly" child be applied to children who: (a) Have committed an offense applicable only to a child (status offenders); (b) Are habitually disobedient of reasonable commands of parents or guardians and are ungovernable; (c) Are habitually truant from school; and (d) Are in need of treatment or rehabilitation for any of the foregoing. (p. 37)

The above criteria for intervention appear on the surface to be reasonable and logical, but they offer little protection from discriminatory and arbitrary decisions by police and court personnel. Because the basis for the police decision of whether or not to arrest the child is not well defined by law, even greater potential exists for abuse. For example, we know from several research studies reviewed in this chapter that juvenile justice practitioners (like any other organization) often make decisions based on social values, and those values often are imbued with class, race, and gender biases.[5]

Sussman (1959) has dramatized the absence of precise criteria that characterized juvenile justice codes during the 1950s and 1960s by compiling the following types of behavior that would qualify as juvenile delinquency under most juvenile statutes during that era:

1. Violates any law or ordinance
2. Habitually truant
3. [Knowingly] associates with thieves, vicious or immoral persons
4. Incorrigible
5. Beyond control of parent or guardian
6. Growing up in idleness or crime
7. So deports self as to injure self or others
8. Absents self from home (without just cause) without consent
9. Immoral or indecent conduct
10. [Habitually] uses vile, obscene, or vulgar language (in public places)
11. [Knowingly] enters, visits house of ill repute
12. Patronizes, visits policy shop or gaming place
13. [Habitually] wanders about railroad yards or tracks
14. Jumps train or enters car or engine without authority
15. Patronizes saloon or dram house where intoxicating liquor is sold
16. Wanders streets at night, not on lawful business
17. Patronizes public poolroom or bucket shop
18. Immoral conduct around school (or in public place)
19. Engages in illegal occupation

20. In occupation or situation dangerous or injurious to self or others
21. Smokes cigarettes (or uses tobacco in any form)
22. Frequents place the existence of which violates the law
23. Addicted to drugs
24. Disorderly
25. Begging
26. Uses intoxicating liquor
27. Makes indecent proposal
28. Loiters, sleeps in alleys, vagrant
29. Runs away from state or charity institution
30. Found on premises occupied or used for illegal purposes
31. Operates motor vehicle dangerously while under the influence of liquor
32. Attempts to marry without consent, in violation of law
33. Given to sexual irregularities (p. 21)

A more current example is provided by Michigan's juvenile code, which includes the following definition for jurisdiction over youth committing a status offense (King, 1980):

> Child has run away without sufficient cause; is disobedient; associates with immoral persons or is leading an immoral life; was found on the premises occupied or used for illegal purposes; is truant; habitually idles away time; repeatedly patronizes a tavern or place which primarily sells alcohol. (p. 16)

Age is the most obvious criterion separating juvenile court from adult criminal court. Although there is a paucity of precise guidelines for juvenile court intervention based on behavior, one still might expect definitive age criteria to define court jurisdiction. Such is not the case. State legal codes exhibit wide variation in the age limitations placed on court procedures from state to state. Minimum age (or the age of original jurisdiction) refers to the earliest age at which the court has jurisdiction over a child. Minimum age restrictions are stipulated in few of the codes, leaving individual courts to develop their own unwritten policies, or to rely on the common law dictum that no person can be held accountable for criminal behavior until the age of 7 years. Maximum age limit refers to that age when a person is defined as an adult and is beyond the jurisdiction of juvenile court.

Currently, 35 states and the District of Columbia set the maximum age for original jurisdiction at 17 years and below (see Table 3.4).

TABLE 3.4   Circumstances Under Which Juveniles May Be Tried in
Criminal Courts

Age at which criminal courts gain jurisdiction of young offenders ranges from 16 to 19

Age of offender when under criminal court jurisdiction	*States*
16 years	Connecticut, New York, North Carolina
17	Georgia, Illinois, Louisiana, Massachusetts, Missouri, South Carolina, Texas
18	Alabama, Alaska, Arizona, Arkansas, California, Colorado, Delaware, District of Columbia, Florida, Hawaii, Idaho, Indiana, Iowa, Kansas, Kentucky, Maine, Maryland, Michigan, Minnesota, Mississippi, Montana, Nebraska, Nevada, New Hampshire, New Jersey, New Mexico, North Dakota, Ohio, Oklahoma, Oregon, Pennsylvania, Rhode Island, South Dakota, Tennessee, Utah, Vermont, Virginia, Washington, West Virginia, Wisconsin, Federal districts
19	Wyoming

SOURCE: *Upper age of juvenile court jurisdiction statues analysis,* Linda A. Szymanski, National Center for Juvenile Justice, March, 1987.

All states allow juveniles to be tried as adults in criminal courts

Juveniles are referred to criminal courts in one of three ways:

> Concurrent jurisdiction—the prosecutor has the discretion of filing charges for certain offenses in either juvenile or criminal courts

---

continued

Eight states (Georgia, Illinois, Louisiana, Massachusetts, Michigan, Missouri, South Carolina, and Texas) set the age at 16 years and below, and 4 states (Connecticut, New York, North Carolina, and Vermont) use age 15 and below. Only Wyoming uses the age limitation of 18 and below. Oklahoma is unique as it uses age 15 for males and 17 for females (Rose Institute of State and Local Governments and the American Legislative Exchange Council, 1987). This variation is due in part to a difference of opinion among the juvenile justice experts concerning the age at which children mature and which age groups should be protected from the potentially more harsh sanctions available from the adult system.

Another age restriction in juvenile codes limits continuing jurisdiction, which defines the maximum age at which the court can

TABLE 3.4   Continued

> Excluded offenses—the legislature excludes from juvenile court jurisdiction certain offenses usually either very minor, such as traffic of fishing violations, or very serious, such as murder or rape

> Judicial waver—the juvenile court waives its jurisdiction and transfers the case to criminal court (the procedure is also known as "binding over" or "certifying" juvenile cases to criminal courts)

12 states authorize prosecutors to file cases in the juvenile or criminal courts at their discretion

This procedure, known as concurrent jurisdiction, may be limited to certain offenses or to juveniles of a certain age. Four states provide concurrent jurisdiction over jurisdiction charge with traffic violations. Georgia, Nebraska and Wyoming have concurrent criminal jurisdiction statutes.

As of 1987, 36 states excluded certain offenses from juvenile court jurisdictions

Eighteen states excluded only traffic, watercraft, fish, or game violations. Another 13 states excluded serious offenses; the other 5 excluded serious offenses and some minor offenses. The serious offenses most often excluded are capital crimes such as murder, but several states exclude juveniles previously convicted in criminal courts.

48 states, the District of Columbia, and the Federal Government have judicial waiver provisions

Youngest age at which juvenile may be transferred to criminal court by judicial waiver	*States*
No specific age	Alaska, Arizona, Arkansas, Delaware, Florida, Indiana, Kentucky, Maine, Maryland, New Hampshire, New Jersey, Oklahoma, South Dakota, West Virginia, Wyoming, Federal districts
10 years	Vermont
12	Montana
13	Georgia, Illinois, Mississippi
14	Alabama, Colorado, Connecticut, Idaho, Iowa, Massachusetts, Minnesota, Missouri, North Carolina, North Dakota, Pennsylvania, South Carolina, Tennessee, Utah
15	District of Columbia, Louisiana, Michigan, New Mexico, Ohio, Oregon, Texas, Virginia
16	California, Hawaii, Kansas, Nevada, Rhode Island, Washington, Wisconsin

NOTE: Many judicial waiver statues also specify offenses that are waivable. This chart lists the states by the youngest age for which judicial waiver may be sought without regard to offense.
SOURCE: *Waiver/transfer/certification of juveniles to criminal court: Age restrictions: Crime restrictions,* Linda A. Szymanski, National Center for Juvenile Justice, February, 1987.

SOURCE: Bureau of Justice Statistics, Report to the Nation on Crime and Justice.

retain control beyond the original age of jurisdiction. For example, if the case of a 17-year-old youth is heard by the juvenile court, it is possible in some states to retain control over that delinquent until he or she reaches the age of 21. In California, youth committed to the California Youth Authority for certain offenses are retained under the jurisdiction of the state up to age 25. In such instances, the youth cannot be tried again for the same crime once he has reached the age of 18, but it is possible for the court to retain its jurisdiction over the individual through probation, parole, or institutionalization. This legal loophole permits adult criminal courts to waive jurisdiction over a person charged with an adult offense if that person still is under juvenile court control. He can be remanded to the juvenile court, which can then inflict a stiffer sentence through continued incarceration or parole supervision stemming from a previous juvenile offense.

To add another level of complexity, some states employ different maximum age limitations for certain offenses. For example, 17 states have lower maximum age limitations for youth charged with status offenses. New York is the only state that allows for different maximum age limitations by sex for status offenses (the age for females is 18 and for males is 16) (King, 1980).

An additional jurisdictional question related to the age criterion, the waiver or transfer of juveniles to the adult court, is undertaken in juvenile cases in which the offense is thought to be especially serious. In many states, the power to transfer a juvenile to the adult criminal court lies with the district attorney's office. The prosecutor's office is allowed to assume control over a juvenile case with or without the consent of the juvenile judge based on the judgment of the district attorney. Predictably, the guidelines used by the prosecutor in making such waivers or transfers are vague. This jurisdictional interface between adult and juvenile courts is widespread, as nearly all states give the judge the right in some cases to waive jurisdiction and transfer juveniles to adult court. The U.S. Supreme Court in the Kent decision (*Kent v. United States,* 1966) attempted to ensure that juveniles could not be waived to adult criminal courts for trial without a formal hearing before a judge, with the assistance of a lawyer. Critics of waivers argue that transferring juveniles to the adult court is in conflict with the juvenile court's treatment philosophy. A common reason given for transfer is that the juvenile court is unable to properly handle the juvenile, but there is no reason to conclude that the adult court is in a better position to provide the desired services. The basic intent of the waiver, despite liberal rhetoric to the contrary, is that adult court has more latitude to impose lengthy sentences than juvenile court, which in most cases must relinquish jurisdiction of offenders beyond the age of 21. Conservative critics of the juvenile system, who complain that the court is too lenient, generally would like to see the use of waivers expanded.

Armed with the threat of transfer to adult court, juvenile authorities are in a strong position to influence a youth's decision to plead guilty to the alleged offense. This is a form of plea bargaining, and serves as an incentive for a juvenile to relinquish his or her full due process rights (Skolnick, 1975).[6] One study uncovered three counties in one state that had established a policy of transferring to adult court any juveniles who refused to admit to the allegations presented in the delinquency petition. Authorities assumed that the reluctance of youths to admit guilt demonstrated incorrigibility and criminal sophistication (National Council on Crime and Delinquency, 1967). Thus, to demand one's legal rights under the present juvenile system may increase the severity of punishment. Some states provide that the judge in a waiver proceeding must consider the suitability of the youth for rehabilitation and the seriousness of the delinquent act, whereas other states require only that the youth be deemed unsuitable for rehabilitation or treatment.[7]

Despite the guarantees provided by the Kent decision, there is no assurance that in waiver hearings the case will be disposed of fairly. In many states, there is no requirement that the youth be present at such hearings, because the court is assumed to act in the best interests of the child. Frequently the transfer of a juvenile is based not on the merits of the individual case, but rather on the discretion of court personnel. It is notable that some states guarantee a juvenile's right to request transfer to an adult court. This alternative typically is used if the juvenile's lawyer feels that the disposition of the case would be more favorable in an adult court with a jury trial and its other constitutional safeguards.

A review of juvenile court laws gives one the impression that the court is empowered to gain control over virtually any youth, for whatever reasons the court chooses. Kittrie (1971) warns that, in view of this enormous discretion, the juvenile court philosophy of *parens patriae* needs to be reexamined so the court does not become overly zealous in its "therapeutic" actions (pp. 167-168). This criticism is not novel, because as a California legislative commission's 1960 evaluation of California juvenile laws concluded (California Governor's Special Study Commission on Juvenile Justice, 1960):

There is an absence of well-defined empirically derived standards and norms to guide juvenile court judges, probation, and law enforcement officials in their decision-making. Consequently, instead of a uniform system of justice, varied systems based upon divergent policies and value scales are in evidence. . . . Basic legal rights are neither being uniformly nor adequately protected under present juvenile court provisions. (p. 12)

The diversity of court practices has led to injustices such as the plight of Gerry Gault, which resulted in the pivotal *In re Gault* (1967) decision. Gerry Gault was arrested at the age of 15 for making obscene phone calls to a neighbor. He was subsequently convicted of the charge and placed in the Arizona State Industrial School for 6 years, during which time the court relinquished its jurisdiction over the case. The juvenile court judge who sentenced Gault stated that Gault was "habitually involved in immoral matters," and that the phone calls were tantamount to "disturbing the peace." Although the complainant in the case neither met with the judge nor attended the hearing, the judge felt justified in sentencing this 15-year-old to a penal institution for 6 years. If Gault had been tried as an adult in the same jurisdiction in Arizona, he would have been sentenced to not more than 60 days in prison with a maximum fine of $50. The Supreme Court decision that resulted was an attempt to provide basic procedural rights for juveniles, including rights to counsel, notice, and cross-examination and safeguards against self-incrimination.

The case of a 14-year-old youth in West Virginia further illustrates how current statutes encourage abuse. In this case, a youth had made a phone call to the local school and falsely reported the planting of a bomb on the premises. Because of the youth's age, he was tried in juvenile court, and was subsequently declared delinquent by the judge and committed to juvenile prison, where he remained for 7 years until the age of 21. Upon appeal to the state supreme court of appeals, the higher court affirmed the decision of the lower court. If the child had been sentenced in a West Virginia adult criminal court, the maximum sentence would have been 30 days in the local county jail (*State v. Mills*, 1959).

Although some might conclude that statutory changes would remedy alleged abuses of court discretion, the Gault case demonstrated that law reform is not the entire answer. Soon after the Supreme Court's decision in Gault, many states rushed to develop ways of encouraging youths to voluntarily forfeit procedural safeguards, thereby bypassing the intended effect of the U.S. Supreme Court ruling. To be effective, reform of the juvenile court must be rooted in principles of social *justice* for children, not merely in easily circumvented procedural safeguards.

Detention: The Jailing of Youth

Detention refers to the period in which a wayward youth is taken into custody by police and probation prior to a petition being filed and an adjudication hearing by the juvenile court. It is analogous in function to pretrial detention for adults but not comparable in terms of its rationale and the level of due process accorded to youth who experience detention.

Various juvenile codes, where they exist, serve as standards for the selective use of detention. However, a 1980 study found that 17 states have no statute governing juvenile pretrial detention (Pappenfont & Young, 1980). And where such statutes exist they are quite general in nature. A recent national survey funded by the U.S. Department of Justice found the most common criteria used by states were as follows (King, 1980):

1. For the juvenile's protection, or for the protection of the person or property of others
2. No parental care available for the juvenile
3. To ensure a juvenile's presence at the juvenile court hearings
4. The seriousness of the offense and the juvenile's record (p. 49)

The Institute of Judicial Administration (IJA) and the American Bar Association (ABA) developed a standard saying that secure detention should be applied only where a minor was charged with a crime of violence for which an adult would face a sentence of 1 year or more, and where other objective risk factors were present (Standard 6.6) (Flicker, 1982). The National Advisory Committee on Juvenile Justice and Delinquency Prevention issued a standard where detention would be limited to youth who were fugitives from other jurisdictions, were charged with murder or another felony, and had a history of demonstrable past misconduct (Standard 3.152). Despite these national standards, few states have implemented them.

Although juvenile court was designed to protect children from the harmful effects of incarceration, the number of juveniles being incarcerated in detention facilities grows each year. The President's

Commission on Law Enforcement and the Administration of Criminal Justice found, in 1965, that two thirds of all juveniles apprehended by police were admitted to detention centers and detained for an average of 12 days. The commission asserted that the excessive number of juveniles being detained was creating a serious social problem because in many jurisdictions juveniles were being housed in adult jails (President's Commission on Law Enforcement and Administration of Justice, 1967, p. 234). The Law Enforcement Assistance Administration (LEAA) reported that on the day of June 30, 1971, there were 11,748 juveniles in detention facilities (U.S. Department of Justice. National Criminal Justice Information and Statistics Survey, 1974).

Three decades later, there have been mixed results in the deinstitutionalization effort. In 1989, only 2,245 status offenders were in public facilities. However, another 6,863 were housed in privately operated facilities, for a total of 9,098. Approximately 416,000 youth were admitted to detention and spent an average of 11.4 days there. And the cost of this system has grown to $240 million (Krisberg, Schwartz, Litksy, & Austin, 1986).

In theory, detention of youth fulfills three primary objectives. First, youth are detained if there is reason to believe that in the absence of such external controls the juvenile would be free to commit additional serious crimes, thereby posing a threat to the safety and security of the community. In this situation the child is incarcerated primarily for the benefit of the community. Second, juveniles also are detained in cases where the bad influences of a home environment necessitate placing the child in a more protective setting. In this case, children are viewed as being endangered, and detention is construed as a temporary measure until a more permanent home placement can be arranged. Finally, detention parallels the function of the bail system in adult criminal court, and ensures the appearance of the youthful offender at subsequent court dates. This goal is consistent with the desires of the court to expedite the processing of criminal matters at both adult and juvenile levels. It is exceedingly efficient and expedient for the court to have defendants readily available at all stages of the adjudication process. Unlike adult court, juvenile court does not necessarily provide an alternative similar to being released on one's own recognizance or on bail. In most states, the child must be released to the guardianship of parents or relatives, who must be willing to assume full responsibility for the child. Beyond these three official rationales for employing detention is one additional function that often is ignored: punishment (Platt, Schechter, & Tiffany, 1968; Sarri, 1974; Sumner, 1968).

A recent Supreme Court decision has brought some clarity to this controversial issue by liberalizing the court's rationale for the use of detention. In *Schall v. Martin* (1984) New York's prevention detention law was challenged by attorneys representing detained youth and their families. The New York statute justified detention for youth as an exercise of the state's *parens patriae* authority over children and asserted that it did not constitute punishment. A federal district court struck down the statute, and this decision was affirmed by the U.S. Court of Appeals. Nevertheless, the Supreme Court reversed these lower court rulings, holding that prevention detention of juveniles for their own protection and to prevent crimes was a legitimate state action.

In most states, the power to detain rests with police and probation officers. Upon the arrest of a juvenile, police may transfer the child to a detention facility until screening procedures are completed by the probation or intake officer. Once the juvenile is received at the detention unit, the probation or intake officer may request that the juvenile be retained in custody for further investigation. If a delinquency petition has been filed, the youth can be detained until the adjudication and disposition hearings are completed, and even after disposition if a delay occurs in placement. For instance, children waiting to be placed in foster homes often are detained several months until suitable homes are located.

Most states allow the child to be released to the custody of parents or guardians so long as these adults promise to bring the juvenile to additional court appearances. However, police may not approve a release if they believe the child's home is incapable of providing the police's notion of proper supervision. Although a few states allow youths to be released upon their own signatures or through the posting of bail, this alternative rarely is exercised.

Once the initial decision has been made by law enforcement officials to incarcerate a child, it becomes the responsibility of the juvenile court to review the detention decision. Many states do not require a formal court hearing, and even in those states requiring a detention hearing few guidelines exist for making the detention decision. Most states require mandatory hearings within 36 to 72 hours, whereas a few states require a hearing within 24 hours (Florida, Idaho, Nevada, New Hampshire, and New Mexico) and only for certain types of offenses. For example, Nevada allows juveniles in cases involving dependency and neglect to be detained for 72 hours before a detention hearing must be held, as opposed to the 24-hour rule for delinquency cases (King, 1980, pp. 55-59). Statutes neither require the court to consider the factual merits of each delinquency petition nor ensure that the authorities show probable cause to believe that the child committed a delinquent act.

Few states have laws to regulate the duration of detention. In those states that do provide standards, maximum lengths of detention range from 3 days to 3 months. Little is known about actual compliance with detention restrictions, as most states have no provisions for monitoring detention practices. Too often, those who are detained for the longest periods are children for whom it is difficult to locate suitable supervision. Thus, it is not true that those in detention facilities for long periods of incarceration are the more serious offenders. More often, status offenders from broken homes are those who become the victims of long periods of detention.

Another important issue is that juveniles who are detained may be placed in adult county jails rather than specially designed juvenile institutions. This is of particular interest because the juvenile justice system was specifically intended to prevent the mixing of adult and juvenile offenders. In 1990, nearly 60,000 juveniles were admitted to adult jails and approximately 2,300 were in jail on any given day (U.S. Department of Justice, 1991).

As in the area of jurisdiction, legal codes generally are inadequate to end the flagrant abuses in the jailing of juveniles. In fact, the absence of legal restrictions may actually encourage abusive detention practices as suggested by the increasing number of children detained. According to the Community Research Associates survey, only a handful of states prohibit the jailing of juveniles. Where such a practice is allowed, the standards generally state that such placement is permissible in those situations where no other suitable facility exists or for those youth who present a "serious security risk" (King, 1980, pp. 94-99).

The Juvenile Court Structure

Following the initiative taken by Illinois in 1899, the states began, one by one, to design their own independent juvenile court systems. The result is that today great diversity exists in both court structures and the roles of relevant participants. The right of appeal for juveniles was virtually ignored by states in fashioning their court systems, due to their paternalistic philosophy. The judge was expected to be sensitive to the specialized needs of youthful offenders, and thus assume a paternal role. This ideology ignores appellate rights for the child, affirming the reluctance of court officials to reform juvenile codes to enable children to challenge court decisions (Dineen, 1974):

> Since the appellate courts, particularly the highest court of any state, make the definitive interpretations of law in the state, issues and cases which do not progress past the inferior courts often are left unpublicized and with little value as precedent setting decisions. Juvenile law has long suffered from this condition of underdevelopment. (p. 2)

Although some states have uniform standards for juvenile courts, other states show considerable internal variation in juvenile court structure. Some courts are far more rigid in their adherence to due process guidelines than others, and avenues for appealing lower court decisions often depend on local policies. In some jurisdictions, two juvenile courts may exist concurrently, with no formal provision to determine which court should initially hear the case. The confusion of juvenile court practice is for attorneys much like playing a high-stakes game without knowing either the rules or who makes them, and this environment often discourages attorneys from taking children's cases.

In view of the ambiguity of court structure, it is remarkable that states even concur that judges should preside over the courts and should possess law degrees. Several states in this respect exceed minimal requirements, specifying that juvenile judges be knowledgeable about family and child problems. An examination of the process by which most juvenile judges are selected may lead one to question their supposed expertise. Because most states provide for the election of judges, justice essentially is linked to the political process. State election boards in many instances fail to indicate that a particular judicial position is on the juvenile court. Typically, a judge elected to a position in an adult court subsequently is transferred to the juvenile court by recommendation of senior members of the bench. In those few states that do not choose judges by election, they are appointed by the governor. Whether elected or appointed, judicial positions may represent political rewards for those who have supported the political party currently in power, and may have no relation to the candidate's skills. In some cases, judges may be transferred to the juvenile court as a penalty for incompetence or unpopular decisions. "In some jurisdictions, for example, the juvenile court judgeship does not have high status in the eye of the bar, and while there are many juvenile court judges of outstanding ability

and devotion, many are not" (President's Commission on Law Enforcement and the Administration of Justice, 1967, p. 216).

Due to heavy caseloads, as well as an unwillingness by local
governments to provide adequate staffing for juvenile courts, some
jurisdictions use referees in lieu of juvenile judges. Referees, too, are
subject to political pressures, as they are appointed by juvenile
judges and serve at the discretion of those judges. Not only do few
states require that referees have law degrees, but also only a slight
majority of states specify any educational or professional criteria that
referees must meet. In those states with educational qualifications,
the requirements are so loosely worded that a referee need have no
formal education or legal experience. Although referees' decisions
are only recommendations to the presiding judge, the heavy caseloads and the necessity of expediting juvenile justice results in virtual blanket approval, with an uncritical review and pro forma
concurrence by the judges.

Juvenile Court Intake, Adjudication, and Dispositions

Once a child has been referred to the juvenile court, the court must
determine the merits of the delinquency petition and seek a disposition of the case. The major function of the intake decision is to
determine whether a petition should be filed against the youth. The
filing of a petition is analogous to a complaint being filed in adult
court. It signifies that the charges appear to be sufficiently valid to
warrant further processing by the court. As shown in Table 3.3, only
52% of the 1.2 million court referrals result in a petition being filed.
Those cases that are not "dismissed" generally result in a referral to
another social service agency or placement on another unique component of the court called "informal probation." The latter represents a state of control where the court maintains jurisdiction and
can violate the youth's informal probation status for behaviors that
are not criminal in nature (i.e., failure to report to the probation
officer, failure to report for services recommended by the court, etc.).
Such technical violations of informal probation in some states can
constitute sufficient reason to refer the child back to juvenile court,
where he or she can receive a more formal and punitive sanction.

The adjudication hearing is the trial stage of the juvenile court
process, in which information is presented before the court concerning the juvenile's alleged delinquent behavior. Youth who are successfully adjudicated are viewed as guilty of the charges presented in the

court and will receive a formal disposition (or sentence). Less than 30% of all court referrals are formally adjudicated (see Table 3.3). Of those cases resulting in a formal petition being filed, approximately 60% receive a formal adjudication (see Figures 3.1 and 3.2).

Whereas adult criminal courts have such standards as restrictions on the introduction of hearsay evidence, protection against self-incrimination, the right to jury trial, the right to cross-examine witnesses, and the requirement of establishing guilt beyond a reasonable doubt, these safeguards are not built into the juvenile court. The defense for the absence of such protections in juvenile court is that the court is designed to protect children, and formalization would make the proceedings more like a junior criminal court. The Supreme Court has not always shared this view. Recent Supreme Court decisions such as *In re Gault* (1967) and *In re Winship* (1970) provide minimal protection of the constitutional rights of juveniles, especially in adjudication hearings. The court did rule in Gault that minors must be afforded the right to notice of all charges, right to counsel, right to confrontation and cross-examination of witnesses, and the privilege against self-incrimination. However, it did not address a youth's right to appellate review, which is the right to the provision of a written transcript or a written statement of the court's rationale for its decision. In the Winship case, the Court ruled that juveniles could be judged delinquent only upon establishment of delinquency in a formal judicial hearing. Although juvenile courts initially used the principle of "a preponderance of evidence" to determine delinquency, the Supreme Court held in the Winship case that juvenile courts must establish delinquency "beyond a reasonable doubt." In *McKiever v. Pennsylvania* (1971), the Supreme Court ruled that juveniles do not have a constitutional right to trial by jury. Jury trials for juveniles can be obtained only in those jurisdictions that specifically provide for them in state constitutions or statutes.

The type of evidence necessary for a court to reach a determination in a delinquency petition varies considerably from one state to another. Many juvenile codes require that social investigations be presented by the probation or intake officers. In many instances adjudications are premised on hearsay evidence contained in such investigations, and therefore would not be admissible in an adult criminal court. Social investigations containing information concerning the child's family, school progress, peer associations, and attitudes may have no bearing on the involvement in an alleged offense. Court personnel claim that such information is vital to a complete picture of the youth's situation and to selection of proper treatment.

Although evidence may be presented by prosecutors, probation officers, or other court personnel, most states allow the judges to determine who argues for the delinquency petition. Although recent Court decisions have provided minimal procedural safeguards to juveniles, considerable resistance to these safeguards still exists on the part of those responsible for the legal control of youths. The International Association of Chiefs of Police expressed fear that the juvenile court may be coming "dangerously close to complete adult court procedures" (Kobetz & Bosarge, 1973, p. 111). The National Council of Juvenile Court Judges (1972) stated that the Supreme Court decisions have excessively formalized juvenile court hearings, thus reducing the possibility of individualized justice. This view was best summarized by Supreme Court Chief Justice Warren Burger in his dissenting opinion in Winship (*In re Winship*, 1970):

> What the juvenile court systems need is not more but less of the *trappings* of legal procedure and judicial formalism; the juvenile system requires breathing room and flexibility in order to survive, if it can survive the repeated assaults from this court. . . . My hope is that today's decision will not spell the end of a generously conceived program of compassionate treatment intended to mitigate the rigors and trauma of exposing youthful offenders to a traditional criminal court; each step we take turns the clock back to the pre-juvenile court era. I cannot regard it as a manifestation of progress to transform juvenile courts into criminal courts, which is what we are well on the way toward accomplishing.

This level of resistance has led some observers to conclude that despite the Court's rulings, considerable abuses still exist in the processing of these youth through the adjudication hearings. Former juvenile court judge H. Ted Rubin (1979) documented a number of administrative actions by the court designed to circumvent the Gault ruling, which led to him to conclude that much more remains to be done:

> The foregoing cases are but a smattering of the abuses of juvenile rights which have occurred in our courts and the juvenile justice agencies since *Gault*. From the defense point of view, actualization of due process and uniformly executed legal safeguards remain today, more rhetoric than reality. (p. 211)

A recent study by Barry Feld (1988a) provided clearer evidence of the lack of conformity by juvenile courts to the legal requirements of Gault as set forth by the U.S. Supreme Court. Using statewide juvenile court data only for cases where a petition has already been filed in six states (California, Minnesota, Nebraska, New York, North Dakota, and Pennsylvania), Feld found that in three states (Minnesota, Nebraska, and North Dakota) only about half of the cases with petitions filed were represented by counsel. More disturbing was the consistent finding across all six states that presence of counsel resulted in a more severe disposition.

Several reasons for these trends were advanced by Feld, including the possibility that judges may reserve the use of counsel for the more severe charges. However, Feld's analysis takes into account the severity of prior delinquent behavior and the severity of the current charge. Nonetheless, the data speak for themselves in that some states are not meeting the need for counsel as envisioned by the Supreme Court in its original ruling: "The juvenile needs the assistance of counsel to cope with problems of law, to make skilled inquiry into the facts, (and) to insist upon the regularity of the proceedings" (*In re Gault*, 1967, p. 36).

Thus despite these landmark court rulings, a wide gulf still remains between the rights afforded juveniles and adults. Adult criminal proceedings are intended to be formal, adversarial hearings, open to the public, in which a judge or jury finds guilt or innocence, based on evidence pertaining directly to the offense in question. Adult defendants are assured the right to legal representation. In contrast, juvenile hearings are informal, and usually closed to the public and to news media. Such hearings are conducted by a referee or judge without a jury, and decisions may be based on information other than evidence related to the case.

If the youth is found delinquent at the adjudication hearing, a disposition hearing is then held. At this stage, the court is principally concerned with determining whether the youth is to be put on probation or placed in an institutional setting such as a foster home, a private institution, a boys' ranch, or a state training school. Disposition hearings are analogous to sentencing hearings in adult criminal courts.

However, as shown earlier, a significant number of cases are handled informally prior to adjudication and dispositional hearings, often without consent of parent or child. Recommendation for a nonadjudicated disposition frequently is made by the probation officer investigating the case, although in some jurisdictions it may require the consent of the prosecutor's office (as is the case in California). Some observers believe that such informal court intervention results if there is insufficient evidence to support the delinquency

petition. Although some interpret the trend toward informal processing as a progressive step that will prevent labelling of youths by
officials, there is an alternative explanation. It is possible that the
court has been forced to sift out certain cases prior to the adjudication
hearing in light of the Gault and Winship decisions, which require
more extensive proof to establish the validity of a petition. In most
cases, judicial approval of "informal probation" is contingent upon
an admission of guilt by the youths. As a result, youths may admit
to delinquent acts of which they are innocent because they fear being
sent to a juvenile institution or feel powerless to assert their legal
rights (Levin & Sarri, 1974):

> This informal probation procedure, even as statutory limited, is of
> dubious merit. The voluntariness of the child's consent and the truthful-
> ness of this confession are questionable, given the possibilities offered
> to the juvenile: fixed period of probation rather than possible institution-
> alization if he chooses the full hearing route. The child must gamble on
> asserting his rights. (p. 53)

For those youth who are adjudicated, the final step in the court's
process is the dispositional hearing itself. Here again, one is im-
pressed by the lack of formal criteria although states have made
some efforts to formalize the dispositional decision-making process.
For example, 21 states have enacted some kind of prohibitions or
regulations governing the placement of youth after adjudication in
adult jails and prisons.[8] Put differently, 29 states have no such
restrictions, which suggests that youth can be placed in such facilities at the discretion of the court. About half of the states still have
the power to sentence youth to an indefinite period of incarceration
up until the age of majority. Conversely, some states (Utah, Washington, and North Carolina) have developed very specific statutes or
administrative guidelines that limit the period of confinement for
youth in state correctional facilities. And 15 states set minimum and
maximum sentence lengths that serve to parallel sentence lengths
one would receive as an adult.

Formal probation is the most common disposition in the juvenile
court followed by placement in a residential facility of some type (see
Table 3.3 and Figures 3.1 and 3.2). Most statutes leave the length of
probation to the judge's discretion, with supervision ending when
the youth reaches the age of majority. Most adult criminal courts set
the probation terms at the time of sentencing. On the other hand,
those few states requiring a fixed length of time for juvenile proba-

tion set a maximum of 2 years, with periodic review every 2 months. If the judge does not choose formal probation, the other dispositional alternatives include placement in a foster home or private institution, commitment to a public juvenile training school, or fines and restitution.

When the youth receives a formal disposition, the court either relinquishes control over the case or shares that responsibility with state and local correctional agencies or a state parole board. In 19 states the court can determine whether a youth will be placed in an institution and what kinds of special programs he will be involved in. Eight states grant that authority to youth corrections agencies, and in the remaining states, the responsibility is shared between the court and corrections agencies. Authority for determining when a youth is no longer under the control of the state is equally diversified among the states. In 9 states the court decides when a youth will be discharged (Connecticut, Georgia, Indiana, Iowa, Maryland, Pennsylvania, Rhode Island, South Dakota, and Wyoming). In the remaining states, the decision is based on sentencing statutes, a shared decision process with the court and correctional personnel or the juvenile parole board. Most states set the maximum length of incarceration at the age of 21 or the age of majority.

The various state juvenile codes, which delineate the statutory provisions for the processing of youth, form the basis of the juvenile justice system. These codes ultimately sanction the decisions made by juvenile justice authorities. The inconsistency and ambiguity of juvenile codes suggest that states do not place a high value on the protection of children. Rather, state laws serve to legitimate pervasive social control over the lives of those children unfortunate enough to be caught in the web of the juvenile system. Although progress is being made in reforming this process, it has been slow in coming and has been resisted by those very agencies charged with the care of wayward youth.

Organizational Factors That Influence the Processing of Youth Through the Juvenile Justice System

To fully understand the juvenile justice system, we must go beyond the inadequacies of the juvenile codes and crude national data. In the following pages, we examine more closely the decisions of those responsible for enforcing juvenile codes—police, probation officers, and court personnel—and those factors that underpin such decisions.[9]

Police and the Decision to Arrest

Police typically are the first officials of the juvenile justice system that a juvenile encounters. Because youths form impressions about the quality of justice they can expect to receive based on this initial contact, the importance of police reaction to delinquency is critical. Police response ranges from a simple warning to arrest and detention. We now examine the complex or extralegal factors that interact to influence police response to youth. Assuming the overriding *parens patriae* ideology, one might expect the police to have developed an especially sensitive approach for dealing with children. On the contrary, evidence suggests that youths are treated as harshly as their adult counterparts and with less respect for their constitutional rights.

In practice, the two conflicting themes in police ideology, social service versus law enforcement, usually are resolved in favor of the more punitive approach. A former policeman has written that police recruits, when leaving the "ivory tower" atmosphere of the training academy, must make a crucial decision upon their first assignments in local precincts. They have to choose between the professional ideals taught in the academy and the pragmatic stance characterized by a "lock-them-up" attitude (Niederhoffer, 1967, p. 52). Neiderhoffer (1967) found that police develop a cynical and authoritarian attitude toward their work as their length of service increases, and that they eventually reject the social service approach: "The cynics deride the soft 'do-gooder' social service philosophy. The authoritarian reliance on strong-arm methods is attractive to them because when respect for men and principles is absent, force is substituted" (p. 227).

Some police officials, recognizing this pervasive cynicism among police officers, have attempted to develop police specialists (i.e., juvenile youth bureaus) to deal solely with youth. But even with this trend, the fact remains that the vast majority of police-juvenile encounters occur between regular officers and youth. Critics of police handling of juveniles attribute the tendency of police to ignore the civil rights of youths to the conflict of controlling crime while attempting to maintain a benevolent treatment approach (Cicourel, 1968):

But the professional orientation of the police department emphasizes the repression and control of criminal activities regardless of age and relies upon typified imputations of "disorganized" or "bad" environments for seeking offenders. For the police, "robbery" or "rape" has little to do with the age of the offender or his life circumstances. (p. 62)

Police often make no distinction between delinquents and adult criminals, although children are not accorded the same legal rights. Officers can utilize interrogation, search and seizure, and arrest tactics that would be clearly illegal if used with adult offenders. Police can take advantage of the fact that restrictions on evidence and due process are not rigidly adhered to in the more informal atmosphere of juvenile courts. Cicourel (1968) offers these conclusions:

> The apprehension of juveniles involves an almost immediate disregard for the procedures of criminal law; adult arrest, and search and seizure rules are seldom followed. There are few formal legal procedures followed, and the problem of evidence seldom poses a serious issue, inasmuch as a presumption of guilt is often an integral part of the investigative process. . . .
>   The police utilize a rather strict social control model for juveniles they feel are guilty and repeaters; the juveniles are handcuffed and treated as adults. (p. 62)

Extensive efforts have been made to educate rank-and-file police officers to adopt enlightened approaches in handling juveniles, but these efforts have had minimal impact. In fact, police officers have spoken out strongly for more punitive approaches to delinquency. In view of the historical role of police in controlling the poor segments of society, there seems little hope that reform efforts can remedy the situation.[10] Many people in poor and Third World communities believe that the relationship of police to juveniles will improve only if there is greater community control over all aspects of policing.

The Police Decision to Release or Refer

We have already noted that over 70% of all juveniles who are arrested by police subsequently are referred to the court. In addition, many contacts between police and youth never are formally recorded by state and federal crime reporting agencies. Informal contacts typically involve offenses such as curfew violations, running away, or trespassing, which usually result in a warning to the youth, although the police sometimes record these informal contacts for future use. Police can use these data to compile a case history of a juvenile, which later can be used if the juvenile commits a more serious crime and the police wish to ensure that the child is judged delinquent.

A study of two police departments in California illustrates the use of such records in generating a history of the juvenile to defend the dispositional decisions of police and probation officers (Cicourel, 1968):

> I have focused upon the significance of officers applying general policies or rules, based upon legal criteria and augmented by a sense of social structure and properties of the interaction scene, to designate acts of delinquency and criminal or ill character structure. The interrogation procedures and written reports constitute oral and written dossiers of juveniles, and provide the conditions for justifying evaluative and dispositional action. (p. 69)

One empirical study reflecting the pervasiveness of unofficial police intervention with youth was Bordua's (1967) analysis of the Detroit police. In 1964, the Detroit Police Department reported a total of 106,000 contacts with juveniles. The youth bureau interviewed 25,645 youths, who were either arrested by them or referred by the patrol division. In addition, 10,157 interviews with minors were conducted for the purpose of gaining evidence. In contrast, the official police statistics recorded only 5,252 juvenile arrests, suggesting that, in Detroit, police had informal contacts with youths nine times more frequently than they actually made arrests (Bordua, 1967).

Police departments vary considerably in formal versus informal processing of youth. A 1971 survey by the International Association of Chiefs of Police in three cities showed wide variations in informal processing of juveniles: The Kansas City, Kansas, police department handled less than 10% of its juvenile cases informally; the Topeka, Kansas, police department settled 20% to 30% informally; and in Des Moines, Iowa, the police settled 50% to 60% informally.

Before discussing the factors that influence whether the police arrest or use other alternatives with youths, let us briefly review the five basic options available to police:

1. Release accompanied by a warning to the juvenile
2. Release, accompanied by an official report describing the encounter with the juvenile
3. Station adjustment, which may consist of (a) release to parent or guardian accompanied by an official reprimand; (b) release accompanied by referral to a community youth services agency for rehabilitation; or

(c) release accompanied by referral to a public or private social welfare or mental health agency
4. Referral to juvenile court intake unit, without detention
5. Referral to juvenile court intake unit, with detention

In determining which option to employ, police are influenced by two conflicting models of law enforcement: the *due process* model and the *crime control* model (Packer, 1968). The crime control model implies that the primary function of law enforcement is to deter and control crime by strict enforcement of criminal laws. In this model, police view themselves as forming the "thin blue line" between civilized society and total anarchy. In contrast, the due process model, which emphasizes the protection of the constitutional rights of all citizens, is often viewed as an obstacle to law enforcement and the apprehension of criminals. In the eyes of police, search and seizure restrictions, limits on interrogation, and the legal presumption of innocence merely serve to protect sophisticated criminals from their just punishment.

For example, the past decade has witnessed a concerted attack by various law enforcement groups and former Attorney General Edwin Meese to remove the limitations imposed by the landmark Miranda decision. Skolnick (1975) summarizes this attitude:

> The ability of known "criminals" to frustrate and harass law enforcement, the commitment of the police department to structures for the apprehending of criminals, and the perceived demands of political superiors for the evidence of the policeman's ability and initiative, all combine, in the context of nontotalitarian norms about the initiative of workers, to bring the policemen to interpret procedural requirements as frustrating the efficient administration of criminal justice. (p. 183)

Coupled with this reliance on a crime control model, police tend to view themselves as self-confirmed experts or craftsmen in the field of law enforcement. The police appear convinced that they are the best qualified to determine whether an act is delinquent, when to release a youth rather than arrest him or her, when to detain a youngster, and when it is necessary to disregard certain individual rights in the interest of the community or the well-being of the delinquent. Without this level of flexibility, police feel it would be impossible to catch criminals (Skolnick, 1975):

> [The police officer] sees himself as a craftsman, at his best, a master of his trade. As such, he feels he ought to be free to employ the techniques

of his trade, and that the system ought to provide regulations contributing to his freedom to improvise rather than constricting it. (p. 196)

The problem of police discretion is not that police are hesitant to
assume responsibility for their actions, but rather that they believe
more specific guidelines would reduce the tools necessary for crime
fighting. Attempts to restrict police discretion have met with little
success. In California, the revised Juvenile Court Law, which Lemert
cites as a revolutionary reform, offers the following ambiguous
standard for police in decisions concerning the arrest of juveniles:
"In determining which adoption of the minor he will make, the
officer shall prefer the alternative which least restricts the minor's
freedom of movement, provided such alternative is compatible with
the best interests of the minor and the community" (California Revised Juvenile Court Law, 1961). Within such a broad framework the
officer maintains his freedom to act as he sees fit.

Additional examples of restrictions on the exercise of police discretion can be drawn from the training manuals of two metropolitan
police departments:

1. "All other cases in which the youth officer feels that the court action is
   the most feasible disposition will be brought to the attention (referral
   or detain decision) of the court" (Chicago Police Department, 1971).
2. "Juvenile officers are told to dispose of all juvenile offenders in the way
   that will be to the best interest of the offender and to society in general"
   (Wichita Police Department, n.d.).

Police guidelines and model standards do not specify the limits of police
discretion, but merely advise the police to act in the best interests of youth
and society. Law enforcement departments use this ideology to build
public confidence that police will act in a fair and unbiased manner.

A large body of research has attempted to isolate the factors
influencing the selective nature of police arrests. In general, these
studies (some of which are presented in the following sections)
indicate that "nonlegal" variables such as the youth's race, class, and
sex and the police's perception of the community's economic status
level have a significant influence on police decision making.[11]

The Influence of Community, Race, Social Class, and
Demeanor on Police Arrest and Court Referral Decisions

There is broad agreement in the literature that minority adolescents are overrepresented at all stages of the juvenile justice system

as compared to their numbers in the general population (Pope & McNeely, 1981). Some of the research suggests an "amplification effect" as minority youths are processed through the juvenile justice system (Fagan, Slaughter, & Hartstone, 1987; Fenwick, 1982).

As shown below, many of these studies are largely descriptive and are unable to reach definitive conclusions simply because the data used for analysis do not permit the researchers to isolate the direct effects of ethnicity on juvenile justice decision making. Although little doubt exists that various ethnic groups are arrested, detained, and sentenced to secure facilities at higher rates than other ethnic groups, it is not always clear whether ethnicity alone is the basis for the disproportionate numbers of minority youth throughout the juvenile justice process. To better understand the level of over-representation of disadvantaged and minority youth, one must first examine the arrest and court referral process typically triggered by law enforcement.

Youth referred to the juvenile court by police and other agencies do not represent the typical U.S. youth population. Numerous studies have shown that these youth are disproportionately male, African-American or Hispanic, and from low-income households headed by women.[12] Based on 1988 court referrals for delinquency cases, 81% were male and 32% were "nonwhite."

Table 3.5 shows court referral rates per 1,000 youth age 10-17 by race, controlling for offense and age. Within the delinquency offense groups, nonwhite court referral rates are two to three times higher for nonwhites. The level of disparities are highest for nonwhite youth charged for crimes of violence and drugs. Only among status offenses are the white and nonwhite rates comparable.

A comprehensive review of the literature since 1970 conducted by Pope and Feyerherm (1990a) found that most, but not all, studies reveal ethnicity as a significant variable in juvenile justice outcome decisions. That is, differences exist in juvenile justice outcomes among the major ethnic groups. However, there is considerable debate on whether the ethnicity effect is direct (i.e., causal), indirect, or spurious. For example, in a study utilizing Florida case records over a 2-year period, examined the effects of social and legal characteristics on detention, intake, disposition, and severity of disposition. They found that race influenced initial detention decisions in that black youths were more likely to be detained than white youths. Further, whether or not a youth was detained influenced all subsequent decisions because detained youths received the most severe dispositions.

One explanation is the perception of law enforcement toward certain communities in which they are deployed to control street

TABLE 3.5   Delinquency and Status Offense Case Rates by Race, Age, and Offense, 1988*

| Age | Person | | Property | | Drugs | | Public Order | | Status** | |
	White	Non-white	White	Non-white	White	Non-white	White	Non-white	White	Non-white
10	0.7	2.1	3.7	7.5	0.0	0.0	0.3	0.6	0.1	0.2
11	1.3	3.9	5.5	11.7	0.1	0.1	0.6	1.3	0.2	0.4
12	2.2	7.8	10.6	20.7	0.3	0.5	1.6	3.3	0.7	1.4
13	4.1	13.8	19.0	33.9	0.7	1.9	3.8	7.3	1.7	3.1
14	6.2	21.5	29.2	49.4	1.9	5.0	7.4	13.1	3.4	5.2
15	7.7	26.9	35.9	58.5	3.5	10.0	11.2	18.8	4.1	5.6
16	9.3	29.4	42.0	65.7	5.7	15.2	14.8	24.1	5.7	4.6
17	10.1	31.0	42.6	65.8	8.1	21.8	17.8	26.4	6.8	2.8
Total	5.2	16.8	23.6	39.2	2.4	6.2	7.1	11.5	3.0	3.0

SOURCE: Juvenile Court Statistics, 1988.
NOTES: * All numbers reflect court referral rates per 1,000 youth population age 10-17.
** Status offense rates reflect petitioned cases only.

crime. Police often make assumptions about communities described as lower class, impoverished, ghettos, or slums with respect to the community's capacity to generate crime and control youth defined as delinquent by police and the court. First, such communities are assumed to fulfill what Cicourel terms the "background expectancies" of delinquency and crime. That is, because police historically have concentrated their activities in lower-class neighborhoods, they have come to expect high crime rates to occur primarily in such areas. Second, poor neighborhoods are assumed to lack the local resources necessary to facilitate informal dispositions by police that would reduce the need for arrest, detention, and court referral. Although community resources for informal processing may or may not exist, police generally presume that poor communities contain only sources of social pathology and are ill-equipped to handle wayward youth without further action by the court. For example, although police often assume that single-parent families are inadequate for child-rearing in poor communities, they do not necessarily reach similar conclusions about divorced or separated parents in middle- and upper-class suburbia.

Carter and Lohman (1968), in a study of middle-class delinquency in California, found significant variations in police decisions to arrest or release informally in two middle-class communities when compared with police on a national basis. They offer the following conclusion:

These data clearly indicate that the "drop-out" rate, i.e., adjustments without the benefit of the formal agencies of juvenile justice, for the middle-class suburban youth at the law enforcement level is considerably above the national and state averages. Almost eighty percent of the youth with residence addresses in Lafayette or Pleasant Hill had their delinquency disposed of in an informal fashion by the law enforcement agency. This phenomenon, which we will later refer to as "absorption," is also found at the probation department level and within the juvenile court structure. (p. 20)

In this instance, the wealth and stature of the community affects the police's decision to arrest and intervene in a youth's life, such that wealthier communities experience more leniency in the processing of youth than less affluent communities. Police, influenced by respect for members of privileged communities, often hesitate to inform upper-class residents about the delinquency of their children.

A second study of police and probation practices in middle-income communities echoes the findings of Carter and Lohman (Cicourel, 1968). In this study Cicourel analyzed how delinquent behavior is conceptualized by various agencies of social control. The research revealed that the wealth and public image of a family determines, to a large extent, the nature of the disposition of a juvenile's case. Middle- and upper-class families were in the best position to project appropriate images, and to provide alternatives such as private tutoring, professional counseling, and private institutionalization. Cicourel (1968) explains the exercise of class influence:

When parents challenge police and probation imputations of deviance, when parents directly question law enforcement evaluators and dispositions, law enforcement personnel find it difficult to make a case for the criminality in direct confrontation with the family resources and a "rosy" projected future. Imputations of illness replace those of criminality, or the incidents reviewed as "bad" but products of "things" done by "kids" today. (p. 243)

Middle-income families, because of their fear of the stigma imputed to incarceration, mobilize resources to avoid this problem. The family's ability to generate or command resources for neutralizing or changing probation and court recommendations, as in adult cases, is a routine feature of the social organization of juvenile justice. (p. 331)

Closely intertwined with the influence of community are the more specific and individual level variables of race, class, and demeanor.

Several criminological studies have suggested that class and race are of primary importance in selective enforcement of juvenile statutes, whereas others conclude that these factors are at best of secondary importance. The latter have argued that the demeanor of the juvenile at the time of arrest or the seriousness of the offense explain why disproportionate levels of minority and low-income youth are caught up in the juvenile justice system. This argument implies that lower-class youth are disproportionately involved in delinquent activity or exhibit inappropriate demeanor more often than middle- and upper-class youth. For example, Gibbons's (1991) survey of studies on the attributes of delinquents makes the following conclusions:

> However, there may be more to the picture than has been indicated. The results which we have examined thus far have been drawn from records of various kinds. They seem to show that demographic characteristics of offenders are related to police disposition, but this is because serious- ness of offense is correlated with background characteristics. At the same time we might find that more subtle social factors operate in police decision-making if we were to examine particular instances of officer- offender interaction. (p. 39)

A significant number of conflicting studies utilize similar data and methodologies, but reach dissimilar conclusions. On both sides, findings are ambiguous, inconclusive, and contradictory, partially owing to the inadequacies of both data and methods employed. For example, Cicourel (1968) points out the weakness of quantitative delinquency research based solely upon police records in generating relationships and conclusions relevant to outside academia. While recognizing the limitations and difficulties inherent in such research, let us briefly examine some of the works that suggest that race and class are significant determinants in police arrest behavior and the subsequent processing of children.

The most recent study on this issue was published in 1987 by Huizinga and Elliott, who used their highly respected National Youth Survey (NYS) data to examine the relationship of self-reported delinquency to official arrest rates (Huizinga & Elliot, 1987). Unlike other studies, the NYS represents a national probability sample of the nation's 11- to 17-year-old population as of 1976. Each year this cohort is questioned with regard to their delinquent and substance use behavior. In subsequent years, the researchers also conducted a search of each youth's arrest records to better understand the rela- tionship of self-report responses and official police contacts. Significantly, they found that only 24% of the youth who commit crimes for which they could be arrested are actually arrested. In other words, a great deal of selectivity is operating between the stages of committing a crime and being arrested.

With respect to race, Huizinga and Elliott also found *no* differences in both the proportion and number of crimes committed by white and African-American youth. However, there is a significant difference in the probability that an African-American youth will be arrested for such behavior compared to a white youth. Specifically, African-American youth are two to three times more likely to be arrested for a serious crime than whites. These national data strongly suggest that criminal behavior is not the primary factor influencing the police's decision to arrest a youth (Huizinga & Elliot, 1987).

Robert Sampson (1986) reached similar conclusions using a methodology similar to that used by Huizinga and Elliott but with a more narrow focus, on the city of Seattle. In this analysis, Sampson used a stratified sample of 1,612 Seattle youth, ages 15 to 18, who had participated in a self-report survey identical to the one used by Huizinga and Elliott. For each youth, the record of official police contacts was also recorded so the amount of self-reported delinquency could be compared with the levels of official police contacts. Furthermore, the socioeconomic status (SES) of both the youth and his or her neighborhood also were measured.

Sampson sought to explain, through multivariate regression analysis, which set of background variables best explained the police's decision to arrest. The results showed that although self-reported delinquency was a significant predictor of arrest, the youth's community economic class rating was inversely and more strongly associated with the arrest decision. In other words, the extent to which youth were located in lower SES communities, the greater the likelihood of arrest even when taking into account the youth's level of self-reported delinquency. The youth's race and individual SES level also showed up as powerful variables, with African-American youth and low SES youth more likely to be arrested than white youth. However, the community SES ranking was dominant. In Sampson's terms these results illustrate the existence of a so-called ecological bias in which police vary their arrest policies according to the class context of the community they are patrolling.

An earlier study of race, class, and police arrest practices reached similar conclusions but used yet a third methodology. Thornberry's comprehensive study "Race, Socioeconomic Status and Sentencing in the Juvenile Justice System" (1979) considers all of the critical points in the juvenile intake process, from arrest to disposition. The data are based on a birth cohort of 9,601 cases collected in Philadelphia by Wolfgang et al. (1972). Holding constant both the seriousness of the offense and the number of previous juvenile offenses committed (recidivism), Thornberry found that the relationships of race and class to police disposition remained intact:

> But unlike the previous studies, the present study shows that when the two legal variables were held constant, the racial and SES differences did not disappear. Blacks and low SES subjects were more likely than whites and high SES subjects to receive severe dispositions. Although these differences were more noticeable at the levels of the police and the juvenile court than at the level of the intake hearing, they are generally observable at all three levels. (p. 97)

Williams and Gold, in their pioneering work entitled "From Delinquent Behavior to Official Delinquency" (1972), make an important distinction between delinquent behavior per se and delinquency that comes to the attention of juvenile authorities. In this work the authors compared the discrepancies between official reports and self-reported delinquent behavior in terms of sex, age, race, and socioeconomic status.[13] They found that although race and class do not affect the overall incidence of delinquent behavior in self-report analyses, upper-class boys surprisingly tend to commit more serious offenses than their lower-class counterparts.

Comparing police action with various levels of decision making and referral, the same authors report that police do not behave in a racially discriminatory manner at the time of arrest. They find instead that juvenile court intake units tend to treat African-Americans more harshly than whites (Williams & Gold, 1972, p. 226): "Differential treatment [of blacks] at that point [intake referral] cannot be attributed to the greater seriousness of their offenses compared to whites; for the seriousness of offenses seems to matter little in the determination of court referrals."

Williams and Gold suggest that discriminatory practices may reflect police response to background expectancies or stereotypes when assessing the adequacy of the juvenile's social milieu. They note that police and other social control agents tend to view poor, working-class families and communities as pathogenic and breeding grounds of crime and they tend to focus their resources on those populations.

In numerous studies of the impact of demeanor on police-juvenile encounters, the central issue is whether demeanor is independent of racial and socioeconomic influences. Piliavin and Briar (1964) suggest that demeanor is closely associated with race, because they found that an "uncooperative demeanor" was recorded for more than one third of African-American juveniles, compared to one sixth of the white youths contacted by police. Although it is conceivable that African-Americans may exhibit poor demeanor toward police, this should not be surprising considering the historical use of law enforcement in lower-class communities. The reluctance of African-American youths to view police as nonthreatening and friendly allows the police to justify an overzealously punitive approach toward African-Americans. Police beatings of African-American citizens often have resulted in victims being charged with "resisting arrest." In the words of one police official (Piliavin & Briar, 1964):

> If you know that the bulk of your delinquent problem comes from kids who, say, are from twelve to fourteen years of age, when you are out on patrol you are much more likely to be sensitive to the activities of juveniles in this age bracket than older or younger groups. This would be good law-enforcement practice. The logic in our case is the same except that our delinquency problem is largely found in the Negro community and it is these youths toward whom we are sensitized. (p. 212)

The self-fulfilling prophesy of "poor demeanor" on the part of poor and minority youths results because police are preponderant in their communities, and are prone to be overly sensitive about behavior that they view as hostile. Increasing resistance from the African-American community to police harassment has helped to reinforce the prejudices of police as well as to intensify police intervention in such communities (Piliavin & Briar, 1964):

> These discriminatory practices—and it is important to note that they are discriminatory, even if based on accurate statistical information—may well have self-fulfilling consequences. Though it is not unlikely that frequent encounters with police, particularly those involving youths innocent of wrongdoing, will increase the hostility of these juveniles toward law enforcement personnel. . . . They thus serve to vindicate and reinforce officers' prejudices, leading to closer surveillance of Negro districts, more frequent encounters with Negro youths, and so on in a vicious circle. (p. 213)

The interaction of race and demeanor helps explain the overrepresentation of African-Americans in official arrest figures. The fact that police tend to view delinquency as strongly related to race was borne out by Kephart (1954), who found in a survey of police officers in Philadelphia that 75% of the officers overestimated the extent of arrests involving African-Americans within their precincts (pp. 94-95).

The Probation Intake Decision

Once police decide to refer a youth to the juvenile court rather than using the informal alternatives available at the time of arrest, the child typically is referred to an intake unit of the court usually staffed by probation officers. The sole function of intake units is to screen the cases referred by police or other individuals to determine whether a formal delinquency petition should be filed in the court. If a decision is made to file a petition, an investigation of the case is made to determine the validity of the allegations in the petition. The intake officer may decide that the allegations are without basis or that the case may be difficult to substantiate, and suggest that the juvenile be informally processed without further court intervention.

Probation officers also are involved in the detention decision. Typically, when a juvenile is arrested, he or she is taken into custody, booked, and often transferred to a local detention unit to await further review by the intake officer. The detention facility can range from the local county jail, where the youth may be mixed with adult offenders, to a specialized juvenile detention unit staffed with counselors and other specialists. In cases where the juvenile is referred to an intake unit, the probation officer immediately must decide whether to further detain the child or release him or her to the custody of an adult.

In theory, probation officers are to represent a more sophisticated or professionalized approach to juvenile delinquency than police. They tend to be college-educated and are required to write numerous reports—essentially mini-legal briefs—arguing for dispositions that serve both the interest of the youth and that of the community. To present intelligent and persuasive arguments before the court, the probation officer must be aware of principles of law relating to jurisdiction, evidentiary restrictions, appeal motions, and dispositional alternatives. The officer also must be a therapist able to diagnose the etiology of the delinquent's problem and administer the appropriate assistance. Although probation officers are expected to possess academic skills and broad knowledge, this professional image invariably is negated by the reality of most probation departments (Cicourel, 1968):

The average probation officer's college degree gives him a broader base from which to claim professional status, but the organizational structure of the probation department leaves him few possibilities for change and little difference in pay. The probation department pyramids faster than the military-like police, so that a regular deputy probation officer is restricted in his internal mobility. (p. 95)

Some have argued that probation officers at the intake and post-adjudication stages function as no more than highly paid clerical workers, whose primary responsibility is to facilitate the processing of juvenile cases with minimal delay. Probation officers often are burdened with excessive caseloads and departmental priorities emphasizing social investigations, court appearances, and report writing, leaving them little time for counseling and supervising juveniles. Newly recruited officers quickly realize that the professional status is rapidly lost in the monotonous task of churning out reports.

Ohlin, Piven, and Pappenfort (1956), in an early study of probation, found three types of probation officers, each type with its own distinct ideology. One is the punitive officer, who reflects the image of a "frustrated policeman" and tends to view his work as law-enforcement oriented, much like the police ideology. In contrast to this type of probation officer is the "welfare worker," who adopts a social service approach. This type of officer, a relatively recent addition to probation departments, typifies the treatment approach that now pervades the juvenile justice system. Although "welfare workers" are trained in social work theory and often possess graduate social work degrees, they must make decisions that do not relate to a treatment perspective. Finally, there is the "protective officer," who tends to vacillate between the approaches of the "welfare worker" and the "frustrated policeman." This officer appears most concerned about not making any waves and remaining employed.

Despite what is known about probation, there have been suggestions that progressive changes in the juvenile system will originate and find support among probation officers. This view fails to recognize that although the perspective of probation officers differs from that of policemen, probation officers often share similar values. Unwin (1974), in his study of probation officers' attitudes in California—considered to be one of the more progressive states—found that probation workers favored increased use of detention:

[O]nly 4 percent of juvenile probation staff felt that minors were detained too often and 52 percent complained that they were not held as often as they should be. This variation is probably due to the fact that probation officers are the ones who request the detention hearing in the first place, but it does question the often-stated belief that probation officers are the most liberal or "soft-hearted" members of the criminal justice system. (p. 27)

For their jobs to be manageable and tolerable, probation officers must work in concert with police, prosecutors, and the courts. As a result, probation staff are influenced by these agencies in handling juveniles, which often stifles the efforts of progressive reformers.

Probation Intake Options

Once juveniles have been referred to the intake unit, several alternatives are available to the intake officer in disposing of cases. The range of alternatives varies from one jurisdiction to another depending upon factors such as community tolerance, the frequency of referrals, existing alternative resources, and resources available within the juvenile court itself. The last alternative includes access to detention facilities, probation resources, and the accessibility of juvenile court staff.

The major decision made by intake is whether or not a formal petition is to be filed. For nonpetition recommendations, three basic disposition alternatives remain: (a) release/dismissal, (b) informal probation, and (c) referral to another agency. As shown earlier in Figures 3.1 and 3.2, the most frequently chosen alternative is dismissal of the case. The cases of first offenders sometimes are dismissed because it is believed that the youths will not recidivate, whereas other cases may lack sufficient evidence to substantiate delinquency. Dismissal also helps reduce the congestion of the juvenile court, and does not so much reflect a lenient intent as a need to quickly process large numbers of cases.

Informal probation essentially means resolving cases without formal court intervention. Informal probation can take on different meanings depending on the attitude of the local court and probation department. Under informal probation, the child is supervised by either police or probation for a designated period of time, ranging from a few months to several years. The regulations of informal supervision may be just as stringent as the conditions of formal probation. If the youth fails to meet these obligations, it is possible to file a petition based on the original offense and begin the process again.

Many critics feel informal probation is an infringement of the youth's constitutional rights. The U.S. Children's Bureau (1966), in its *Standards for Juvenile and Family Courts*, states that

> no action which would deny or abridge the rights of a child or parent should be undertaken unless a petition is filed and a hearing held: probation has been defined as a legal status which to a certain extent limits the rights of the child and the parent and, therefore, should only be created by a formal court order. (p. 24)

But a youth who has been placed on informal probation still is vulnerable to having a petition filed. This is particularly noteworthy because one of the primary conditions of informal probation is an admission of guilt. One study notes that most courts impose informal probation only for those children who admit to the offense. Every case in which the juvenile denies guilt is automatically referred to formal adjudication or has a petition filed (Ferster & Courtless, 1969). Thus those children on informal probation have little defense available to them should they fail to meet the conditions of probation (Ferster & Courtless, 1969):

> Any child on informal probation, even under the model laws, faces the risk that for a considerable period of time formal court action on the original charge will be activated if he violates his probation conditions. Thus, under the present practices, a juvenile may be informally restricted for months, then taken to court on his original petition and again placed on probation or even committed to an institution. (p. 131)

The intake alternative used least often is the referral of youth to non-law-enforcement or private agencies. In 1984, only 8% of all court referrals were disposed in this fashion. Although it is difficult to determine what types of cases are handled in this manner, one can assume that youth from more affluent families, who have the necessary resources, are more likely to be sent to such agencies.

In cases where the decision to file a petition has been made, the intake officer has determined that existing community resources or the youth's family are insufficient, and that the case is of a sufficiently serious nature that it must be resolved by formal adjudication. This decision often involves consultations with law enforcement agents, especially the district attorney's office, to determine whether the case can be prosecuted. The increased discussions with the district attorney's office reflect recent requirements that juvenile court proceedings ensure the basic due process rights of youth. Questions are raised with the district attorney's office concerning the strength of the evidence and potential problems caused by police methods of arresting and detaining the youth. The impact of recent Supreme Court decisions on probation officers is viewed by Unwin (1974) as follows:

> The Gault and other decisions which have mandated many legal safe-guards for juveniles, the tightening of rules of evidence and the degree of proof necessary to make a finding, the provision almost routinely of defense counsel, and the general emphasis throughout society on protecting individual rights have vastly altered the traditional "parental" or equity nature of juvenile court to that of an adversary system which is, in many areas, almost identical to that of the criminal courts. The knowledge of the more stringent demands on "proving" a case to obtain a finding has doubtlessly influenced the decision making of the juvenile probation staff at every level. (p. 31)

It should not be assumed that those juveniles who have petitions filed against them necessarily commit the most serious delinquent acts. Although current data are not available, national figures in 1984 reveal that youth charged with "status offenses" had petitions filed in 73% of the cases, whereas the filing rate for youths charged with specific crimes was considerably lower, ranging from 39% for person crimes to 53% for drug-related behavior (Snyder, Finnegan, Nimick, Sickmond, Sullivan, & Tierney, 1984, p. 34).

If the decision is made to file a petition, the court must decide whether to continue to detain the youth. The detention hearing is similar, in principle, to bail hearings in adult criminal court; the decision to release turns on the likelihood of the youth's appearing for subsequent court hearings. It is not uncommon for police to use the threat of informal detention to obtain a confession from the youth (Cicourel, 1968). Probation officers also may rely on detention to gain additional information from a youth who would be less available if not in custody.

With these diverse alternatives, the correct option is left largely to the personal preference of the intake officers. Few states provide statutes or written court policies to govern intake decisions. According to the President's Commission on Law Enforcement and Administration of Justice (1967), many intake units set policies via "word of mouth" (p. 396). Because informal policies are not made public, there is a danger of arbitrary and unjust decisions, with few opportunities to review such probation determinations (Burns & Stein, 1967):

TABLE 3.6 Juvenile Court Processing Rates by Decision Point, by Race per 1,000 Youth Population

	White	Nonwhite	Total
Secure Detention			
Delinquency process	11.7	24.8	10.6
Status offenses	0.4	0.9	0.6
Disposition*			
Petitioned cases	20.2	37.6	23.9
Probation	9.6	15.5	10.4
Placement	5.0	9.8	4.9

SOURCE: U.S. Department of Justice Children in Custody Survey (1989).

> Few formal guidelines are available to those who are responsible for exercising discretion in determining which youngsters should be sent deeper into the judicial process. Where these guidelines do exist, their relevance and justice is open to question.... Without a system for the periodic review and correction of criteria and decision making practices in this area, such practices are infrequently refined and frequently arbitrary. (p. 396)

Influences on Probation Petition and Detention Decisions

As with the studies of police, research reveals associations between the race and socioeconomic status of youth and juvenile court dispositions. At the national level, nonwhite youth experience significantly higher rates of detention, petition filing, and placements than do white youth (Table 3.6).

In a review of the literature by Gibbons (1991, pp. 61-67), which includes such studies as Lemert and Rosenberg (1948), Shannon (1963), Terry (1967), Axelrad (1952), Cohn (1963), Cross (1948), and Alexander (1964), the author acknowledges evidence that probation recommendations made at the intake level are based on the race or class position of the child:

> What are we to conclude from these studies of probation disposition? ... Youths who have been involved in offenses which arouse members of the community, who commit law violations which result in sizable financial suffering to the victims, and who are repeaters, are the ones who most often get placed on the transmission belt to the training school. Ethnic characteristics, sex, age, and other demographic variables seem to be related to dispositions through their variances. (Gibbons, 1991, p. 38)

Cohen (1975), in a study of dispositions of three juvenile courts, draws an even stronger conclusion:

> Our study has yielded no empirical evidence to sustain the charge that youth of lower socioeconomic status are systematically accorded the most severe treatment by agents of the juvenile court. Similarly, there is no direct evidence to suggest minority youths are the objects of discriminatory treatment. (pp. 53-54)

But certain methodological problems are inherent in such conclusions. Variables such as "demeanor" or "community status" rarely are captured by quantitative studies of juvenile court decision making. Furthermore, we have already presented several studies that show that discrimination within the juvenile justice system occurs at the law enforcement level of arrest and court referral. Consequently, at the stage of juvenile court intervention one is left with a relatively homogeneous population with respect to race and socioeconomic status. As Cohen found in his study, it is statistically difficult to account for significant levels of intraclass variation in court dispositions because the vast majority of youth appearing in court are from African-American, Latino/Hispanic, or lower-class backgrounds. But, despite the problems associated with analysis of court decisions, some studies do illustrate the relationship of race and class to intake dispositions.

Gibbons cites Cohn's study as an explanation for the absence of demographic variables in intake dispositions, but that study in fact reports that young women and African-Americans were sent to institutions more often than white boys. Cohn explains that a high incidence of sexual misconduct in young woman was responsible for their commitments, whereas African-Americans were institutionalized more often due to the seriousness of their delinquent acts and because they tended to be defined as coming from socially deprived backgrounds. Cicourel (1968), Figueria-McDonough (1987), and Harari and Chwast (1964) also have shown that young women, lower-class, and African-American youth are often stereotyped in such a way that they appear to social control agents as delinquents and thus as requiring greater levels of juvenile court control and intervention.

Thomas and Sieverdes (1975) sought to clarify the confusion and contradiction resulting from these studies of probation intake. In their study of 346 juvenile case dispositions, they attempted to isolate the most significant legal and nonlegal variables affecting juvenile court dispositions. Their initial analysis showed that the seriousness of the most recent offense had the strongest relationship to court disposition. However, "nonlegal" factors such as age, number of codefendants, race, family stability, and gender also exerted an influence on the disposition. When these variables are controlled for, the power of the seriousness-of-offense variable is diminished for certain types of youth. For example, it was found that the seriousness-of-offense factor was most powerful for an African-American male from a lower-class background and with a prior record (Thomas & Sieverdes, 1975):

> These findings lead us to conclude that both legal and extralegal factors are being taken into consideration in the determination of whether to refer a given case for a formal [petition] hearing in the juvenile court. Indeed some social factors appear to provide an "insulation" which may inhibit such referrals. (p. 425)

Another valuable study on the impact of race and socioeconomic status in juvenile court decisions was conducted by Thornberry (1979). While controlling for both the seriousness of the offense and "recidivism" (i.e., prior delinquent history), Thornberry found that the bivariate relationships of race and socioeconomic status with the court decision points of intake and final disposition, though weakened, did not disappear. In other words, African-American youth and youth from disadvantaged backgrounds continued to receive the more severe dispositions while taking into account the youth's current charges and prior delinquent history. Thornberry (1979) concludes:

> Finally, the present findings should be related to the assumption often found in the theoretical realms of criminology, namely, that blacks and members of low SES are treated more harshly than whites and high SES subjects in the juvenile justice system. Clearly, the findings of the present study are in agreement with that assumption. (p. 98)

In summary, studies exist that both support and negate the presence of race and class in influencing intake and disposition decisions. After reviewing previous research findings that conflict with his own results, Thornberry believes there are no overt methodological reasons to account for these discrepancies. One could perhaps conclude that findings are relevant to only the courts being studied, as diverse policies are in effect throughout the nation's numerous and largely locally operated juvenile courts.

The Role of the Court Decisions

Although the number of youths affected by formal court proceedings is relatively small (see Table 3.3) due to screening by police and intake staff, this stage of the juvenile justice process has grave consequences for the child. Labelling theorists view the role of the court as critical, because it can impose a stigma that will remain with the youth throughout adult life. Although the term *delinquency* was envisioned as a means of reducing the stigma of youthful crimes, it has come to be synonymous with adult crimes in the eyes of many. State and federal crime reporting agencies may maintain complete files on all arrested youth, which crime control agencies routinely use in evaluating cases and selecting appropriate dispositions. Thus a determination of delinquency often is redefined by other agencies to infer criminal behavior for which a youth eluded significant punishment only because of his age.

Apart from the inherent assumptions of *parens patriae,* benevolence, and paternalism, the court has a latent goal of expeditious processing of youth with minimal interagency conflict. Due to the burden of excessive caseloads, the court is forced to function as a coordinating unit in order to keep abreast of its statutory obligations. The emphasis is upon harmonious relationships, as was envisioned by early advocates of the public defender system (Barak, 1974).

> The defense of the accused under a public defender law would require no more time nor effort than is now consumed. Indeed quite the contrary, for orderly arrangement of cases for trials would be far better effected between opposing offices than between a district attorney and a dozen lawyers with conflicting business. (Foltz, 1897, p. 400)

> The proper duty of the prosecuting attorney is not to secure a conviction, but to convict only after a fair and impartial trial. Upon the same principle it is not the duty of the public defender to secure acquittals of guilty persons, but to endeavor to ascertain the true facts and go to trial upon those facts, *the aim of both officials would be to go to work in harmony* to bring out a just administration of the law. (Rubin, 1979, p. 708, emphasis added)

A study of a public defender agency showed that all the actors in the court's adjudication and dispositional processes were highly dependent on each other's cooperation for the court to function in an orderly manner (Platt et al., 1968, pp. 12-17). Juvenile defendants usually met with their assigned lawyers for a few minutes prior to the formal hearing, with the bulk of negotiation taking place outside the courtroom. The ability of the public defender and the prosecutor to play their roles and maintain the atmosphere of justice depended on their willingness to accept unreasonable decisions, with the assurance that in the long run such cooperation would ensure stability and a more tolerable work atmosphere (Platt et al., 1968):

> [The public defender's] performance is judged by his superiors in a variety of ways. . . . He is expected to be properly prepared in court, not to ask for an unreasonable number of continuances, not to antagonize unnecessarily the state's witnesses, and not to offend the judges by requesting a change of venue on the grounds of prejudice. The public defender knows that assessments of his competence by judges will ultimately reach his boss. (p. 14)

Similar pressures are imposed upon all members of the juvenile court, and the need for such compromises has increased with the expansion of juvenile procedural rights. The prosecutor and public defender are obliged to consult with one another prior to making appearances in court. This consultation extends to the intake unit, as the probation officer routinely consults with the district attorney's office prior to filing a petition (Unwin, 1974):

> By law the district attorney is given no decision-making power in juvenile court. Only the probation officer can file a petition to bring a minor before the court. However, because of the almost routine presence of defense counsel in contested cases [in California] and the more rigorous demands on the type and sufficiency of evidence needed to sustain an allegation many probation departments consult regularly with the district attorney as to whether or not they have evidence to file a petition and, if so, what charges should be filed. (p. 42)

The interlocking interests of defense and prosecution have not resulted in more equitable treatment for children. Some authors, such as Lemert (1970, pp. 171-195), advance evidence to support the positive effect of attorneys in gaining favorable dispositions for young clients. A closer analysis of Lemert's data reveals that lawyers have been most successful in negotiating dispositions, but have had negligible impact in avoiding the court's control over youth. Moreover, youth represented by counsel are more likely to be detained than those without attorney representation, because they are viewed as contesting the court and disrupting normal procedure (Lemert, 1970, p. 148).

Although some have expressed fear that the presence of lawyers introduces an adversarial character to juvenile court proceedings, little data exist to support this concern. Although the court process may appear adversarial in nature, attention is focused primarily on the efficient handling of children with minimal conflict and delay (Platt et al., 1968):

> Mutual cooperation by all court personnel makes possible the management of large caseloads. . . . The public defender must be careful not to obstruct the efficient processing of cases, for the other court functionaries are depending upon him to help finish or expedite the court call for the day. . . . Aside from the role cooperation plays in facilitating the mechanics of the proceeding, it also makes the entire process more personally tolerable for everyone involved. Court interaction is intensely focused upon deciding the fate of other's lives and this responsibility is made impossible if conflict is the norm underlying the task at hand. The court functionaries see themselves as colleagues rather than adversaries, for "the probability of continued future relations and interaction must be preserved at all costs." (pp. 8-9)

This emphasis on the efficiency of the system is far removed from the ideal of the court acting on behalf of the child.[14]

Court Dispositional Options

The court has two basic alternatives: either to find the child "not delinquent" and remove him or her from the jurisdiction of the court or to find the child "delinquent" and make a dispositional judgment. Some states provide for special adjudication hearings, whose primary intent is to ascertain the legitimacy of the petition's allegations. In many instances, the judge is advised informally about a case by both prosecutor and public defender, so that the decision is made with involvement on the part of the youth. If the child is found delinquent, a separate dispositional hearing may be held at a later date, depending upon the policies of the court in a particular locale. Many states combine dispositional and adjudication hearings in the interest of saving time. Judges and referees have been known to base their findings on assessments of the child's social history made by probation officers, which may resemble hearsay evidence.

If the child is found delinquent, the court has a narrow range of dispositional alternatives available from which to select an appropriate treatment. The primary alternatives are formal probation or incarceration for an indeterminate period perhaps followed by a period of parole or aftercare supervision. In some courts, fines, restitution, and informal supervision also are used. It also should be noted that in some states a growing number of youth are placed in privately operated facilities or supervised in the community by privately operated organizations.

As previously noted in our discussion of legal codes, the juvenile system is unique in that the period of court supervision is continuous through the age of maturity. Those youths placed on probation, in foster homes, or on informal probation may have their disposition reviewed any time the court feels the child has violated the terms of the original disposition. This control is virtually unlimited, because a new hearing is not required to revoke prior decisions. Revocation is not necessarily predicated on subsequent delinquency, but may result from a youth's failure to maintain regular contacts with probation officers, from family difficulties, or from school truancy. There is no requirement that facts in a revocation request be verified, and often such cases receive informal disposition based on the probation officer's interpretation of the case.

One of the primary factors believed to influence the court's dispositions is the seriousness of the delinquent act. Even critics of juvenile justice have assumed a positive correlation between the seriousness of the offense and the disposition (Kittrie, 1971):

> In the case of minor first offenders, a warning and release are the usual disposition. Probation is more typically used for the second-time offenders or when the offense is more serious. . . . Institutional commitment, on the other hand, is described as reserved for the recidivists and hardcore offenders whose response to milder treatments is predictably unfavorable. (pp. 133-134)

However, a study of juvenile court dispositions in New York during 1965 (Lerman, 1971) refutes assumptions about the relationship between the seriousness of delinquency and disposition, and concludes:

1. Persons in need of supervision (PINS), such as status offenders, are more likely to be detained than serious delinquents (54% versus 31%).
2. Once detained, PINS are twice as likely to be detained for more than 30 days than serious delinquents (50% versus 25%).
3. The length of incarceration in juvenile prisons is 2 to 28 months for the serious delinquents versus 4 to 48 months for PINS. The mean length of imprisonment is 10.7 months for serious delinquents versus 16.3 months for PINS.

4. PINS are more likely to receive harsh dispositions and be sent to juvenile prisons than serious delinquents (26% versus 23%).

5. Nationally, Lerman (1971, pp. 28-29) estimates that 40% to 50% of the residents of juvenile institutions are status offenders or PINS, who are warehoused with the "more serious" offenders.

If, as Lerman's data suggest, the seriousness of the delinquent act is not the primary influence on the court's decision, it is necessary to ascertain the main factors. Platt et al. (1968), in their study of the public defender's office, suggest four criteria that are employed by the defender's office to determine how a case will be pleaded:

1. Does the juvenile claim to be innocent?
2. Is the alleged offense of a serious nature?
3. Does the juvenile have a criminal record?
4. Is the juvenile a "good kid" or a "bad kid?" (pp. 8-9)

The authors illustrate how these factors intertwine and affect whether the public defender will plead the case guilty or innocent. They conclude that the public defender's decision is based largely on a subjective character judgment of the juvenile (Platt et al., 1968): "The determination of whether a client is 'good' or 'bad' is, thus, crucial to the public defender's consideration of a case. How does he decide to apply these judgmental labels? To a great extent, he looks for criteria which positively indicate moral and social propriety" (p. 10). Here, once again, the notion of demeanor plays a crucial role in criminal justice decision making. These authors conclude that racial and economic discrimination does not result simply because most of the defendants are from the lower socioeconomic classes. Rather, judgments of character are derived from stereotypes prevalent in the dominant culture. Thus, the child treated most favorably by the court is the one who most successfully projects characteristics, such as charm and personality, that are viewed as positive traits in the white culture. Even the outward appearance of the client may be crucial in determining how a public defender responds to a given case (Platt et al., 1968, p. 10).

It is undeniable that because of discrimination based on race and class, a disproportionate number of African-American, Latino, and poor people are involved at the court adjudication stage. Although the impact in sheer numbers may not be as significant as at earlier stages, racial and class biases continue to operate at the court hearing. Thornberry's (1979) study previously reviewed here lends empirical support to this position. Examining dispositional institution-alization and probation placement, Thornberry sought the discriminating variables that explain variance in court dispositions. Using controls for both the seriousness of the delinquent act and prior record, Thornberry found that, at the court disposition stage, African-Americans are treated more severely than whites, and juveniles of low socioeconomic status are treated more harshly than those of high socioeconomic status.

Two more recent studies have produced similar results. Reed (1984) found that not only were African-American youth more likely to be detained by police but also they were more likely to receive the most severe court dispositions even while controlling for relevant offense and prior record characteristics. McCarthy and Smith (1986) found that although the expected influence of severity of offense and prior record on court dispositions were of primary importance, race and class also influenced the decision-making process, with minority and lower-class youth more frequently receiving the most severe dispositions.

Conclusion

We set two goals for this chapter. First, we intended to familiarize the reader with the juvenile court system—its philosophy, the various state juvenile laws, and the practitioners who make the system work. Second, we wanted to offer a critical perspective on the juvenile justice system. Our analysis paints a discouraging picture. Juvenile laws are vaguely worded and inconsistently applied, permitting extensive abuses in the handling of children by social control agencies whose discretion is largely unchecked. Instead of protecting children from injustices and unwarranted state intervention, the opposite effect frequently occurs. The practices and procedures of juvenile justice agents mirror our society's class and racial prejudices and fall disproportionately on African-American, Latino, and poor people.

These conclusions are not new. Many practitioners within the juvenile court share this critical perspective. The vital question is, "What is to be done?" Most critics of the juvenile court continue to offer narrow reform measures that do not confront the relationship between inequities in the juvenile justice system and inequities within society. Present innovations consist primarily of diversion, deterrence, decriminalization, and de-institutionalization. Although these reforms also embrace a critical perspective on the present justice system, they imply that through policy and program innovation alone, the juvenile justice system can be transformed into a humane and equitable process.

Although we would not discourage such efforts, our analysis suggests that correcting the injustices of this system will come about largely through broad changes in society. The quest for juvenile justice is tied inextricably to the pursuit of social justice. Reforms will continue to fail, as they have in the past, if they do not address the maldistribution of wealth, power, and resources throughout society.

Notes

1. Juveniles frequently are held in facilities servicing multiple client populations. Many facilities are necessary to provide suitable confinement for a wide range of custody objectives.

2. Much of the data for this section on juvenile laws were taken from Mark Levin and Rosemary Sarri, *Juvenile Delinquency: A Comparative Analysis of Legal Codes in the United States;* National Conference of State Legislatures, *Legal Dispositions and Confinement Policies for Delinquent Youth;* and Community Research Associates, *An Analysis of State Juvenile Codes.* The last report was based on a national survey of existing juvenile codes as of 1980 and subsequently updated in 1987. It is probable that many laws have since changed, but there has not been another major national survey to update these findings.

3. For excellent critiques of liberal conceptions of law, see Richard Quinney, *Critique of Legal Order,* and Isaac Balbus, *The Dialectics of Legal Repression.*

4. A review of the conflict perspective can be found in the works of Richard Quinney, *Crime and Justice in Society, The Social Reality of Crime,* and *Criminology: An Analysis and Critique of Crime in America;* Austin Turk, *Criminality and Legal Order* and "Conflict and Criminality"; and George Vold, *Theoretical Criminology.* An excellent summary and critique of the conflict theorists is provided by Ian Taylor, Paul Walton, and Jock Young in *The New Criminology.*

5. Aaron Cicourel, *The Social Organization of Juvenile Justice;* Robert Emerson, *Judging Delinquents: Context and Process in Juvenile Court;* Irving Piliavan and Scott Briar, *Police Encounters with Juveniles;* Terence Thornberry, *Race, Socioeconomic Status, and Sentencing in the Juvenile System;* and Meda Chesney-Lind, *Judicial Paternalism and the Female Status Offender,* are but a few of the numerous studies documenting such biases.

6. Plea bargaining involves an agreement whereby the defendant enters a plea of guilty in return for a promise from the district attorney that some charges will be dropped, or that the sentence will be less harsh. Most adult criminal cases are settled through plea bargaining.

7. Most states do not require that the juvenile court establish "probable cause" that the youth is guilty of the alleged crime prior to transfer to adult court.

8. The data presented in this section are taken directly from National Conference of State Legislatures, *Legal Dispositions and Confinement Policies for Delinquent Youth.*

9. Many credit the labelling perspective for encouraging research on criminal justice practitioners. See, for example, Howard Becker, *Outsiders: Studies in the Sociology of Deviance;* Edwin Lemert, *Social Pathology;* and Richard Quinney, *The Social Reality of Crime.*

10. The presence of professional and state-organized police forces is a recent phenomenon. Until the middle of the 19th century, metropolitan areas in the United States were guarded by contingents of community volunteers who worked in a watch system. During the first decades of the 19th century industrialization expanded, triggering a massive migration of U.S. workers from rural to urban centers. Waves of European immigrants fulfilled the need for a ready supply of cheap labor, thus adding to the rapid urbanization of the United States. It was feared by those in the upper classes that traditional police tactics would be ineffective in controlling the large working-class section of large cities. Protection was felt necessary due to the possibility of increased militancy and insurrection by workers. As Roscoe Pound noted in *An Introduction to the Philosophy of Law,* a central theme of progressive era reformers, which remains intact in current policy ideology, was the necessity for more effective social control forces to meet problems posed by society's increasing complexity and diversification. Professional police forces promoted the assimilation of the poor into the economic and social roles envisioned by those in *power.* The major concepts of police reform to emerge from the Progressive Era were centralization, crime prevention and deterrence, professionalism, the use of technology, and scientific approaches to law enforcement. For a detailed historical analysis of U.S. police forces see Center for Research on Criminal Justice, *The Iron Fist and the Velvet Glove: An Analysis of the U.S. Police.*

11. It has been well established in a number of studies that the adult arrest decision is selective and based, in part, on nonlegal variables. For a good summary of these reports see Douglas A. Smith, Christy A. Visher, and Laura A. Davidson, "Equity and Discretionary Justice: The Influence of Race on Police Arrest Decisions."

12. See Barry Krisberg and Ira Schwartz, "Rethinking Juvenile Justice," and H. Snyder, T. Finnegan, E. Nimick, M. Sickmond, D. Sullivan, and N. Tierney, *Juvenile Court Statistics, 1985,* for summary data on the attributes of youth referred to the juvenile court.

13. This study is in the tradition of self-report studies of delinquency, such as I. Nye, J. F. Short, and V. Olson, "Delinquent Behavior"; Lamar T. Empey and Maynard L. Erickson, "Hidden Delinquency and Social Status"; John P. Clark and Eugene P. Wenninger, "Socio-Economic Class and Area as Correlates of Illegal Behavior Among Juveniles"; and Albert J. Reiss, Jr., and Albert Lewis Rhodes, "The Distribution of Juvenile Delinquency in the Social Class Structure."

14. G. Barak, *The Public Defender,* shows that the purpose of the public defender movement was not so much to help the poor by providing counsel. Rather the public defender idea was designed to make the court process more efficient, and to unburden lawyers from the financially unrewarding task of representing indigent defendants under the old assigned counsel system.

4

Taking Youth Into Custody
and the Influence
of Gender and Race

Introduction

In Chapter 3, we reviewed how the contemporary juvenile court operates in terms of processing the more than 1 million youth who are referred each year. Although the nature of the crime and the youth's prior record heavily influence the court's decision-making process, we also noted the influence of so-called nonlegal factors such as social class, gender, and race. In this chapter we examine in more detail the influence of gender and race, especially regarding those decisions that result in the most punitive and controlling actions the court can take with a youth—taking a youth into custody.

One form of custody—detention—which occurs prior to a petition being filed, already has been discussed in some detail in Chapter 3. However, other forms of custody can occur after the youth has been adjudicated and has been given a "placement" disposition. In such instances, the court may commit the youth to either a private or public operated facility. Choices also exist to either commit the youth to a local or county-operated custody system or a state-operated system. And the court may even commit the youth to a facility originally designed for detention purposes only.

TABLE 4.1   Juveniles in Public and Private Correctional Facilities, 1979-1989

	1979	1983	1985	1987	1989	% Change 1979-1989
A. Private facilities						
Total admissions	69,507	88,806	101,007	125,954	141,463	103.5
Male	40,251	54,439	59,928	74,701	84,251	109.3
Female	29,256	34,367	41,079	51,253	57,212	95.5
1-Day counts	28,688	31,390	34,080	38,143	37,822	31.8
Male	20,512	22,242	23,844	26,339	26,602	29.7
Female	8,176	9,148	10,236	11,804	11,220	37.2
B. Public facilities						
Total admissions	568,802	530,200	527,759	590,654	619,181	8.9
Male	453,342	423,844	423,135	472,893	506,309	11.7
Female	115,460	106,356	104,624	117,761	112,872	-2.2
1-Day counts	43,234	48,701	49,322	53,503	56,123	29.8
Male	37,167	42,182	42,549	46,272	49,443	33.0
Female	6,067	6,519	6,773	7,231	6,680	10.1
C. Public and private facilities						
Total admissions	638,309	619,006	628,766	716,608	760,644	19.2
Male	493,593	478,283	483,063	547,594	590,560	19.6
Female	144,716	140,723	145,703	169,014	170,084	17.5
1-Day counts	71,922	80,091	83,402	91,646	93,945	30.6
Male	57,679	64,424	66,393	72,611	76,045	31.8
Female	14,243	15,667	17,009	19,035	17,900	25.7

SOURCES: The 1979-1989 Census of Public and Private Juvenile Dentention, Correctional and Shelter Facilities: Admissions for Calendar Years 1978, 1982, 1984, 1986, 1988; and 1-Day Counts for December 31, 1978; February 1, 1983, and 1985; February 3, 1987; February 14, 1989.

Since 1979, the number of youth incarcerated in public and privately operated facilities increased by 31%, from 72,000 to nearly 94,000 by 1989 (see Table 4.1). Significantly, youth committed to privately operated facilities more than doubled while the public facility population increased by 30%. In total, there were over 760,000 admissions to these facilities in 1989 with most of the admissions being to detention centers for relatively short periods of time. The total operating cost of this system is nearly $3 billion, or approximately $31,000 per youth per year.

Considerable variation exists among the states in their use of custody as either a court disposition or for detention purposes (Table 4.2). The nation's overall custody rate is 367 per 100,000 youth population age 10-17. Nevada and California rank 1 and 2 (700 and 666 custody rates per 100,000 population), whereas Hawaii has the lowest rate, which is one seventh that of California (103 per 100,000).

(text continued on page 116)

TABLE 4.2 Rate* of Juveniles in Custody (1-Day Counts) by Reason for Custody by Region and State, 1989

	All Facilities			Public Facilities			Private Facilities**		
	Delinquent Offenses	Status Offenses	Non-Offenders	Delinquent Offenses	Status Offenses	Non-Offenders	Delinquent Offenses	Status Offenses	Non-Offenders
U.S. Total	259	36	73	207	9	3	51	27	70
Northeast	228	51	89	137	3	3	91	47	87
Connecticut	184	40	150	115	9	0	69	31	150
Maine	215	0	41	194	0	0	21	0	41
Massachusetts	142	17	57	47	0	0	95	17	56
New Hampshire	136	36	29	114	0	0	22	36	29
New Jersey	230	16	28	227	10	10	4	6	17
New York	221	90	127	171	0	0	50	89	127
Pennsylvania	297	52	90	85	3	2	212	50	88
Rhode Island	173	66	143	117	13	0	56	53	143
Vermont	84	5	161	39	0	0	44	5	161
Midwest	226	60	93	171	19	5	54	41	88
Illinois	174	9	28	165	0	0	9	9	28
Indiana	204	90	98	157	34	12	46	56	86
Iowa	214	149	168	104	26	12	110	123	145
Kansas	329	58	199	244	10	10	85	48	189
Michigan	241	34	74	165	11	5	76	23	69
Minnesota	221	49	87	132	3	0	89	45	87
Missouri	148	87	121	144	59	5	4	28	116
Nebraska	219	105	229	159	4	2	59	101	227
North Dakota	171	76	100	97	27	0	73	49	100
Ohio	272	77	85	237	30	5	36	47	80
South Dakota	357	125	75	231	38	0	126	86	75
Wisconsin	232	44	115	128	2	0	104	43	114
South	185	19	61	164	7	4	22	12	57
Alabama	173	35	13	161	17	1	12	19	13

Arkansas	99	5	54	88	1	1	11	4	52
Delaware	227	0	14	206	0	0	21	0	14
D.C.	939	59	27	773	29	6	165	31	20
Florida	214	4	65	220	11	2	16	9	63
Georgia	237	19	63	189	1	3	25	3	60
Kentucky	122	44	72	112	22	4	9	22	69
Louisiana	239	29	30	222	6	3	17	23	27
Maryland	197	17	68	162	1	2	35	15	65
Mississippi	121	11	2	119	10	2	1	1	0
North Carolina	173	29	64	156	5	4	18	24	60
Oklahoma	119	29	102	77	3	8	42	26	94
South Carolina	201	18	24	197	10	1	4	7	22
Tennessee	171	15	47	157	8	6	14	7	41
Texas	160	12	77	129	2	1	30	10	76
Virginia	243	28	113	229	12	17	14	15	96
West Virginia	115	24	30	76	0	0	39	24	30
West	441	22	58	377	5	2	64	17	56
Alaska	453	54	234	324	0	0	129	54	234
Arizona	342	12	55	273	5	1	69	7	54
California	595	15	56	526	2	1	69	12	55
Colorado	246	39	88	158	6	0	88	33	88
Hawaii	75	16	12	71	7	1	4	9	12
Idaho	119	17	25	84	1	0	35	16	25
Montana	220	40	111	190	4	28	30	35	83
Nevada	594	67	39	447	49	14	147	18	24
New Mexico	310	24	49	277	4	3	34	21	46
Oregon	321	26	71	208	0	0	113	26	71
Utah	100	35	31	72	11	2	28	25	29
Washington	238	8	44	230	0	6	7	8	38
Wyoming	190	248	140	98	119	0	92	129	140

SOURCE: 1989 Census of Public and Private Juvenile Detention, Correctional and Shelter Facilities; and the U.S. Bureau of the Census Population Estimates (unpublished).
NOTES: * Rates are calculated per 100,000 youth age 10 to the upper age of original court jurisdiction in each state for 1989.
** May include some out-of-state placements in some jurisdictions.

115

As indicated above, youth can be committed to either a public or privately operated facility. Table 4.3, which compares the attributes of youth placed in public versus private facilities, shows that youth placed in private facilities tend to be disproportionately young women, white, and charged or adjudicated more for less serious property and person crimes. Public facilities, because they include detention facilities, have far larger numbers of youth being admitted each year and a much shorter length of stay. They also tend to be crowded and include many large training school facilities.

These differences, especially with respect to gender and race, have raised concerns that private facilities are increasingly reserved for white and young woman delinquents, while minorities are increasing being placed in the more crowded and more secure public facilities. The remainder of this chapter focuses on those court actions that contribute to disparities among the states and decisions to place a youth in a public versus a private facility. In particular, we examine the controversial issues of race and gender in terms of their relative contribution to the growing number of youth placed in juvenile correctional facilities.

The Influence of Race

There has been growing national concern about the overrepresentation of minority youth (traditionally defined as blacks, Native Americans, Hispanics, and Asians) confined in secure facilities. Unquestionably, minority youth, and in particular African-American males, are confined in public correctional facilities disproportionately to their representation in the general population. Moreover, this trend has been increasing.

Table 4.4 summarizes the number of youth in juvenile facilities from 1985 through 1989 by traditional ethnic/racial categories. The numbers of white youth who were taken into custody during that period *declined* from 29,917 to 22,127 (a 26% decline). The same trend persists if the focus is solely on youth in secure juvenile facilities (from 23,568 in 1985 to 16,712 by 1989, for a 29% decline). Conversely, a substantial *increase* occurred in the numbers of black, Hispanic, and Asian youth so confined. Numerically, the largest increase was for blacks, from 18,247 in 1985 to 23,707 by 1989 (a 30% increase), followed by Hispanics (a 32% increase) and Asians, who in percentage of growth experienced the highest rate (a 104% increase). These data, however, provide little insight as to why the nation's public juvenile facilities increasingly are being filled with minority youth.

TABLE 4.3   Characteristics of Public and Private Youth Populations, 1989

	Public	Private
Total population	56,123	37,822
Total facilities	1,100	2,167
Male	88%	70%
Female	12%	30%
White/Non-Hispanic	40%	60%
Black	42%	29%
Hispanic	16%	8%
American Indian	1%	2%
American Asian	1%	1%
Person crime	27%	19%
Serious property crime	29%	26%
Other property crime	14%	28%
Alcohol and drug crime	12%	14%
Public order crime	5%	2%
Technical violations	9%	2%
Other	3%	9%
Total admissions	619,181	141,463
Average length of stay	33 days	98 days
Percent overcrowded	2%	25%

SOURCES: 1989 Census of Public and Private Juvenile Detention Correctional and Shelter Facilities: Admissions for CYA 1988; and 1-Day Counts for February 15, 1989.

Research conducted to date has been contradictory as to the nature and extent of the problem. For example, is the problem attributable to (a) minority youth being more involved in delinquent behaviors; (b) a juvenile justice system that treats minority and white youth differentially in its decisions to arrest, detain, adjudicate, or sentence; or (c) a combination of these and other external factors? If one believes the juvenile justice system is a major contributor to the problem, exactly where in the process is this most apparent, for which ethnic groups, and how can it best be corrected?[1]

Definitions of Minority Youth

When referring to the various minority groups, the literature, including reports, statistical summaries, and census data, commonly use the terms *White (non-Hispanic), Hispanic, Black, Asian & Others.* These terms, however, can be misleading and often inaccurate. The parenthetical "non-Hispanic" following the category "White" has only been a recent addition in census surveys. This addition was an

TABLE 4.4   Juveniles in Custody, One-Day Counts for All Public
             Facilities by Race/Ethnicity, 1985-1989

	1985**		1987		1989	
	N	Percentage*	N	Percentage	N	Percentage
White	23,418	(48.00)	23,375	(44.00)	22,201	(40.00)
Black	18,269	(37.00)	20,898	(39.00)	23,836	(42.00)
Hispanic	6,551	(13.00)	7,887	(15.00)	8,671	(16.00)
American Indian	706	(1.43)	774	(1.00)	637	(1.00)
Asian American	378	(0.76)	569	(1.00)	778	(1.00)
Total	49,322	(100)	53,503	(100)	56,123	(100)

SOURCE: 1985-1989 Census of Public Juvenile Detention, Correctional and Shelter Facilities
NOTES: * Figures may not add up to 100% due to rounding.
** For 1985 the number of whites and blacks were estimated due to some overlapping in those categories. For that year, blacks and whites were indistinctively included in the Hispanics category.

attempt to address the complications created by the assumption that the present categories are mutually exclusive, when in fact they are not. In fact, "White" or "Caucasoid," "Black" or "Negroid," and "Asian" or "Mongoloid" are the three main accepted anthropological races. "Hispanic" is an ethnicity, not a race.

Ethnicity refers to cultures of common language, custom, and social views. An ethnic group can include more than one racial group, and a race will definitely include several ethnicities. For example, there are people who are "white," "black," and "Asian" Hispanics, and the "Asian" race includes many ethnicities, such as Chinese, Japanese, and Korean. Although the parenthetical "non-Hispanic" was intended to solve the confusion, the definitional problem still remains.

Using only ethnic labels avoids the confusions of race and ethnicity. For these reasons, the following ethnic group terms may be more precise as well as historically current:

1. Anglo-American (or Euro-American, traditionally referred to as white)
2. Latino (traditionally referred to as Hispanic)
3. African-American (traditionally referred to as black)
4. Asian-American (traditionally referred to as Asian)[2]

Studies on the Influence of Race

A number of studies have been conducted during the past decade attempting to determine the extent to which race or ethnicity influence juvenile court decisions to place youth in secure facilities. Researchers tend to disagree as to the most appropriate explanation for the high rates of confinement of minority youths. One view is that minority incarceration rates can be explained by the disproportionate involvement of minority juveniles in serious and violent youth crime.

For example, Hindelang (1982) reported that African-American youth have higher rates of arrest for offenses such as robberies, rapes, aggravated assaults, and simple assaults. Similarly, studies by Blumstein (1982) and Wolfgang et al. (1972) have shown higher rates of criminal involvement for African-American males. Victimization studies conducted by the U.S. Department of Justice, where the ethnic background of the offenders was determined, showed extremely high rates of offending by African-American males. From this perspective, the higher incarceration rates for blacks is simply a reflection of these youth committing more serious crimes, which results in decisions to detain and, ultimately, to institutionalize these youth at much higher rates.

In the only study of national trends in 1977, 1979, and 1982, Krisberg, Schwartz, and Fishman (1987) found that minority youth are incarcerated at a rate three to four times that of Anglo-Americans, and that minority youth tend to be confined in secure facilities, whereas Anglo-American youth represent the majority of those confined in private facilities. Once again, the rates of overrepresentation were most pronounced for African-American males. The data also show differential treatment across time periods. From 1977 to 1979, when rates of youth incarcerations were declining, minority rates did not decrease as sharply as Anglo-American rates. Anglo-American rates accounted for 75% of the entire decline. From 1979 to 1982, when rates of youth incarceration were increasing, minority youth bore the brunt of the increase, representing 93% of the entire increase. Thus, over time, the disproportionate rate of incarceration has become more pronounced when examined on a national level.

A unique feature of the above national study is a state-by-state calculation of Anglo-American and minority arrest rates in 1979. These data reveal large disparities among some states and few differences among others. The researchers conclude (Krisberg et al., 1987):

> These data reveal that there are a number of states where minority youth incarceration rates are close to those for [Anglo-Americans]. In other jurisdictions, however, rates of minority incarceration are four to five

times greater than rates of [Anglo-American] incarceration. These interstate differences are intriguing and suggest the need for a much more
localized analysis of differential incarceration patterns. (p. 190)

Krisberg et al. (1987) also tested the hypothesis that higher rates of
incarceration for certain minority groups were simply the result of
higher delinquency and arrest rates. Using Uniform Crime Report
juvenile arrest data and self-report delinquency data collected by Elliott
and Ageton (1980) via the National Youth Survey, Krisberg et al. found
that although African-American males have higher rates, these higher
rates are not of such a magnitude as to explain the much higher
incarceration rates:

> Data on arrests and self-reported delinquency were examined to evalu-
> ate the hypothesis that high rates of incarceration of minority youth were
> a function of their greater involvement in serious criminal behavior. This
> hypothesis was not supported by the best available data. Rather, the data
> on arrests and self-reported crime raise further questions about juvenile
> justice decision-making processes that may be consciously or unwit-
> tingly exacerbating minority youth incarceration. (p. 200)

To further test whether arrest and incarceration rates are a reflection
of crime rates, more recent results from the National Youth Survey were
examined by Huizinga and Elliott (1987). They analyzed a nationally
representative cohort of youth who were tracked from 1976 through
1980. Their research found slightly higher rates of delinquent behavior
among ethnic groups. However, there were significant differences in
the likelihood of arrest according to ethnic group. African-Americans
are arrested seven times more often than Anglo-Americans for minor
offenses, and twice as often for the more serious index crimes (homicide, robbery, assault, rape, burglary, theft, and auto theft). For the same
type and amount of crime involvement, minorities also tend to be
charged with more serious offenses than Anglo-Americans, even
though there are "no racial differences in the severity of offenses as
indicated by . . . greater physical injury to victims or the use of weap-
ons" (Huizinga & Elliott, 1987, p. 220). Huizinga and Elliott's (1987)
conclusions are similar to those of Krisberg et al. (1987):

> [A] summary of the findings would suggest that differences in incarcer-
> ation rates among racial groups cannot be explained by differences in
> offense behavior among these groups. The assertion that differential
> incarceration rates stem directly from differences in delinquency in-
> volvement is not supported by these analyses. There is some indication

of differential arrest rates for serious crimes among the racial groups, but further investigation of the relationship of race to arrest and juvenile justice system processing is required if reasons underlying the differences in incarceration are to be more fully understood. (Huizinga & Elliot, 1987, p. 221)

Other studies have been conducted at specific jurisdictions across different regions of the United States, and over different time periods, and have found ethnicity to have a pervasive and systematic effect on juvenile court decisions. This effect has been noted in a 1976 study by Fenwick (1982) of a major eastern city, in a 1983 study of a western state by Fagan et al. (1987), and in a 1982 study of the southeast metropolitan areas by McCarthy and Smith (1986).

The McCarthy and Smith study concluded that ethnicity and class become more important, and legal factors become less important, at later stages in the juvenile court process. In other words, minority youth increasingly receive custody placements at the referral, adjudication, and disposition stages of the court process. This "cumulative effect" of race also was found to be true in California and Florida during 1985 by Pope and Feyerherm (1990a). Pope and Feyerherm (1990a) found that minority youth receive more severe dispositions than Anglo-American youth, though the differential treatment is more pronounced at the earlier decision points, such as intake and detention. They also found that the pattern of differential treatment is not the same in all California and Florida counties, and county patterns can differ from the overall state pattern.

Finally, in a recent study by Peterson (1988) of New York juvenile court waivers to adult courts, race surfaced as having an independent effect in the court's decision-making process. In New York, youth who are age 16-18 may be tried in adult court or may receive a "youthful offender" (YO) designation indicating a more lenient sentence. In this study of 6,453 youthful defendants processed by the state's felony courts, the probability of receiving a YO disposition was reduced for black and Hispanic youths by 12% and 10%, respectively, while controlling for the offender's charges, prior record, and other background factors.

Other studies also using multivariate statistics have examined the interaction of ethnic status and legal factors, and have found similar evidence to support the bias theory although the effects often are reduced (Fagan et al., 1987):

[When] controlling for offense severity, other offense characteristics, and extralegal factors in addition to race . . . the results show racial disparities

TABLE 4.5   Juvenile Custody Rates for Juveniles in Public Facilities by
Three Major Offense Groups, United States, and California, 1989

| | Rate per 100,000 Juveniles | |
Offense Group	United States	California
Criminal offenders	207	463
Status offenders	9	2
Non-offenders	3	1

SOURCE: Children in Custody Survey, 1989, U.S. Department of Justice, Juveniles in Public
Facilities (secure and nonsecure).

at each point, with minorities consistently receiving harsher dispositions. . . . Race was a direct, indirect, and interactive influence at various
decision points. (p. 224)

Some studies, however, contradict these findings. For example,
Cohen and Kluegel's (1979) study of juvenile court adjudication decisions in two metropolitan juvenile courts (Denver and Memphis) found
no support for the conclusion that race and class exert an independent
and residual effect on court dispositions resulting in secure placement.
Instead, they conclude that sex, court philosophy, and type of offense
have the greatest influence on court decision-making.

The 1991 California Study

To help the reader better understand the dynamics of this issue,
the following section summarizes the results of a major study undertaken by National Council on Crime and Delinquency (NCCD) for
California. California is significant because of its relative size and the
fact that it has the highest juvenile custody rate among all the states.
As shown in Tables 4.5 and 4.6, California has a very high rate of
custody compared to the national averages and represents nearly
30% of the entire juvenile custody population.

The ethnic pattern of distribution for these incarcerated juveniles
is somewhat different in California than for the nation as a whole.
California incarcerates a much lower share of Anglo-American youth,
a slightly lower share of African-American youth, but a much larger
share of Latino youth compared to national figures (Table 4.6). The
higher proportion of Hispanic/Latino youth is due primarily to
California's large Latino youth population, which exceeds that of
most states.

TABLE 4.6   Juveniles in Public Facilities by Ethnicity, California, and U.S. One-Day Counts, 1989

Ethnicity	United States		California	
	N	%	N	%
Anglo-American	22,201	40	4,193	26
African-American	23,836	42	5,862	37
Latino	8,671	16	5,205	33
American Indian	637	1	77	1
Asian/Pacific Islander	778	1	532	1
Total	56,123	100	15,869	100

SOURCE: Children in Custody Survey, 1989, U.S. Department of Justice, one-day counts of juveniles in public facilities (secure and non-secure).

More significant, the incarceration of minority youth has increased over the past few years. Between 1985 and 1989 the absolute number of white youth in custody actually declined by 10% (Table 4.7), whereas the numbers of black and Hispanic youth increased by 48% and 38%, respectively. The largest growing population was Asian/Pacific Islander, although their numbers are relatively small compared to the other groups.

As in most states, African-Americans (and particularly African-American males) are heavily overrepresented in California's juvenile facilities.[3] Of the 13,767 California incarcerated youth, 5,093 or 37% were African-American, as compared to their 8.7% representation in the total youth population (Table 4.8). Not surprisingly, African-Americans have the highest custody rates (1,950 per 100,000 and 4.25 index score), followed by Latinos (430 per 100,000 and .94 index

TABLE 4.7   Number of California Children in Custody, Ages 10 to 17, in Public Juvenile Facilities, 1985-1989

Ethnicity	1985		1987		1989		% Change
	N	%	N	%	N	%	
White	4,597	66.7	4,556	31.2	4,140	26.5	−9.9
Black	3,879	31.2	5,096	34.9	5,747	36.8	+47.9
Hispanic	3,706	29.8	4,458	30.6	5,125	32.9	+38.3
American Indian	87	0.7	166	1.1	76	0.5	−12.6
Asian/Pacific Islander	178	1.4	307	2.1	521	3.3	+192.7
Total	12,447	100.0	14,583	100.0	15,599	100.0	

SOURCE: National Council on Crime and Delinquency. (1985, 1987, 1989). *Children in Custody Survey.* Author

TABLE 4.8   California Juveniles in Custody by Ethnicity and Sex, Secure Public Facilities Only, 1989

Ethnicity	State population[a] N	%	Juveniles in Custody[b] N	%	Custody Rate Per 100,000 Youth[c]	Index Score[d]
Anglo-						
American	1,405,369	46.6	3,701	26.8	263	0.58
Male	719,840	23.8	3,231	23.5	449	0.99
Female	685,529	22.8	470	3.4	69	0.15
African-						
American	261,118	8.7	5,093	37.0	1,950	4.25
Male	130,922	4.5	4,739	34.4	3,620	7.64
Female	130,196	4.5	354	2.6	272	0.58
Latino	1,036,403	34.4	4,458	32.4	430	0.94
Male	525,677	17.4	4,188	30.4	797	1.75
Female	510,726	17.0	270	2.0	53	0.12
Asian-American						
& other	309,985	10.3	515	3.7	166	0.36
Male	158,022	5.2	466	3.4	295	0.65
Female	151,963	5.0	49	0.4	32	0.08
Total	3,012,875	100.0	13,767	100.0	457	NA
Male	1,534,461	50.9	12,624	91.7	823	1.80
Female	1,478,414	49.1	1,143	8.3	77	0.17

NOTES: a. Source: California Department of Finance Population Estimates, 1989, Ages 10-17
b. Source: 1989 "Children in Custody" Census of Public Juvenile Detention, Correctional and Shelter Facilities
c. Rates per 100,000 were computed by dividing the number in custody by the number of youth population for each gender and racial/ethnic group, and multiplying by 100,000.
d. Index score is percentage in custody divided by percentage of state population.

score).[4] In sharp contrast, Anglo-American and Asian-American juveniles are underrepresented in California secure public facilities (index scores of .58 and .36, respectively).

It also should be noted that female juvenile offenders have consistently lower rates and indices of incarceration than males, both in total and for each ethnic group. In fact, an often neglected fact is that an index for sex overrepresentation would produce high levels of overrepresentation. For example, although males constitute approximately 51% of the youth population, they represent 92% of the secure facility population (or an index of 1.80). Conversely, the young female index score is .16. This trend of extremely low indices of young women persists for the various minority groups. However, as among the males, young female African-Americans have the highest rates and Asian-American young women have the lowest rates of incarceration.

The remainder of the research sought to identify those juvenile justice and offender factors that produce these results. The first step was to see whether overrepresentation occurs at the various decision points of the juvenile justice system (from arrest through disposition). For example, it may be that the decision to arrest is more important than subsequent decision points in explaining ethnic bias. Table 4.9 shows the ethnic distribution of juveniles in the state population, as well as the distribution (number, percent, and rate) by ethnic group of juveniles at five stages of processing, from arrest through detention, placement, and secure commitment using aggregate data (see Table 4.5).

African-American youth are overrepresented at arrest (2.2 times their share of the youth population) but their index *continues to rise* at each decision point until, at the deep end of the system—commitment to the California Youth Authority (CYA)—they are overrepresented by a factor of 4.6. By contrast, Anglo-American youth are proportionately filtered out of the juvenile justice system as the severity of the sanction increases; their rate of representation at arrest is .85, dropping to .65 among those juveniles committed to secure county facilities and to .41 among those committed to the CYA. Latino youth show little variation in their rates of representation in the state youth population whereas Asian-American youth maintain their low rates of representation.

The next issue is whether these ethnic disparities at each of the major decision points persist after statistical controls are applied. Table 4.10 shows the percentage of juveniles in each ethnic group who were *detained,* cross-referenced to other factors such as offense, age, sex, probation status, and prior offense history. Here one can see that African-Americans have higher detention rates even when controlling for relevant background attributes. For example, within the class of juveniles referred for violent felony offenses in 1989, 64.7% of African-Americans with violent felony referral offenses were detained, versus 47.1% of Anglo youth in this offense class and 60.7% of Latino youth in this offense class.

The same results, shown in Table 4.11, emerge when one examines *commitments* to the state's training school system (CYA). For example, among juveniles with violent felony offenses, 11.4% of African-American youth with violent felonies were committed to CYA in 1989, versus 3.4% of Anglos, 9.4% of Latinos, and 8.6% of Asian/other youth with these offenses. For every offense class except "misdemeanor drug," blacks had the highest percentage of CYA commitments.[5]

TABLE 4.9   California Juvenile Population, Arrests and Admissions to Secure Detention, Private Facilities, Secure County Facilities and CYA, 1989

	N	%	Rate per 100,000[c]	Index[e]
Population[a]				
Anglo-American	1,405,369	46.65	—	—
African-American	261,118	8.67	—	—
Latino	1,036,403	34.40	—	—
Asian-American/other	309,985	10.29	—	—
Total	3,012,875	100.00	—	—
Arrest[b]				
Anglo-American	94,782	39.78	6,744.28	0.85
African-American	45,960	19.29	17,601.24	2.22
Latino	81,639	34.27	7,877.15	1.00
Asian-American/other	15,860	6.66	5,116.38	0.65
Total	238,241	100.00	7,907.43	—
Secure detention[b]				
Anglo-American	17,759	34.07	1,263.65	0.73
African-American	13,660	26.20	5,231.35	3.02
Latino	17,006	32.62	1,640.87	0.95
Asian-American/other	3,706	7.11	1,195.54	0.69
Total[d]	52,131	100.00	1,730.27	—
Private facility[b]				
Anglo-American	2,148	43.79	152.84	0.94
African-American	1,219	24.85	466.84	2.87
Latino	1,325	27.01	20.55	0.79
Asian-American/other	213	4.34	427.44	0.42
Total[d]	4,905	100.00	162.80	—
Secure county facility[b]				
Anglo-American	4,128	30.14	293.73	0.65
African-American	2,908	21.23	1,113.67	2.45
Latino	5,885	42.97	567.83	1.25
Asian-American/other	774	5.65	249.69	0.55
Total[d]	13,695	100.00	454.55	—
CYA[b]				
Anglo-American	660	19.20	46.96	0.41
African-American	1,380	40.17	528.50	4.63
Latino	1,210	35.23	116.75	1.02
Asian-American/other	185	5.38	59.68	0.52
Total[d]	3,435	100.00	114.01	—

NOTES: a. Source: California Department of Finance, Population Estimates, 1989, Ages 10 to 17.
b. Source: California Bureau of Criminal Statistics, 1989, Ages 10 to 17.
c. Rates per 100,000 were computed by dividing the number in custody by the number of youth population for each ethnic group, and multiplying by 100,000.
d. Youth of unknown ethnicity omitted from these totals.
e. Indexes are based on the racial/ethnic groups' proportions in the general populations. Calculations are made by dividing the ethnic group's percentage representation at the legal point of interest by the ethnic group's percentage of the total youth population. An index value over 1.00 indicates over-representation; an index value under 1.00 indicates that the group is under-represented.

TABLE 4.10   California Juveniles With Court Dispositions, Percentage Detained by Ethnicity Controlling for Other Factors

Characteristics	Anglo-American	Latino	African-American	Native American	Asian/Others	Total
			Ethnicity			
Number of youths	60,539	47,564	26,982	906	8,591	144,582
Overall % detained	30.6	35.9	48.5	43.0	38.8	36.3
Referral offense felonies						
Felony violent	47.1	60.7	64.7	59.6	58.0	11,629
Felony property	38.8	38.4	49.5	47.4	49.4	35,880
Felony drug	43.1	59.9	71.9	37.5	61.8	7,704
Felony sex	37.2	44.4	50.3	—[a]	39.1	1,716
Felony weapons	32.7	36.5	56.7	55.6	46.8	2,081
Misdemeanor assault & battery	33.6	31.0	35.8	37.5	35.5	11,517
Misdemeanor property	15.9	18.9	22.8	27.1	15.1	18,626
Misdemeanor drug	0.8	28.1	29.4	36.7	23.2	3,660
Misdemeanor sex	30.8	17.1	31.4	75.0	20.0	654
Misdemeanor alcohol	14.0	24.2	24.4	39.2	12.1	6,838
Misdemeanor weapons	20.4	28.4	47.2	—[a]	39.6	1,733
Status offense	35.1	35.1	40.5	32.9	42.6	10,044
Probation violation	65.3	57.6	62.9	69.7	52.8	7,997
Probation-CYA status						
On probation or CYA	59.5	58.4	67.2	62.4	61.4	29,950
Not probation or CYA	24.9	29.9	40.9	36.2	34.1	115,032
Sex						
Male	30.3	36.7	50.3	42.5	40.4	115,551
Female	31.6	31.6	39.9	44.5	29.2	28,031
Age						
Ages 10-15	28.4	31.8	44.3	39.6	36.9	73,581
Ages 16-17	31.5	38.3	52.8	46.9	40.8	74,718
Number of offenses						
One only	24.6	30.4	40.5	38.8	32.9	81,960
More than one	39.5	43.0	56.3	47.5	47.5	62,622

NOTE: a. Indicates where the number of cases available for statistical analysis is less than 30. Consequently, there are insufficient cases to compute reliable percentages.

In broad terms, this analysis unveils a picture of persistent, differential treatment for some minority groups after having accounted for pre-referral factors such as offense and prior record. This leads one to the observation that some ethnic disparities in detention and sentencing outcomes are limited to African-Americans and cannot be fully explained by the juvenile justice attributes of that ethnic group.

TABLE 4.11 California Juveniles With Court Dispositions, CYA Dispositions by Ethnicity Controlling for Other Factors

Characteristics	Anglo-American	Latino	African-American	Native American	Asian/Others	Total
			Ethnicity			
Number of youths	64,300	49,800	28,401	926	8,760	152,187
Overall % to CYA	0.9	2.1	4.0	1.1	1.6	1.9
Referral offense						
Felonies						
Felony violent	3.4	9.4	11.4	3.7	8.6	12,555
Felony property	1.6	2.0	3.0	2.0	1.3	37,506
Felony drug	1.0	4.1	7.2	—[a]	5.0	7,886
Felony sex	1.7	2.8	3.4	—[a]	0.0	1,798
Felony weapons	0.6	1.8	5.6	—[a]	0.6	2,214
Misdemeanor assault & battery	0.4	1.0	1.1	0.0	1.1	11,695
Misdemeanor property	0.1	0.1	1.1	0.0	1.1	20,388
Misdemeanor drug	0.8	2.1	1.2	0.0	0.0	4,764
Misdemeanor sex	1.0	0.0	2.7	—[a]	0.0	677
Misdemeanor alcohol	0.0	0.2	0.7	0.0	0.0	6,897
Misdemeanor weapons	0.4	1.7	2.3	—[a]	0.0	1,836
Status offense	0.1	0.0	0.2	0.0	0.0	10,548
Probation violation	1.9	2.1	3.9	0.0	1.5	8,320
Probation-CYA status						
On probation or CYA	4.2	7.2	9.4	3.8	5.4	30,180
Not probation or CYA	0.2	0.8	1.9	0.2	0.8	122,007
Sex						
Male	1.0	2.4	4.7	1.5	1.7	122,480
Female	0.3	0.3	1.1	0.0	0.8	29,707
Age						
Ages 10-15	0.4	1.0	2.2	0.4	0.7	74,179
Ages 16-17	1.3	3.1	5.9	1.3	1.9	78,008
Number of offenses						
One only	0.6	1.3	2.8	0.8	1.1	87,495
More than one	1.3	3.2	5.2	1.3	2.4	64,692

NOTE: a. Indicates where the number of cases available for statistical analysis is less than 30. Consequently, there are insufficient cases to compute reliable percentages.

A major objective of the California study was to elicit from juvenile justice officials (law enforcement, probation, judges, and community service providers) their "perceptions" of the causes and remedies to overrepresentation of minority youth. This was accomplished by holding a series of "town meetings" in several key counties to elicit their perceptions of why minority youth, and especially African-American males, are so overrepresented in juvenile correctional facilities.[6] What follows is a summary of what they said were the primary causes of the overrepresentation and their solutions to the problem.

Institutional Racism Within the Juvenile Justice System

The thrust of this observation is that racism, in the form of negative stereotypes, is historically embedded in U.S. culture and is reflected in the institutions of the justice system. One such stereotype is that African-Americans are expected to act violently; when this stereotype is held by law enforcement officers and other juvenile justice officials, it leads to selective over-arrest and over-incarceration of minority youth and especially black youth. One judge admitted that when he adjudicates a black youth he views that youth very differently from other youth even if the youth is charged with a similar offense. Specifically, black males are seen as less controllable and with limited family support if returned to the community. In the same vein, many black and Hispanic youth are labelled as gang members simply because of their race and residential location. Conversely Anglo, and even more so Asian, youth were viewed by decision makers as having more family and institutional resources, which is seen as reducing their risk for further involvement in the justice system.

Staffing Within Law Enforcement Agencies, Probation Departments, and Juvenile Courts

Staffing within law enforcement agencies, probation departments, and juvenile courts is largely Anglo-American and does not reflect the ethnic distribution in the society as a whole. Lack of ethnic balance and Anglo-American dominance of high-level juvenile justice jobs contribute to the overrepresentation of certain minority groups in secure juvenile justice facilities. The assumption is that by increasing the numbers of minority staff at the executive levels, law enforcement and the juvenile justice system would become more attuned to the special needs and problems of lower-class ethnic youth and their communities.

Poverty and Joblessness

Poverty and joblessness affecting minority youth are largely to blame for high offense and incarceration rates for these individuals.

Most officials expressed concern about the social and economic conditions that precede and contribute to delinquent conduct. In particular, African-American youth have poor job prospects and economic opportunities and thus turn to nonlegal economic pursuits, such as selling drugs. Poor social and economic circumstances also lower self-esteem, thereby contributing to misconduct. It was viewed as no coincidence by the participants that neighborhoods with high crime and arrest rates also have the highest rates of poverty.

Different Family and Cultural Values

Different family and cultural values explain both over- and under-representation of certain ethnic groups in the juvenile justice system. This relates to the relationship between family and cultural values and involvement with the juvenile justice system. Some participants believed that Asian-American families were best equipped to handle youth conduct problems within the structures of home and community; however, some officials qualified this observation by suggesting that "old-line" Asian families were better at controlling youth misconduct than were newer, immigrant Asian families, especially Southeast Asians. Others noted that Latino families, as well as Asian, tended to be two-parent families with relatively strong disciplinary values. Nearly all officials singled out African-American families as more often dysfunctional than those of other ethnic groups, with a greater proportion of single-parent/absent-father families and with a less consistent ability to resolve youth behavior problems when they first arose.

Minority Youth's Understanding of the Juvenile Justice System

Minority youth being processed in the juvenile justice system, as well as their parents, do not always understand how the system works. This problem is intensified when language barriers are present. The suggestion here is that many youth lack familiarity with the legal process and do not understand the "mumbo-jumbo" court jargon that goes on among attorneys, judges, and probation officers, especially in formal juvenile court proceedings. Juvenile justice personnel, in turn, may not be able to communicate effectively with parents and children from different cultural backgrounds. Latinos and some Asians, especially new immigrant youth and their parents, may have an inadequate command of English as well as insufficient translator support in official proceedings. This lack of communication and understanding may have a negative effect on sentencing decisions and may foreclose options that are open to youth and parents who are more conversant with the system.

Lack of Resources

The juvenile justice system lacks the resources needed to respond effectively to delinquency in general and to minority youth problems in particular. Diversion and alternative disposition programs that used to be available have disappeared, leaving juvenile justice decision makers with fewer options and contributing to higher incarceration rates for some minority groups. Frustration and disappointment were expressed in all focus groups over the declining base of resources for juvenile justice programs and services. The reduction in service level has had a disproportionately strong effect on minority groups, contributing in turn to disproportionately high arrest and incarceration rates for some minority youth. Some participants expressed concern that no resources were available for efforts to discourage first-time offenders from reentering the criminal justice system. Many youth on probation supervision, for example, were "banked," receiving little or no attention or service. When sanctions are ineffective, kids learn that they can ignore the justice system until it comes down hard on them. When services are absent, situations that contribute to delinquency get worse. All county groups underscored the need for more youth services, including family counseling, community recreation centers, and basic support (including food and shelter) for poor families.

Failure of Schools

Schools have failed to provide minority youth with the educational and personal development needed to overcome adverse social and economic conditions. Some participants singled out schools for failing to rescue minority youth, who already were suffering difficult circumstances from educational failure and eventual delinquency. Some suggested that Anglo-American youth had preferred access to good schools, and that Latino or Asian youth with language problems failed to receive adequate attention to special needs. African-American youth, some suggested, were likely to be classified early as behavior problems and to be forced out of the classroom or otherwise discouraged from succeeding in school. Schools (and other public agencies) were blamed for failing to experiment sufficiently with school-based, coordinated service models that could deliver help where needed directly to children attending school.

Drug Involvement

Drug involvement often leads quickly to arrest and prosecution, especially for African-American youth. The lack of substance-abuse prevention and treatment programs at the local level means little can be done to stop the growth of minority arrests for drug-related crimes. Some participants noted that African-American youth were often apprehended for drug-related offenses, both selling and using. Where local programs for drug-involved youth are lacking, judges may order commitments to the California Youth Authority because CYA has drug treatment slots.

Recommendations

Based on the above findings, these same juvenile justice officials offered the following suggestions to correct these ethnic-based biases.

1. Increase the ethnic balance in law enforcement, probation, and court agencies that administer the juvenile justice system
2. Institute and require cultural sensitivity training for police officers, beginning at the recruit stage
3. Address the root causes of crime with programs designed to improve social and economic conditions that contribute to delinquent behavior
4. Implement programs to help African-American youth develop self-esteem
5. Increase the involvement of minority communities and citizens in the making of juvenile justice policy
6. Establish new family support services in minority communities
7. Change school policies toward minority youth who are at high risk of dropping out; implement coordinated, school-based service plans creating a multiagency service capability at school sites
8. Establish drug treatment programs where needed
9. Institute objective risk-screening criteria and objective needs assessments in juvenile justice systems to reduce system bias where it may exist
10. Expend local funds to address the disproportionate representation of minorities in the juvenile justice system in the following ways:

- Require cultural sensitivity training for police, probation officers, and judges
- Establish community-based agencies providing family counseling and support services to minority clients
- Implement voucher service systems allowing youth and families to redeem vouchers for needed services with public or private providers
- Provide social workers and case advocates to help minority youth and families navigate the juvenile justice system and to develop alternative-to-institution dispositions
- Make drug treatment programs readily available, including residential treatment options
- Build mentoring programs to link positive role models to high-risk youth and to build self-esteem and responsibility among these youth
- Create job training and placement programs for minority youth
- Establish police diversion and other pre-adjudication diversion programs; fund these programs in proportion to local minority representation in the justice system
- Dedicate assets captured in the war on drugs to minority programs in proportion to rates of minority representation in the juvenile justice system

In summary, the California study showed that race does play at least an indirect role in juvenile court decision making, which in turn affects the rates of confinement for various ethnic groups. Among minority groups, African-American males are those being overrepresented at extremely high rates from the point of detention through commitments to the state training school system. Although a significant proportion of this overrepresentation can be attributed to a high rate of arrest, even when this and other relevant factors are controlled for, African-American males continue to receive more severe dispositions than their counterparts.

Similar to the results reported earlier, differences in incarceration rates among racial groups cannot be explained by differences in offense behavior among these groups (Pope & Feyerherm, 1990a). More important, juvenile justice officials themselves believed that institutional racism, and all of its attending consequences, is the primary cause of overrepresentation. Thus, although some important reforms can be made within the juvenile justice system itself, addressing the preconditions and social framework for such overrepresentation is far more important than attempting to reform juvenile justice. As long as African-American youth have higher rates of poverty, single-parent families, high school dropouts, and unemployment rates, these same factors should be counted in the calculus of possible causes for minority youth overrepresentation in crime and thus incarceration. Reducing minority overrepresentation requires fundamental changes in the larger social environment that forms the basis for these disparities (Duster, 1987).

The Influence of Gender

Unlike with race, concern over the influence of gender has a very different context. Virtually all research has showed that young women are far less involved in criminal activities as compared to their male counterparts. Elliott, Ageton, Huizinga, Knolwes, and Canter (1983), using national self-report data, found that males were involved in serious delinquent activities at a ratio three to six times that of young women. Consequently, young women have much lower rates than males of arrests, and their representation in the juvenile court process and correctional populations also is significantly lower. The most recent Uniform Crime Reports (UCR) data show that of the 1.6 million arrests of juveniles, only 23% were of young women. Similarly, of the 1.2 million juvenile court referrals, only 20% were young women (U.S. Department of Justice, 1990). As illustrated in Table 4.12, the per capita juvenile court referral rates for young women by offense group are systematically higher than for males. And, of all the youth in custody, only 19% in 1989 were young women (U.S. Department of Justice, 1989). The per capita rates for young women are one fourth that of males (see Figure 4.1). But despite these trends, the white male-dominated field of criminologists has given relatively short shrift to the fact that sex is the single most important factor in explaining variation in crime rates.

Only in the area of status offenses do the female court referral and custody rates begin to reach parity with those for males. For example, little difference exists between males and females in the status offense category (Table 4.12). Were it not for liquor-related crimes, young women would have a higher court referral rate than males. Table 4.13 shows the proportion of males and females in custody by each offense group. For both private and public facilities, a greater proportion of young women is incarcerated than males for status and "nonlegal" offenses. And it is the status-offense behaviors that have received the most attention concerning the effect of gender on juvenile court decision making.

Meda Chesney-Lind (March 1988) has argued that status offenses pose a unique "threat" to juvenile females. It is for these behaviors

TABLE 4.12   1988 Court Referrals by Sex, Age, and Offense*

Age	Person		Property		Drugs		Public Order		Status**	
	Male	Female	Male	Female	Male	Female	Male	Female	Male	Female
10	1.6	0.3	7.5	1.2	0.0	0.0	0.6	0.1	0.2	0.1
11	2.8	0.6	11.2	2.1	0.1	0.0	1.2	0.3	0.4	0.1
12	5.0	1.5	20.0	4.9	0.4	0.1	3.0	0.9	0.9	0.8
13	8.9	2.9	34.4	8.9	1.5	0.4	6.5	2.3	1.8	2.2
14	13.7	4.5	52.0	13.3	3.9	1.0	12.5	4.4	3.5	4.2
15	17.6	5.1	64.2	15.3	7.9	1.5	19.3	5.8	5.2	5.2
16	20.4	5.0	74.6	17.1	12.6	2.1	26.4	6.4	6.5	4.3
17	22.6	4.6	75.3	16.8	18.0	2.6	31.9	6.2	8.9	3.2
Total	11.6	3.1	42.8	9.9	5.3	0.9	12.5	3.3	3.4	2.5

SOURCE: Juvenile Court Statistics, 1988.
NOTES: * All numbers reflect court referral rates per 1,000 youth population ages 10-17.
** Status offense rates reflect petitioned cases only.

that the greatest proportion of young women are arrested and processed by the juvenile court. Several authors have found that young
women are more likely to be arrested, detained, and adjudicated for
status offenses as compared to males. Teilmann and Landry (1981)
found in their analysis of six metropolitan sites some evidence that
young women were disproportionately arrested for status offenses
as compared to their self-reported status offense behavior. Specifically, Teilmann and Landry found a female overrepresentation of 10%
for runaways and a 31% female overrepresentation rate for incorrigibility. However, the researchers concluded that this bias emanated
more from parental actions than from police or the courts. The
findings that females and males are similarly involved in status
offense crimes were confirmed by Figueira-McDonough (1985) and
Canter (1982).

    Chesney-Lind (1988) and Sussman (1959) offer the following ex-
planation for the basis for these discrepancies:

> The most persuasive explanation for such differences between unofficial
> and official rates of young woman delinquency is that the juvenile justice
> system's commitment to the notion of the state as parent has encouraged
> abuse of the offense category. The language of status offense provisions
> invites "discretionary" application that "allows parents, police, and
> juvenile court authorities, who ordinarily decide whether PINS proceed-
> ings should be initiated, to hold girls legally accountable for behavior—
> often sexual or in some way related to sex—that they would not consider
> serious if committed by boys." (pp. 146-147)

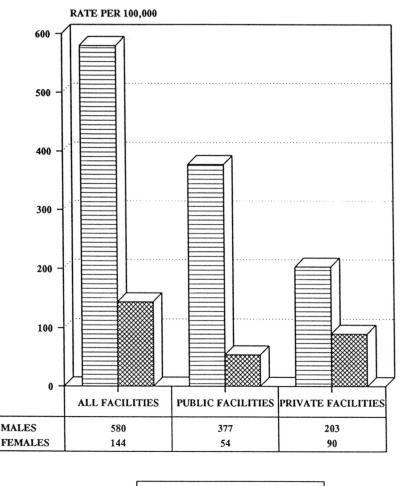

RATE PER 100,000

	ALL FACILITIES	PUBLIC FACILITIES	PRIVATE FACILITIES
MALES	580	377	203
FEMALES	144	54	90

☐ MALES   ▦ FEMALES

Figure 4.1. U.S. Juveniles in Custody by Gender, One-Day Count Rates in Public and Private Facilities, 1989

SOURCES: 1989 Census of Public and Private Juvenile Detention, Correctional and Shelter Facilities. Unpublished 1989 Census Population Estimates from the 1980 Population Census.
NOTE: Rates are calculated per 100,000 youth age 10 to the upper age of original court jurisdiction in each state for 1989.

Once young women are referred to the court, several studies have shown a systematic bias against them for status offenses while also showing a leniency for delinquent crimes. Bishop and Frazier (1992)

TABLE 4.13   Juveniles in Custody in Public and Private Juvenile Facilities,
One-Day Counts by Reasons for Commitment and Gender, 1989

	Public Facilities	
	Males (N = 49,443) Percentages	Females (N = 6,680) Percentages
Delinquent offenses	96.7	77.7
1. Violent	16.1	8.8
2. Other personal	10.6	7.9
3. Serious property	28.5	16.0
4. Other property	13.6	13.0
5. Alcohol offenses	1.1	1.5
6. Drug related offenses	11.1	6.2
7. Public order offenses	4.9	5.7
8. Probation/parole violations	8.0	14.6
9. Other	2.8	4.0
Status offenses	2.3	16.7
Nonoffenders	0.6	3.8
Voluntary commitments	0.4	1.7

	Private Facilities	
	Males (N = 26,602) Percentages	Females (N = 11,220) Percentages
Delinquent offenses	43.8	13.0
1. Violent	2.7	0.5
2. Other personal	6.0	1.4
3. Serious property	12.1	1.75
4. Other property	11.7	4.8
5. Alcohol offenses	1.2	0.7
6. Drug related offenses	4.8	1.15
7. Public order offenses	0.7	1.0
8. Probation/parole violations	0.8	6.3
9. Other	3.8	1.4
Status Offenses	14.8	25.8
Nonoffenders	25.2	37.4
Voluntary commitments	16.1	23.8

SOURCE: 1989 Census of Public and Private Juvenile Detention, Correctional and Shelter Facilities: Census day 2/15/89.
NOTE: Offense categories include the following offenses:
Violent: murder, non-negligent manslaughter, forcible rape, robbery, aggravated assault.
Other Personal: negligent manslaughter, assault, sexual assault.
Serious Property: burglary, arson, larceny-theft, motor vehicle theft.
Other Property: vandalism, forgery, counterfeiting, fraud, stolen property, unauthorized vehicle use.
Part II: alcohol offense, drug related offenses, public order offenses.
Status: offenses not considered crimes if committed by adults
Non-offenders: dependency, neglect, abuse, emotional disturbance, retardation, other.

found in Florida that young women were more likely to be referred to the court for status offenses but less likely for delinquent crimes. Horowitz and Pottieger (1991) found in their study of the Miami juvenile court that black young women were less likely than black males to be arrested for similar drug crimes and that males in general were more likely to receive a disposition resulting in incarceration than were similarly charged young women. However, young women were more likely to be adjudicated for prostitution than males. Datesman and Scarpitti (1980), in their study of an eastern juvenile court, found that young women were treated more leniently for more serious crimes but received more punitive dispositions for "non-criminal status offenses."

Where girls are found to be detained and incarcerated at higher levels than males for certain offenses (generally status offenses and prostitution crimes), the official justification for such actions echoes the original *parens patriae* ideology of the juvenile court with the added touch of chivalry. Specifically, the court must intervene more frequently and more intensively with young women for these nonviolent and nonexistent behaviors because they are less able than males, simply by virtue of their status as young women, to fend for themselves.

This perspective, shared by the white male-dominated juvenile court system, has resulted in considerable resistance from the juvenile justice system to support and implement federally required mandates to de-institutionalize status offenders, most of whom are young women. Chesney-Lind and Shelden (1992) point out that court officials heavily lobbied the federal government to water down reforms that would effectively restrict efforts to remove status offenders from secure facilities. For example, a spokesperson for the National Council of Juvenile and Family Court Judges testified before Congress that the proposed legislation to modify the Juvenile Justice and Delinquency Prevention Act of 1974 would have serious consequences for the court's ability to control wayward boys and girls who were not conforming to traditional family values and behaviors (U.S. House of Representatives, Committee on Education and Labor, 1980):

> The effect of the Juvenile Court Act as it now exists is to allow a child ultimately to decide for himself whether he will go to school, whether he will live at home, whether he will continue to run, run, run, away from home, or whether he will even obey orders of your court (p. 1980).

This type of testimony led to modifications in the proposed legislation that allowed the courts to incarcerate status offenders who violated court orders such as attending school or attending a drug treatment program. Known as "contempt citations," these actions allow the court to declare the youth as "delinquent" without he or she having committed any delinquent acts.

One study of the effects of contempt citations by Bishop and Frazier (1992) found that girls referred to the court had a significantly higher rate of petitions filed than girls charged with criminal actions. Moreover, the probability of incarceration increased from 5% to 30% for girls charged with contempt citations. Similar findings occurred for males, which led the researchers to conclude that a double standard still existed within the Florida juvenile court system.

In a national study of girls in juvenile facilities conducted by the American Correctional Association (ACA, 1990), found that 61% of the girls reported having been physically abused in the past. Another 54% reported being sexually abused with the majority stating that the abuse was not an isolated incident. Another 54% said they had attempted suicide at least once, and most had been using drugs on a regular basis. Finally, they tended to be more sexually active than other girls of their own age, which often resulted in pregnancies, abortion, or birth. These difficulties underscore the need to develop specialized programs not found in traditional juvenile facilities, where programs have been designed for a predominantly male population. In particular, these girls require specialized medical and social services that are unique to their problems.

The issue is not whether these girls are in need of intervention. Clearly, most of them share the same disadvantaged attributes of their male juvenile court counterparts. Instead, one must question the argument that girls in particular can best be served in overcrowded and secure detention centers and training school systems that often are ill-suited for meeting their needs. For example, numerous reports and lawsuits have been filed on behalf of girls who when housed in detention centers, adult jails, and training schools are required to undergo repeated pelvic examinations and vaginal searches, sometimes in the presence of male custody staff. Because these facilities often were designed for male offenders, girls often are confined to jail-like cells or housing units that are segregated from the male population and that allow minimal access to recreational, educational, and vocational programs.[7]

Summary

In this chapter we have examined the special issues of how race and gender status affect the quality of juvenile justice. Although legal factors such as severity of offense and prior record heavily influence the court's decision-making process, it is equally clear that race and gender also play significant and pervasive roles in these deliberations. African-American males, in particular, are increasingly being arrested and incarcerated in public facilities. These trends cannot be fully explained by those who argue that black youth are simply more delinquent. Juvenile court officials themselves acknowledge that their own personal biases often cloud their decisions.

With respect to gender, young women continue to be arrested and incarcerated for behaviors that would not trigger a similar response for young males. The court has been reluctant to minimize its use of incarceration for these girls even though the facilities they are sent to are ill-equipped to handle their special medical, mental health, and social service needs. For these reasons, we continue to see the inappropriate use of the court's powers to control such wayward girls.

It always will be difficult to have a juvenile justice system free of the same forces that exist in our larger society. Indeed, one can argue that in a society with racist and sexist attributes, a large and powerful justice system is required to maintain order and to control the "disadvantaged." Nonetheless, reforms can be instituted, along the lines of those suggested here, that will help minimize these unwarranted and undesirable features of juvenile justice.

Notes

1. The issues raised above led the U.S. Congress to amend the federal Juvenile Justice and Delinquency Prevention Act (JJDPA) to require participating states to evaluate and address the overrepresentation of minorities in their incarcerated juvenile populations. The federal goal, according to the federal Office of Juvenile Justice and Delinquency Prevention (1991), is that states should:

> develop and implement policies and practices which are racially and ethnically neutral and which produce unbiased, neutral results. . . . The ultimate goal is for each state to improve the juvenile justice and youth services system by creating a comprehensive community-based service system that provides services for all youth equally . . . ragardless of race or ethnic background. (p. 148)

2. These changes are in label only and do not change the way data are collected or interpreted. It is common to no longer use "Negro" because "black" was the group's chosen name. The world continues to change, and the self-chosen name is now "Afro-American" or "African-American" to reflect the group's cultural heritage and not its skin color. "Hispanic" was imposed by the larger society onto the referent

group, and denies the Indian heritage. Many of this group have chosen "Latino" to be more accurate and to reflect their cultural background. To refer to the dominant society in this country as "White" is inaccurate. The majority of Latinos also are "White." In this country the descendants of Germanic and English settlers often are referred to as "Anglo-American." The alternative designation "Euro-American" also might be used. "White" refers to the anthropological race; "Anglo-American" refers to the ethnicity.

3. The definition of "secure facility" used here is the federal (Office of Juvenile Justice and Delinquency Prevention) definition. The California definition or understanding of "secure facility" is not necessarily the same as the federal. Juvenile camps and ranches, for example, may be either secure or nonsecure by federal standards, but are most often counted as "secure county facilities" by reporting county agencies.

4. Index score is percentage in custody divided by percentage of state population.

5. A logistic analysis also was completed and showed that a residual ethnic effect persisted even after statistical controls are applied. However, the effects of race clearly are diminished.

6. The counties selected for these meetings were San Francisco, Sacramento, Merced, and Los Angeles.

7. See M. Chesney-Lind and R. G. Shelden (1992). *Girls: Delinquency and Juvenile Justice*, pages 141-165, for an excellent summary of these studies and legal actions.

5

What Works With
Juvenile Offenders

The Massachusetts Experiment

A central concern of juvenile justice practitioners has been the search for interventions that would direct delinquent youngsters away from criminal careers. In the mid-1970s the influential work of Robert Martinson (1974) seemed to support the conclusion that "nothing works" with offenders. Martinson and his colleagues found that no particular intervention seemed any more effective than others in reducing recidivism. His review of existing evaluation studies was employed by those urging more punitive responses to crime as well as those urging that more youngsters should be diverted from the juvenile justice system. Others such as Finckenauer (1984) have demonstrated that fads, "pop psychology," and untested clinical insights have shaped juvenile corrections programs far more than have careful research studies.

More recently, some researchers have questioned the empirical validity of the "nothing works" conclusion. Interestingly, Martinson (1974) himself recanted his initial views and reported data that seemed to confirm the value of rehabilitative programs. Canadian researchers Gendreau and Ross (1987) have compiled an impressive number of studies showing the positive effects of correctional interventions. Others such as Greenwood and Zimring (1985) and Altschuler and Armstrong (1984) have identified what they believe are the critical components of successful juvenile corrections programs. These include (a) continuous case management, (b) careful emphasis on re-integration and reentry services, (c) opportunities for youth achievement and program decision making, (d) clear and consistent consequences for misconduct, and (e) a diversity of forms of family and individual counseling matched to individual adolescent needs. Greenwood and Zimring (1985) highlight the potential of private sector programs such as VisionQuest, the Associated Marine Institutes, the Eckerd Foundation, and Homeward Bound that are alternatives to traditional public juvenile correctional facilities.

A substantial body of evidence indicates that many incarcerated youths can be effectively treated in well-structured community-based programs. The existing research indicates that highly structured community programs produce recidivism rates comparable to, or in some instances better than, traditional large-scale correctional facilities (Krisberg, 1992b). The community alternatives also are considerably less expensive than total confinement.

The Massachusetts Experiment in Juvenile Corrections

No jurisdiction has more clearly demonstrated the value of a more community-based response to juvenile crime than the State of Massachusetts. The organization and programs of the Massachusetts Department of Youth Services (DYS) increasingly are becoming the standard of care for juvenile offenders that many other jurisdictions are examining and emulating.

In the early 1970s, Massachusetts sent shock waves through the world of juvenile justice by removing nearly 1,000 youngsters from state training schools and placing them in a diverse array of community programs. The state training schools had been severely castigated by state and federal agencies for abusive and inadequate treatment programs. Legislative hearings revealed major breakdowns in management and operations. The initial response was agency reorganization, and Jerome Miller was hired as commissioner to do the job.

Under the leadership of DYS Commissioner Jerome Miller, the state training schools were closed. Miller (1991) and his associates first had attempted to humanize the Massachusetts correctional facilities, trying to transform them into "therapeutic communities."

But stiff staff resistance and sabotage of the new, more humane policies led Miller to conclude that only the complete shutdown of existing training schools would reform juvenile corrections practices.

Many juvenile justice professionals welcomed these bold steps and urged replication in other jurisdictions. They argued that the closures were supported by extensive evidence that traditional, large-scale, congregate training schools did not deter crime and actually might create violent and antisocial behavior among inmates (Bartollas, Miller, & Dinitz, 1976; Feld, 1977).

Others claimed that DYS had chosen an imprudent course that endangered public safety and threatened the well-being of the children committed to its care. It was alleged that after the closures DYS youths were unsupervised, wandering the Massachusetts countryside. Critics charged that youths were being transferred to adult courts, which typically resulted in harsher punishments. Others asserted that crime rates were skyrocketing. Miller (1991) and DYS were roundly condemned by many corrections officials. Later in this chapter we review the evidence for these claims.

Four subsequent DYS commissioners succeeded in consolidating the dramatic Massachusetts reforms. Although the original reforms have been subject to several important refinements, the vast majority of Massachusetts juvenile justice professionals and children's advocates remain committed to the goals and philosophy set forth by Jerome Miller. Even the state's staunchly conservative Governor William Weld has been unable to garner much political support to change the DYS model. After 20 years of successful experience with community-based juvenile corrections, the Massachusetts system is no longer an experiment.

In the next section we provide more details about how the DYS system works and summarize the research on youth outcomes. Finally, we briefly discuss attempts at replicating the Massachusetts experiment in other states.

How Does the Massachusetts DYS System Differ From Traditional Youth Corrections Systems?

Each year an average of 810 youths are committed to the DYS by the courts. Upon commitment, juveniles are immediately assigned to a case manager from one of five regional offices around the state. The case managers are responsible for devising a treatment plan for the youth, based on clinical and educational evaluations as well as

Average Daily Population	1,700
Average Number of New Commitments	810
Average Length of Stay	2.2 years
Age of Jurisdiction	7-17 years*
Number of Secure Beds	
Secure Treatment	184
Secure Detention	134
Additional Residential Beds	
Shelter Care Detention	143
Group Care	350
Foster Care	87
Forestry Camp	36
Total Beds	934
Public	222
Private	712
Average Annual Cost Per Youth	$23,000

*   *The youngest commitment has been age nine. Adult court jurisdiction begins at age 17.*
DYS may retain indefinite supervision of youths beyond 18 by seeking an extension from the
committing court.

Exhibit A. Overview of the DYS Commitment Population

family history and the severity of the current offense. As the youngster approaches the completion of a residential placement, the case
manager arranges for the youth to participate in community services, such as drug and alcohol treatment or counseling, as a prerequisite to his or her conditions of release. Exhibit A provides an
overview of the DYS system.

Of the 810 youths annually committed to DYS, approximately
15% are initially placed in a locked treatment program based on a

OFFENSE CATEGORY	AGE LIMIT	TIME ASSIGNMENT
MANDATORY REFERRALS: CATEGORY A Murder: First Degree Murder: Second Degree Attempted Murder Voluntary Manslaughter Involuntary Manslaughter Homicide by Motor Vehicle	13-16 years	A minimum of twelve months to a maximum indeterminate stay. Length of time subject to periodic evaluation by treatment staff and legislation, mandating release at age eighteen years, unless extension is granted by the court.
MANDATORY REFERRALS: CATEGORY B Armed Robbery Asssault and Battery with a Dangerous Weapon (causing serious bodily injury) Arson of a Dwelling Place Kidnapping Possession of a Firearm Sexual Offenses (involving victim)	13-16 years	A minimum of six months to a maximum of fourteen months possible. The length of time wil be based on an examination of the circumstances associated with each individual case. Case conference can lead to early release or extension of maximum.
OPTIONAL REFERRALS Any juvenile whose offense behavior presents a risk and danger to the community and/or to himself/herself or who exhibits a persistent and escalating pattern of delinquency.	14-16 years	A range of months between a minimum of four months to a maximum of twelve months. Case conference can lead to early release or extension of maximum.
REVOCATION REFERRALS: Any juvenile who has violated his/her Grant of Conditional Liberty as determined by a Revocation Hearing and referred by the Hearing Officer.	14-17 years	A range of months between a minimum of four months to a maximum of twelve months. Case conference can lead to early release or extension of maximum.

The Classification Grid shown above shall be used for all juveniles committed or recommitted to DYS and those whose liberty has been revoked to determine whether or not such juveniles will be referred to the Classification Panel for possible placement in security.

Exhibit B. Classification of Offenders by Offense and Offense Behavior

classification system that weighs the severity of the current crime and the extensiveness of the youth's prior court involvement. Exhibit B gives an example of how the security classification process is structured. If the youth meets the classification system's criteria for secure confinement, a departmental panel reviews the case in more detail and makes the final residential assignment.

The largest share of DYS commitments are placed in a wide range of community-based programs, including group homes, forestry programs, day treatment programs, outreach and tracking programs, and foster care. Unlike other states that operate a limited number of large correctional facilities and few community programs, DYS employs a broad diversity of highly individualized options for placing its youths. For example, DYS operates 13 small secure treatment programs, totaling 184 beds; 16 short-term detention programs for those awaiting trial; a broad range of group homes; and a 36-bed forestry camp, as well as contracts for family placements with seven different foster care agencies. In addition, DYS maintains many of its young wards in their own homes supported by outreach and tracking and family preservation services. Other youths live at home but attend day treatment services at a central location.

The hallmark of Massachusetts programs is their small size. No residential program houses more than 30 youths. Community programs and supervision caseloads likewise are kept very small to facilitate the individualization of care that is key to the Massachusetts DYS philosophy. Although the small residential programs are expensive in comparison to large-scale programs in other states, DYS is able to operate efficiently because of its limited use of expensive residential care. Whereas juvenile services in most states are run primarily by public agencies, most juvenile correctional programs are operated by private not-for-profit agencies under contract with DYS. The successful privatization of juvenile services in Massachusetts led state officials to contract for many other aspects of care of the mentally ill, the disabled, and the frail elderly.

The DYS uses secure confinement in a unique and cost-effective manner compared to other corrections systems. As noted earlier, DYS places approximately 15% of their commitments in high security treatment facilities. The average stay in these facilities is between 8 and 12 months, followed by a transfer to a less secure residential or nonresidential program. DYS has found that utilizing "phased reentry" or gradual return to community living permits a shorter stay in locked programs. Failure of youths in community programs may result in revocation whereby the youngster is returned to a more secure setting, usually for a very short length of time. For the less serious offenders, DYS relies on intermittent and short periods of confinement followed by longer stays in community programs.

A more traditional approach to juvenile corrections generally involves longer periods of confinement (9-12 months) for most offenders sent to the state corrections agency. Violent offenders may stay even longer in locked programs. After confinement in most jurisdictions, the youths are returned to parole or aftercare supervision.

Violations of parole may lead to further extended periods of incarceration (see Exhibit C for an illustration of differing corrections
practices). By contrast, 85% of DYS clients experience a very short
period of secure confinement (usually up to 4 weeks) during a
diagnostic stage and then are placed in a variety of community
programs. DYS regional case managers closely supervise and moni-
tor placements. Serious rule violations by youths managed in the
community may result in secure confinement for DYS youths lasting
for 1 or 2 weeks or as long as necessary to return the youngster to a
more structured community placement. These DYS sanctions are
intended to be timely and proportionate to the severity of the rule
violation. In more traditional youth corrections systems, parole violations often are allowed to accumulate and must be adjudicated in
formal hearings, which typically results in lengthy stays in locked
facilities. The DYS actually retains legal jurisdiction over its wards
for at least as long as most other states. However, compared to other
states the DYS youths spend a much larger proportion of their
correctional dispositions in the community albeit under close DYS
supervision.

What Have Been the Impacts
of the Massachusetts Reforms?

Two major evaluation efforts have been aimed at measuring the
impact of the DYS reforms. The first study was conducted by a
Harvard University research team led by Lloyd Ohlin and reported
on results in the early years after the training school closures (Coates,
Miller, & Ohlin, 1982). A second study, completed by the National
Council on Crime and Delinquency (NCCD), examined reform out-
comes after the new system had been in place for over a decade
(Krisberg, Austin, Joe, & Steele, 1988).

The Harvard researchers planned to chronicle many aspects of the
Massachusetts reforms. Initially, the research goals were set to measure
the implementation of the "therapeutic communities" within the existing training schools. The closures required that the researchers change
their design and shift focus to the more dramatic changes that were
under way. Interestingly, the Harvard research focused far more on the
process and politics of reform rather than on outcome measures.

Coates et al. (1982) compared the outcomes of a sample of youths
who were released from the newly established community-based
programs in 1974 with another group of youths who had exited

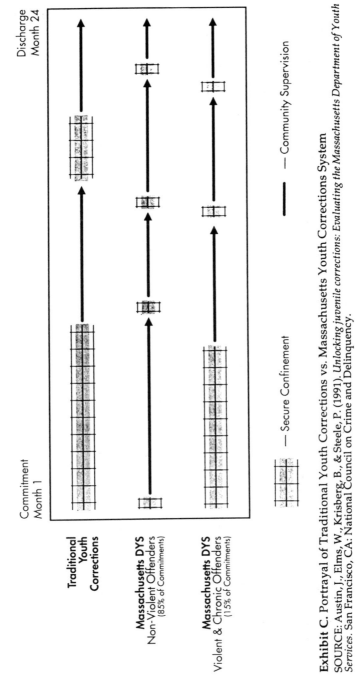

Exhibit C. Portrayal of Traditional Youth Corrections vs. Massachusetts Youth Corrections System

SOURCE: Austin, J., Elms, W., Krisberg, B., & Steele, P. (1991). *Unlocking juvenile corrections: Evaluating the Massachusetts Department of Youth Services*. San Francisco, CA: National Council on Crime and Delinquency.

Massachusetts training schools in 1968. The researchers measured the proportion of youngsters who were referred back to court within 1 year after their return to the community. Significantly, the Harvard group reported that the average recidivism rates for youths who spent the majority of their commitments in community programs were actually *higher* than the rates for youths who had been placed in the training schools (74% versus 66%).

On the surface these results seemed discouraging for the Massachusetts reforms. However, closer inspection of the data revealed a more complex picture. First, the training school sample contained a number of status offenders who subsequently were not placed in training schools. Put differently, the community-based group contained a higher proportion of more serious offenders, for whom one might predict a slightly higher recidivism rate. Second, the Harvard researchers found wide differences in recidivism rates among the various DYS regions. These regional differences were very much related to the successes or failures of each area to faithfully implement the full range of community-based supportive services that were envisioned by Jerome Miller and his associates. "Regions that most adequately implemented the reform measures with a diversity of programs did produce decreases in recidivism over time" (Coates et al. 1982, p. 177). These early DYS data revealed that the costs of the new system of community-based care were roughly equal to the costs of operating the large training schools. DYS had decided to operate very small, secure facilities that were significantly more expensive to run than the training schools. But, by placing the majority of youths in less costly community programs, DYS compensated for the higher expenditures for secure placements.

The NCCD Study

Despite the somewhat ambiguous results of the Harvard study, many within the juvenile justice profession continued to believe that Massachusetts represented a major new paradigm for juvenile corrections. As is discussed later, several jurisdictions attempted partial replications of the Massachusetts experiment. The most faithful attempt to follow the Massachusetts approach was undertaken in Utah. As part of a major federally funded study of the Salt Lake County juvenile court, the NCCD was asked by Utah officials to examine the outcomes of youths handled by the new community programs. Based on a 1-year follow-up, it appeared that the serious and chronic juvenile offenders managed in the new community programs experienced a significant decline in the incidence of reoffending. Moreover, those who committed new offenses seemed to commit less serious crimes (Krisberg et al., 1988).

The encouraging, albeit limited, Utah results suggested the value of reexamining the Massachusetts system. NCCD and DYS sought the financial support of the Edna McConnell Clark Foundation to undertake a comprehensive assessment of DYS as it was operating nearly 15 years after the closure of the training schools. It was expected that this study (Krisberg, Austin, & Steele, 1991) would offer a revealing portrait of a "matured" reformed system of community-based corrections. NCCD both assembled aggregate crime data for Massachusetts and conducted an in-depth study of more than 800 youths who passed through DYS programs in the mid-1980s. The NCCD report organized its findings around the alleged failures of the DYS approach.

Did the Reforms Produce a Crime Wave?

The critics of Jerome Miller prophesied that juvenile crime rates would soar after the training school closures. This was not the case. Compared to other states, Massachusetts continues to enjoy a very low rate of juvenile crime. For instance, in 1985 Massachusetts ranked 46th in juvenile arrest rates among the 50 states and the District of Columbia.[1]

Historical trends in Massachusetts juvenile crime showed substantial declines from the mid-1970s through the 1980s. Fluctuations in Massachusetts juvenile crime rates were quite similar to those in other states such as California that have greatly increased their rates of juvenile incarceration. A substantial body of evidence suggests that crime rates are influenced primarily by demographic trends and other social factors such as unemployment, urbanization, and the prevalence of drug abuse (Blumstein, 1988).

In 1978, 28,419 juveniles were arraigned in Massachusetts.[2] During the next 5 years, arraignments declined by 36%. Since 1984, juvenile arraignments have increased by 2% but are still well below the figures of the late 1970s (Figure 5.1). Similar to trends seen in other states, juvenile crime in Massachusetts was rising prior to the 1970s and then declined. No sudden rise in juvenile crime occurred after the training school closures. Nor can one conclude that the DYS reforms "caused" the later decline in juvenile crime.

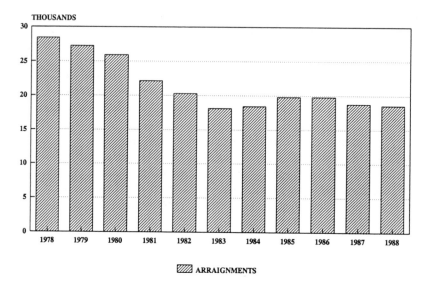

THOUSANDS

Figure 5.1. Number of Arraignments, DYS, 1978-1988

What Are the Recidivism Rates
for Youths Committed to DYS?

There is no standard measure of recidivism. Studies measuring the success of juvenile correctional efforts have employed a number of different indicators to gauge the extent of subsequent criminality. The most widely utilized recidivism measures include: (a) the portion of youths who are crime free during a specified follow-up period, (b) the incidence or frequency of reoffending before and after commitment, and (c) the severity of crimes committed before and after the correctional intervention. Because each of these measures has certain limitations, it is best to examine multiple indicators of subsequent law violations.

Because most DYS youths reside in community placements soon after their commitment to DYS, the follow-up period for assessing recidivism starts as soon as the youth leaves secure custody. The follow-up period covers the time when the youth is in the community and therefore "at risk" to commit new crimes. Due to the intermittent use of secure confinement, the follow-up periods were extended to account for the amount of time the youths were under DYS jurisdiction.

Another difficult research issue was the question of the appropriate comparison groups. The NCCD study examined an entire state system and there was no practical possibility of "randomly assigning" Massachusetts offenders to training schools or to no services. The one obvious possibility is to compare the NCCD results to those reported by Harvard in its previous study (Coates, Miller, & Ohlin, 1982). Another descriptive option pursued by NCCD was to compare the Massachusetts recidivism data with data assembled from other states. These latter comparisons are extremely problematic and must be regarded with great caution. However, the results of these comparisons produced remarkably consistent conclusions.

NCCD examined the criminal histories of all youngsters who left DYS jurisdiction in 1985. Because this "exit cohort" contained a relatively small number of those who had been in secure confinement, the NCCD also compiled information on all youths who exited DYS in 1984 and who had been placed in a secure custody program. In all, the group that was studied consisted of 819 youths. The subsequent criminal involvement of these youths was tracked for at least the next 36 months.

The first indicator of recidivism measured by NCCD was the proportion of DYS youths who continued to violate the law during the 12 months after returning to community living. This is a very conservative measure of success or failure. The analogy in the health field would be the standard of absolute cure. This first indicator is an appropriate measure if criminal behavior is conceptualized as a "critical illness"—one that you either succumb to or survive. On the other hand, if crime is thought of more as a chronic event, then the frequency and severity of reoccurrence are equally valid measures of recovery. Several researchers including Murray and Cox (1979) have argued that the "absolute cure" standard of measuring recidivism may actually mask a good deal of program success.

Of all the youths committed to DYS, approximately 51% were rearraigned within 12 months of their return to community living. This percentage is considerably lower than in the Harvard study. It should be recalled that youths released from the old training schools had a rearraignment rate of 66% and youngsters in the new community programs were rearraigned at the rate of 74% (Figure 5.2). Moreover the overall rearraignment rate for the youths released from DYS in 1985 equalled that of the best regions in the original Harvard study. This suggests that recidivism rates improved as DYS came closer to its stated reform goals: a rich diversity of community-based services permitting youths more normal experiences in school, work, and family settings.

The only alternative explanations for the lower recidivism rates of the 1985 DYS cohort compared to the groups studied by Harvard

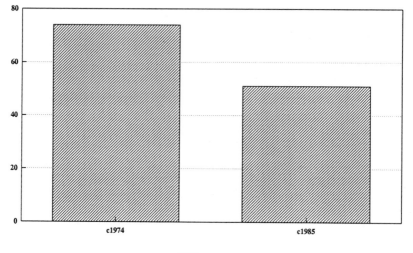

Figure 5.2. DYS Rearraignment Rates, 12-Month Follow-Up, 1974 and 1985

might be that DYS was handling less serious offenders in the later period or that somehow the police were less likely to arrest juvenile offenders. Neither of these explanations are plausible. The proportion of serious and violent juvenile offenders sent to DYS had steadily increased over the years. The personal attributes of the youths in the Harvard and NCCD studies were quite similar except that the NCCD group contained more serious property offenders and less status offenders than the Harvard samples. Further, NCCD found no evidence of changed law enforcement practices since the Harvard study was completed.

NCCD's efforts to compile comparable recidivism data from other juvenile corrections systems revealed that most states do not even collect these data. Other states used an assortment of measures including the proportions of youths who were re-arrested, re-referred to court, or reincarcerated during specified follow-up periods. No other jurisdictions routinely measured the frequency and severity of offending of their clients.

Comparing recidivism rates between jurisdictions poses formidable analytic problems due to (a) differences in the types of youths handled, (b) differences in state juvenile justice practices, and (c) differences in juvenile justice reporting standards as well as a host

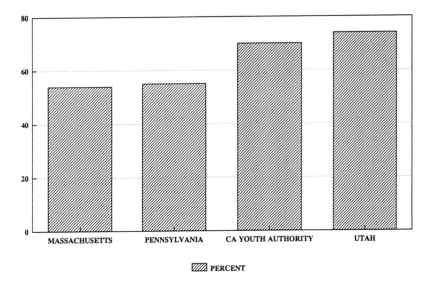

Figure 5.3. Proportion Re-Arrested Within 12 Months

of environmental factors such as urbanization, drug use, unemployment rates, and so on. Nonetheless, NCCD reviewed data from eight separate studies of youths released from juvenile corrections programs. Literature reviews were conducted to identify potential studies and each study was carefully reviewed to assess the validity of the research methods employed. In addition, NCCD contacted a number of states to gather unpublished data on recidivism. The goal of this effort was to look for the accumulated weight of evidence based on a number of studies conduced by independent researchers. Although interstate comparisons are not entirely valid, the cumulative results were very consistent. NCCD cautioned readers to interpret the results conservatively due to the methodological constraints discussed above.[3]

Figures 5.3 through 5.5 present data on three basic measures of recidivism (12-month follow-ups on re-arrests and reconviction, and 36 months for reincarceration) from Massachusetts, Pennsylvania, Utah, Florida, Texas, Illinois, Wisconsin, and California. Both state and county correctional systems were used for California. On all three measures, DYS youths showed recidivism rates equivalent to, and in some cases lower than, youths from the other states. Although some of these jurisdictions operate systems that are quite similar to Massachusetts (notably Pennsylvania and Utah), the others rely far

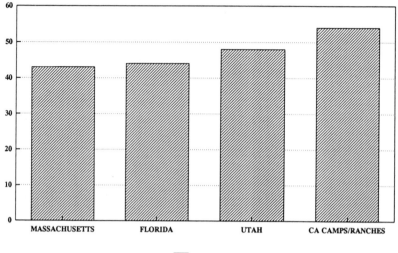

Figure 5.4. Proportion Reconvicted Within 12 Months

more on large-scale training schools.[4] At a minimum these comparisons lend further evidence that the limited use of secure confinement in Massachusetts as compared to other states does not endanger public safety.

NCCD was able to conduct a more detailed comparison between California and Massachusetts recidivism rates. In an earlier project, NCCD had collected recidivism data on over 2,200 youths released from the California Youth Authority (CYA) during 1981-1982. The CYA youths had experienced an average of 14 months of confinement in large training schools compared to the 5 months for Massachusetts youths. Whereas the 12-month recidivism rate for the DYS group was 51%, the comparable rate for the CYA group was 70%. However, the two groups differed in that the California group contained a higher proportion of youngsters who were male, were minorities, were committed for more serious crimes, and had more extensive criminal records than their DYS counterparts. Because these factors often are associated with recidivism rates, NCCD employed statistical techniques to adjust the DYS data to reflect the differences between the groups on these key variables.

First, NCCD computed recidivism rates based on all 819 cases from Massachusetts, which contained a disproportionate number of

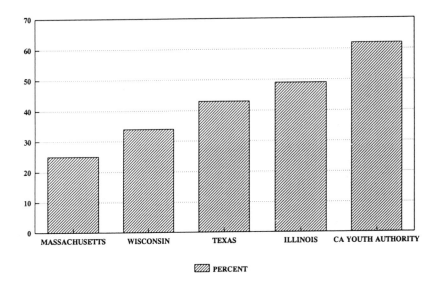

Figure 5.5. Proportion Reincarcerated Within 36 Months
NOTES: * Covers incarceration instate adult or juvenile facilities
** Juvenile commitments only, 24 month follow-up

youths who had been placed in secure residential programs. This DYS sample then was statistically reweighted on the key variables to make it similar to the CYA sample. This produced an adjusted 12-month rearraignment rate for the DYS group of 62%, which still is below the CYA re-arrest rate of 70%.

The statistical procedures used in comparing data from two states are not equivalent to random assignment of youths into two different correctional programs. Dissimilarities in justice system practices, data recording, and other situational and historical factors could influence these findings. Still, the comparisons between CYA and DYS are consistent with other data—the DYS youths performed comparably to and on some measures better than those processed through a more conventional youth corrections program.

How Many and What Types of Crimes Do the DYS Youths Commit?

Several researchers have argued that focusing only on the proportion of youths who are crime free is a misleading measure of rehabilitation.

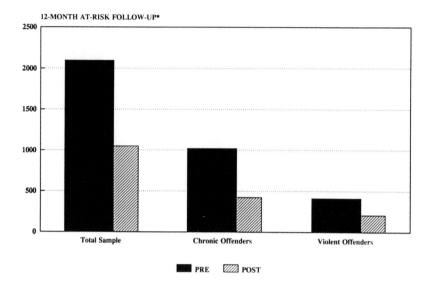

Figure 5.6. Total Number of Arraignments Pre- and Post-Commitment to DYS
NOTE: * Youth not in secure custody; at risk

The criterion of absolute desistence from offending may actually mask significant reductions in the number and severity of crimes committed by program clients (Empey & Lubeck, 1971; Murray & Cox, 1979). This observation was especially true in the case of the DYS youths studied by NCCD.

Figure 5.6 compares the total number of arraignments amassed by the DYS youths during the 12-month periods prior to and after their commitments to DYS. These data reveal a dramatic decline in the number of arraignments after DYS involvement. For example, the cohort selected for study by NCCD collectively accounted for 2,098 arraignments in the year before their entry into DYS programs. This number was cut in half for the first 12 months that the cohort was under DYS supervision (and living in a community setting). This major drop in arraignments was sustained for the next 2 years.

NCCD also examined these offense trends for two key subgroups of DYS clients: (1) those admitted to DYS for a violent crime (N=108) and (2) chronic offenders, who were youths with five or more prior arraignments before their entry into DYS programs (N=249). Figure 5.6 shows that for both offender groups the number of arraignments dropped by half after DYS commitment.

TABLE 5.1 Nature of Offenses Pre- and Postcommitment, Total Sample
($n = 819$)

Offense Type	12 Months Pre		1 - 12 Months Post		13 - 24 Months Post		25-36 Months Post	
	N	%	N	%	N	%	N	%
Part 1 violent	354	10.2	172	10.0	171	9.4	166	10.2
Part 1 property	1,491	43.0	684	39.9	579	31.9	482	29.7
Other person	281	8.1	110	6.4	114	6.3	141	8.7
Other property	385	11.1	194	11.3	245	13.5	187	11.5
Drugs	132	3.8	65	3.8	107	5.9	96	5.9
DUI	14	0.4	5	0.3	236	1.3	26	1.6
Other crime	770	22.2	472	27.5	555	30.6	510	31.4
Juvenile status	10	0.3	5	0.3	0	0.0	1	0.1
Missing	31	0.9	7	0.4	20	1.1	15	0.9
Total Number of Offenses	($N = 3,468$)		($N = 1,715$)		($N = 1,814$)		($N = 1,624$)	

Besides committing far fewer offenses after entering DYS supervision, these youths showed a tendency over time to commit less serious crimes (see Table 5.1). During the pre-DYS period 53% of the offenses were for Part 1 crimes, whereas in the last year of the 36-month follow-up period 40% of the charges were for Part 1 offenses. For violent offenders the trend to commit less serious crimes was even more pronounced. Whereas 60% of their pre-DYS charges were for violent crimes, in successive follow-up periods only one third of their offenses were crimes against persons. The large declines in offenses associated with the DYS youngsters are very encouraging. Even those who continued to reoffend did so less frequently and engaged in less serious law breaking over a sustained period of time.

A critical question is whether the observed declines in offending can be tied directly to the rehabilitation or deterrent effects of DYS programs. There are two other plausible explanations for the observed declines: (a) A predictable slowdown occurs immediately after the frequent and serious offense episodes that led to the initial commitment to DYS (referred to statistically as "regression to the mean"), and (b) there is a hypothesized tendency for youthful offenders to engage in less crime as they grow older. Both of these explanations would account for the findings without the assumption that DYS caused the decline in reoffending. NCCD conducted a number of statistical analyses to test the alternative explanations for the declining offense rates among DYS clients. The available data suggest that regression to the mean and maturation are operating to some extent, but that these factors cannot completely explain the sustained declines in criminal behavior after DYS supervision.

The NCCD research design did not permit precise measurement of all of the factors related to recidivism. To provide such conclusive answers would have required a complex classic experimental design that included random assignment of large numbers of serious offenders to a broad range of interventions, including no services. Moreover, because DYS clients receive multiple placements as part of highly individualized treatment plans, the task of linking particular interventions to specific outcomes is very difficult. The ability of DYS staff to quickly and flexibly shape and change their placement decisions may be as important to successful outcomes as the particular services received by DYS youths.

What is certain is that the volume and severity of crime committed by the DYS youths were far less during and after DYS intervention than before. For those who might argue that enhanced incapacitation might have spared Massachusetts citizens the crimes that were committed, it is worth noting that the crimes committed by the DYS youths under community supervision constituted a very small faction of the state's crime problem. Figure 5.7 shows that in a typical year, approximately 1% of all arrests in Massachusetts (adults and juveniles) involve youngsters who are currently under DYS supervision. Few of the offenses committed by these youths involve personal confrontations with victims (less than 10%)—the majority of their crimes were minor property offenses. These data lend little credence to claims that the community-based approach adopted by DYS has compromised public safety.

What Are the Costs
of the Massachusetts System
Compared to Other Juvenile Corrections Systems?

Another important question about the DYS reforms has to do with the relative expense of implementing a community-based system of care. We have already shown that DYS recidivism rates are comparable to or better than those of other states. What would it cost those states to convert to a Massachusetts model?

Although no national figures are available on the average costs of training schools, a variety of states have reported spending $100-

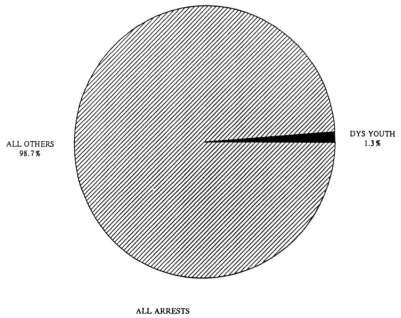

ALL OTHERS
98.7%

DYS YOUTH
1.3%

ALL ARRESTS
(N = 126,769)

Figure 5.7. Massachusetts Arrests, DYS Youth and Others, 1984

$125 per day to hold a youth in a traditional training school (Allen-Hagen, 1991). In Massachusetts, DYS operates a range of dispositional options that include physically secure treatment programs costing $170 per day, staff secure placements at $127 per day, community-based group care averaging $95 per day, day treatment programs at $50 per day, and nonresidential outreach and tracking services costing $23 per day.

The DYS spends more per day to operate its secure units than most states due to the small size of these programs (15-18 beds) and the extensive investments in educational and clinical services. However, DYS administrators argue that these expenditures are cost-effective because they are selective and apply to only a very small portion of the committed population. DYS estimates that its average annual cost per youth is roughly $23,000, which is significantly less than many states that are spending $35,000-45,000 per youth per year.

Although these aggregate numbers favor the DYS approach, a more rigorous cost estimate is needed to determine the relative fiscal merits of the Massachusetts system. As with the data on recidivism, it is extremely difficult to compare budgets across jurisdictions because juvenile corrections programs often are supported through multiple funding sources, and detailed budgetary analyses would be required to reconcile the figures of different states. Instead, NCCD chose to examine these issues for Massachusetts by computing the alternative capital and operating costs that would be required if DYS adopted other correctional policy scenarios.

These calculations are summarized in Table 5.2. The first column illustrates DYS placement practices for youths who exited the system in 1985. The average stay in secure confinement represents a composite for the entire cohort. For example, about 25% of the group spent an average of 6.4 months in the most secure treatment settings. A much larger group spent 2 to 3 months in post-adjudication detention or staff-secure shelter care. Almost all of the DYS youths spent some time in community-based residential programs or under the supervision of outreach and tracking programs. The cost figures in Table 5.2 are averages of the daily costs of actual placements experienced by the group.

The next three columns illustrate the fiscal consequences if DYS were to increase its use of secure confinement and decrease its use of community-based alternatives. Consider scenario II, which represents the national average training school stay in 1985 (Bureau of Justice Statistics, 1987). This analysis reveals that it would cost Massachusetts an additional $10.6 million in operating funds to finance this level of youth incarceration. There also would be the need to create 287 new secure beds. Scenario III projects the costs if Massachusetts placed all of its committed youths in secure programs for 360 days—which was typical of many states in 1988. This would require an additional $16.8 million in operating funds and the state would have to triple its number of secure beds.

Table 5.2 also estimates the maximum annual reductions in statewide juvenile arraignments that might result if DYS increased its use of secure confinement. These estimates are based on the actual number of offenses committed by DYS clients while they were in community placements. At best, Massachusetts might realize a 2% to 4% reduction in juvenile arraignments. The bulk of these crimes would be nonviolent and minor property offenses.[5]

It should be stressed that this analysis is theoretical in nature. Actual trends in statewide arraignments might not reflect the projected increase or decrease in youth crime. As noted earlier, community forces such as demographics, teenage unemployment, family

TABLE 5.2 Comparative Cost of Various Policy Scenarios for the Massachusetts DYS* Sample, 1985 Discharges (*n* = 690 Youth)

	Current	Scenario I	Scenario II	Scenario III
Average stay in secure confinement	118 days	180 days	270 days	360 days
Assuming $156/day cost for secure confinement	$12.7 million	$19.4 million	$29.1 million	$38.8 million
Less costs for unused community placement at $56/day	N/A	<2.4 million>	<5.8 million>	<9.4 million>
Additional costs over current expenditures of increased secure confinement	N/A	$4.3 million	$10.6 million	$16.7 million
Need for secure beds in DYS	223 beds	340 beds	510 beds	681 beds
Additional expenditures (capital & operating) over next 30 yrs. assuming no inflation**	N/A	$164.1 million	$404.1 million	$638.4 million
Estimated annual percentage reduction in Massachusetts juvenile arraignments	N/A	1.0	2.4	3.9

NOTES: *These scenarios assume a constant LOS within DYS, but a shifting of resources from community care to secure confinement.
**The 30-year amortized cost of a new secure bed is assumed to be $300,000.

stability, and drug use are far more important than corrections policies in determining overall youth crime rates.

This analysis suggests that DYS does operate in a cost-effective* manner, balancing fiscal concerns with the imperatives of public safety and rehabilitation. The NCCD cost analysis shows that expanded youth incarceration would require a large investment in public funds, but would achieve little expected reduction in crime rates. An alternative use of tax dollars to reduce crime might entail neighborhood-based crime prevention efforts aimed at curbing child abuse, school dropout rates, youth unemployment, and drug trafficking.

Does DYS Meet the Needs
of Child Supervision?

A major goal of the juvenile court is to provide supervision for children brought under its jurisdiction. Critics of de-institutionalization often have pointed to closures of state mental hospitals as an example of how benign public policies create havoc. There have been many allegations that youths are less well protected in Massachusetts since the closure of the training schools.

One such rumor suggested that the training school closures caused many youths to be transferred into adult courts because judges lacked confidence in the community-based system. The data on transfers from juvenile to adult court refute this allegation. For example, in 1973, 129 youngsters were bound over for adult court hearings. Yet, in the past 15 years the number of juveniles tried in adult courts has steadily declined. By 1980 there were only 43 such transfers; in 1987 the number was down to 14. This reduction in court transfers is partially attributed to the court's confidence in DYS's ability to handle serious juvenile offenders, and the decline occurred despite a national trend in the opposite direction. In the late 1970s nearly half the states enacted legislation making it easier to move juveniles into adult courts. Between 1979 and 1984 the number of youths under age 18 who were residing in prisons nationwide increased by 50% (Krisberg, 1988).

Another concern was that Massachusetts was allegedly shipping many delinquents to residential programs in other states. Although statistics on out-of-state placements have not been available since the early 1970s, several knowledgeable Massachusetts officials estimated that well over 100 youths were annually placed in out-of-state programs in the past. By contrast, in 1987 DYS placed only 27 youths in other states. These were primarily youths on parole who were returning to live in their home communities in New England.

Other indicators of effective supervision reflect positively on DYS. Youth are not released to minimal supervision. NCCD found that over 80% of the DYS youths were given some community-based residential placement during their commitments. Most DYS clients enter community-based programs after a brief stay in detention or shelter-care detention. This short period of confinement permits DYS to complete its diagnostic work and to locate suitable program options for each youngster. Further, youths who violate program rules often are given very short stays in secure programs before they are reassigned to other community-based programs.

The case managers provide a close check on the progress of each youth under DYS care. Moreover, DYS possesses a comprehensive computerized system that tracks each youth's location for every day that he or she is under DYS jurisdiction. This permits DYS management to examine placement trends for each individual youth as well as providing aggregate data for agency planning. The DYS central office sets standards for all programs and strictly monitors contract compliance and legal mandates. Although it is always possible that some youths will "fall between the cracks" of any social service system, DYS is focused on preventing that occurrence. It is far more likely for individual needs to get lost amid the mass processing of people that characterizes the larger training schools.

Can the Massachusetts System Work Elsewhere?

The Massachusetts reforms already have become the standard against which many states are reevaluating and reorganizing their response to youthful offenders. In the mid-1970s, Illinois and Pennsylvania recruited Jerome Miller to revamp their approaches to juvenile crime. In both states considerable progress was made in reducing the number of youths in training schools and in expanding the number of community-based options, although the changes were not as dramatic as in Massachusetts. The most significant replication of the Massachusetts system occurred in a most unlikely place: Utah.

There are few places as different in politics, geography, and culture as Massachusetts and Utah. Yet, a blue ribbon task force appointed by Utah Governor Scott Matheson recommended that the juvenile corrections system pursue de-institutionalization and the less of the least restrictive alternatives possible for rehabilitative care (Van Vleet, Rutherford, & Schwartz, 1987). The task force responded to a legislatively commissioned study conducted by the John Howard Association revealing very serious problems such as over-incarceration, jailing of juveniles, abuses at the state training school, and the virtual absence of community-based alternatives.

A second high-level juvenile justice policy group produced a master plan that recommended the creation of a Division of Youth Corrections that would closely follow the path defined by Massachusetts reformers. The Utah model envisioned closure of the state's century-old 450-bed Youth Development Center and its replacement with three 30-bed regional secure facilities. Interestingly, Utah operated effectively for a decade with only two small secure facilities and is only now reaching the number of secure beds envisioned by the master plan.

As in Massachusetts, the majority of Utah juvenile offenders are managed in community-based programs that are organized in regions of the state. Utah has made effective use of staff secure observation and assessment programs that hold youngsters for up to 90 days before their transfer to group homes or outreach and tracking programs. Many of the Utah programs resemble community-based programs in Massachusetts. Although the state runs the secure treatment units, all of the community-based programs are run by private agencies that are under contract with the Division of Youth Corrections. In 1983, the old Youth Development Center buildings were remodeled and converted to a vocational training center.

As noted earlier, an NCCD study of youths committed to the Utah Division of Corrections in the early 1980s found that there was a significant decline in the frequency of offending of these youths in the 12 months after entry to the community-based programs, compared to the year prior to their commitment. The NCCD study (Austin, Krisberg, Steele, & Joe, 1990) concluded that Utah was successfully able to manage highly active and serious juvenile offenders under appropriate community-based control strategies. Utah officials also report that the new, smaller secure facilities have experienced no runaways, even though as many as 25% of the residents of the old training school were AWOL at some point in their correctional stays (Van Vleet et al., 1987, p. 13). Similar to Massachusetts, the Utah officials found that the new network of correctional services could operate at the same expenditure level as the former training school. They also report that incidents of staff abusing their youthful clients have virtually disappeared.

Another state that has attempted to closely approximate the Massachusetts model is Missouri. As in Utah, it was litigation against the training schools that stimulated action in Missouri. For instance, a federal lawsuit was resolved in 1975 by the closure of a major unit of the state training school for boys. While the lawsuit focused public attention on the failures of the traditional system, staff from the Missouri Division for Youth were building the foundation for a reformed system. The division began to move in the direction of smaller, decentralized facilities, regional management, and the expansion of a full range of alternative community placements.

Today the residential programs in Missouri have units housing 10 or fewer youths. The remaining secure units hold a maximum of 70 youths. Most youngsters are placed in wilderness programs, community group homes, proctor homes in which youths live with college students, day treatment programs, or individual supervision programs.

Missouri's reforms evolved slowly over a period of years. The state benefitted from the expertise of reformers in Utah and Massachusetts as well as from the planning assistance of private foundations interested in juvenile justice reform. Although no research has been done on the Missouri programs, state policy makers continue to strongly support the reformed system. For example, when the division experienced a recent large increase in the number of new commitments, state policy makers convened a statewide conference to explore how the community-based system could be expanded. This conference was well attended by the juvenile court judges and a significant contingent of state legislators. There was virtually no discussion of building new secure facilities or expanding locked programs. The conference identified a number of new community programs that would be developed over the next several months, especially new programs serving the major cities of St. Louis and Kansas City.

Interestingly, Missouri has accomplished its reforms without contracting with the private sector. The strong tradition of publicly operated services was marshalled by juvenile justice officials to replicate many of the private sector programs operating in Massachusetts and Utah. Missouri also has made great strides in expanding home-based services for its foster care population, and many of these home-based prevention services are available to families involved in the juvenile justice system.

Another major state that attempted a significant reform of its youth corrections system was Maryland. Beginning in 1988 the state closed the 250-bed Montrose School and significantly reduced the population at the remaining Charles Hickey School. Between 1985 and 1990 the average daily population in Maryland training schools went from 728 to 206 (Lerner, 1990). Similar to the situations in Utah and Missouri, a lawsuit against the Montrose School brought pressures for reform. As early as 1976 a federal government study criticized Maryland for excessive use of institutionalization for juveniles. Several years later a report by the National Association for the Advancement of Colored People (NAACP) charged that many children in Maryland facilities could be better managed in the community. A 1986 study by the Maryland Department of Health and Mental Hygiene concluded that at least 50% of the Montrose residents should be in community placements. These studies brought little real action by state officials.

Following two tragic suicides in 1986, members of the University of Maryland Law School filed a lawsuit against the Montrose School alleging unconstitutional conditions of confinement. Another lawsuit by the Sierra Club charged that the Montrose School was illegally dumping its sewage. There were estimates that it would take at least $12 million to renovate the Montrose School to remedy its most immediate problems.

Linda D'Amario Rossi, a nationally respected juvenile corrections administrator, was recruited to become director of the Department of Juvenile Services (DJS). Rossi had been a top official in the Texas Youth Commission, where she resolved many similar institutional problems and led a major effort to transfer youngsters from training schools to community-based programs. Rossi persuaded Maryland's Governor William Donald Schaefer to close the Montrose School and to support the expansion of community programs throughout Maryland. She also was able to enlist the strong support of Maryland's Supreme Court chief justice as well as that of several influential legislators.

Working with the Center for the Study of Youth Policy and NCCD, Rossi convened a series of key conferences to build a consensus for closing the Montrose School. The $9 million annual budget that supported the Montrose School operation was recycled into contracted community-based services. The National Center for Institutions and Alternatives (NCIA), headed by Jerome Miller, was tapped to review each youth housed at Montrose and to develop an individualized plan for returning that youngster to community programs. NCIA also was responsible for monitoring those new placements. Other well-known national private agencies such as the North American Family Institute (NAFI), the Associated Marine Institutes (AMI), and the Glen Mills School were brought in as contractors to quickly provide alternative residential and nonresidential programs for Maryland's serious juvenile offenders.

NAFI took over a former forestry camp, the Thomas O'Farrell Center, and created a very innovative and successful residential program for chronic property offenders, many of whom had serious drug problems (Krisberg, 1992a). The AMI established the Fort Smallwood Park Marine Institute, a day treatment program that utilizes specialized educational services and boating and scuba-diving experiences for delinquent youths. Another excellent program called Choice is modeled after the outreach and tracking services in Massachusetts. This program provides high-quality supervision and home-based services to youngsters in several Maryland communities. The DJS also has expanded placements in wilderness programs such as Outward Bound. Maryland's probation workers have become more like the case managers in Massachusetts, involved in brokering services and providing continuity of care for youths moving through various programs. An evaluation of the early community programs created as alternatives to the Montrose School is being completed by the Center for the Study of Youth Policy. The DJS also is planning a more in-depth assessment of all of its programs in the next year.

Although Maryland officials lowered the population of the Charles Hickey School, the last remaining traditional training school, there was no effort to completely close it. DJS worked hard to humanize and improve the operations at Hickey, but to no avail. In response to another investigative report castigating the care of children at the Hickey School, the governor and legislature decided to convert the operation of the facility to a private agency. Within a very short period, hundreds of state employees were given termination notices and a Colorado-based organization, Rebound, Inc., was selected to transform the quality of care at the training school. This move caused great controversy within Maryland. At this writing there is not enough information to determine whether Maryland's bold use of privatization will succeed.

The Massachusetts reforms also have influenced juvenile justice reforms in several other jurisdictions. States as diverse as Texas, Louisiana, Kentucky, Oklahoma, New Jersey, Florida, and Delaware all have significantly lowered their training school populations. Other states including Alabama, Georgia, Arizona, Arkansas, Indiana, Colorado, Michigan, Rhode Island, South Carolina, Tennessee, Washington, and Nebraska have adopted policy positions favoring community-based placements in lieu of more training schools. Only California, the national leader in juvenile incarceration, seems dedicated to building more large training schools, even though California's "edifice complex" seems unrealistic given the state's massive fiscal problems.

Most of these states have confronted the costly and controversial reality of increased litigation over state juvenile facilities. Public officials either must face the harsh imperatives of massive investments into expanding state training schools, with little guarantee of reducing youth crime, or they can explore the path pioneered by Massachusetts. Given the documented and persistent failures of large training schools to advance public safety or protect child welfare, it is not surprising that many jurisdictions are implementing the principles embodied in the Massachusetts DYS approach.

Notes

1. For this comparison, juvenile crime rates were computed by dividing the total number of persons under age 18 arrested for Part 1 offenses (as reported by the FBI Uniform Crime Reports) by the number of youths age 5-17 years in each state's population.

2. An arraignment means a youth has been arrested, taken before a magistrate, and charged with an offense. This is the equivalent of a juvenile court referral in other jurisdictions. The 1978 data represent the first year Massachusetts collected standardized arraignment data. Ideally, it would have been desirable to have such data for 5 years prior to the training school closures to allow time series analysis. Unfortunately, such data simply do not exist.

3. For more details about the data sources for the interstate comparisons see Barry Krisberg, James Austin, and Patricia Steele, *Unlocking Juvenile Corrections* (1991), pages A1-A2.

4. The 12-month re-arrest rate for Utah youths seems unusual given that the state runs programs very similar to those in Massachusetts. Two factors may account for this finding. First, the Utah data come from youths who were placed in the earliest community-based programs in Utah. The results in Utah thus are quite similar to those reported in the Harvard study of Massachusetts. Second, Utah traditionally reports a very high juvenile arrest rate. The youths in Utah had many more prior arrests than did their Massachusetts counterparts. The reader should note that the percentage of Utah youngsters with sustained delinquency petitions in the follow-up period was closer to the Massachusetts percentage.

5. The complete detail for these crime reduction estimates are reported in James Austin, Patricia Steele, and Barry Krisberg (1991). *Evaluating the Massachusetts Department of Youth Services: Final Report.*

6

Future Directions
for Juvenile Justice

Opportunities and Barriers

The Emerging Context of Juvenile Justice

The juvenile justice system will face major social and economic pressures during the coming decades. First and foremost, demographic forces will alter the context of juvenile justice.

In the recent past, the teenage population was shrinking. Between 1980 and 1990 the number of persons ages 10-17 declined by 11.4%. This was the resulting effect of the "baby bust"—the decline in U.S. birthrates that occurred in the late 1960s and into the 1970s. Despite the fewer number of adolescents in the society, the proportion of young people processed through the juvenile court and the juvenile corrections system continued to grow. This increase was due to more formal and punitive juvenile justice policies that produced more court referrals and expanded use of detention and juvenile incarceration.

Beginning in the 1990s, the children of the baby boom generation will reach their teenage years. By 1995 there will be another peak in the adolescent population, although not of the same magnitude as during the mid-1970s, when juvenile crime rates soared. Still, it is highly likely that the currently overloaded and underfunded juvenile justice system will face even higher caseloads in the next few years.

In addition to the growing number of youths, juvenile justice agencies will be asked to manage youngsters reared in extreme poverty who have had extensive involvement in drug use. The proportion of children raised in single-parent families living below the poverty level has increased in the 1980s. Increasingly, urban neighborhoods have become concentrations of impoverished women and their children. The exodus of more successful families has left behind few positive role models of upward mobility (Wilson, 1987).

The plight of the "truly disadvantaged" has been exacerbated by problems of homelessness and drug addiction. For example, in New York City alone over 10,000 children are living in shelters or welfare hotels; less than half of these children are attending school on a regular basis. Drug abuse, particularly addiction to a form of cocaine known as "crack," has increased among minorities and the poor, even as drug abuse among the middle class has declined sharply (National Institute of Drug Abuse, 1989).

A large number of babies have been born addicted to crack. The Center for Disease Control has estimated that there are already over 300,000 babies who were born drug-addicted. It is feared that these children will experience severe developmental problems and will have enormous difficulties in conventional school settings. The Los Angeles Unified School District has created special preschool programs for the children of drug addicts to forestall greater problems when these children enter kindergarten.

Another ominous social trend can be seen in the changing labor market. The job prospects of low-income adolescents are much darker than in the past. The transformation of the economy away from industrial production and manufacturing toward the service sector makes successful continuous employment more tenuous for those without at least a college degree. Yet, urban school dropout rates remain at record high levels (Duster, 1987). Sociologist Troy Duster suggests that whereas adolescents once dropped out of school into factory jobs, today's urban youngsters leave school to enter the world of drug trafficking and crime. The U.S. economy faces a startling contradiction: many high technology jobs with no potential candidates and many youths locked out of the labor market because of inadequate education and training. These economic forces are likely to heavily impact adolescents enmeshed in the juvenile justice system. These young people have low educational attainments and have virtually no access to the limited community-based job training resources now available.

These dire social facts are further complicated by severe cutbacks in governmental funding for programs designed to assist poor families and children (Currie, 1987). Declining resources in the child welfare system have propelled more troublesome adolescents to the juvenile justice system. As we have shown, the demand for institutional beds and out-of-home placements is growing. For example, in several large California counties large proportions of youths held in detention centers are awaiting the availability of foster or group home beds. Because many juvenile justice clients and their families also are served by child welfare agencies, the shrinking social service budgets reduce the juvenile court's already meager treatment resources.

These demographic, economic, and fiscal forces mean that the juvenile justice system will handle many more deeply troubled adolescents in the next several years. Juvenile correctional facilities are increasingly overcrowded. Over half of the youths in training schools reside in chronically overcrowded facilities. Due to the enormous problems of prison and jail overcrowding faced by virtually all states, it is highly unlikely that juvenile corrections administrators will be able to successfully compete for scarce public revenues to construct new facilities. Moreover, the nation's experience with prisons and jails demonstrates that sole reliance on building new beds rarely solves overcrowding.

Besides problems with overloaded and antiquated buildings, the juvenile justice system will face the urgent need to recruit and train new personnel. The juvenile justice system, like most corporations, will compete for a declining pool of skilled workers in the next 2 decades. Salaries in the juvenile justice system traditionally have been lower than comparable salaries in the adult justice system and well below salaries in the for-profit private sector. Training funds are extremely limited for juvenile justice personnel. What little training is provided is heavily subsidized through federal funding.

These trends portend very difficult times ahead for the already beleaguered juvenile justice system. Some would question whether the juvenile court has any future. Increasing numbers of liberal and conservative critics advocate eliminating the separate justice system for children.

With its reduced caseload of status offenders, the juvenile court has lost much of its traditional preventive mission. Moreover, the growing tendency to transfer very serious juvenile offenders to the adult system also has truncated the court's workload. The main clientele of the juvenile justice system now typically are repetitive property offenders, drug offenders, assorted minor offenders, and those who have failed in child welfare placements. These youths have very high recidivism rates—making the juvenile court's effectiveness look quite bad.

Models for the Future

Within this hostile policy and societal environment the court needs a revitalized mission to bolster its image and public support. A number of broad proposals have surfaced about directions in which the juvenile court might be reformed. One proposed direction for the juvenile court would be to reintroduce status offenders into the court's mainstream. There are those who believe that status offenders who are not given effective court sanctions will "grow" into more serious offenders, although little or no research exists to support this conclusion. It is alleged that the de-institutionalization movement has failed and that youths are being victimized and exploited due to lack of proper court supervision. For example, during the Reagan administration well-financed public awareness campaigns were conducted about missing children and the sexual exploitation of runaway children who become involved in prostitution and child pornography. The public also is becoming aware of growing numbers of teenagers who are at great risk of contracting and transmitting HIV and AIDS. The symbol of the child as victim is a powerful justification to strengthen the court's role in regulating family conflicts. National concern over both adolescent and parental drug use also has been used as a rationale for greater governmental intervention with troubled families.

It is undeniable that severe service gaps continue to exist for troubled youngsters. Many communities failed to provide adequate funding for the alternative community programs that were called for by the de-institutionalization movement. Yet returning status offenders to court hearings and expanding utilization of secure confinement to manage these youngsters remains an inappropriate and potentially disastrous response to their very real needs.

Any proposal to reintroduce status offenders to the juvenile court in large numbers must answer serious policy concerns about (a) commingling status offenders with more serious and violent offenders, (b) the court's traditional overreliance on institutional placements versus home-based services, and (c) dangers that status offenders will be unnecessarily drawn further into the juvenile justice process. Moreover, it is crucial to ask where the already underfunded juvenile court will find the necessary funding to handle a new set of clients. Further, the handling of status offenders in the court system always has raised important concerns about equitable treatment, especially for young women.

Another group of conservative reformers have argued for a more punishment-oriented juvenile court. They argue that juveniles must be held accountable for their criminal behavior. Even the National Council of Family and Juvenile Court Judges, an advocate of the traditional juvenile court philosophy, has proposed that "just deserts" play a much larger role in juvenile justice practice.

The calls for enhancing juvenile penalties have led to a partial expansion of determinate sentencing for young offenders. As noted above, there also have been many efforts to make it easier to try juveniles as adults. Some would argue that as the juvenile court moves toward a retributive mission, more attention must be paid to issues of due process, equal protection, and proportionality of sanctions.

The comprehensive reform of the Washington State juvenile code represents the most extensive movement toward determinate sentencing for youngsters. Soon after the new Washington code was implemented, the number of youths in detention centers and training schools rose dramatically. The state juvenile corrections authorities quickly began early release policies to avert severe overcrowding in state juvenile facilities. Today, there remains a lack of consensus in Washington State as to whether the sweeping code revisions have created greater equity in sentencing or whether the tougher sentences have had any positive effect on reducing youth crime.

The political environment supporting harsher juvenile court penalties exists in several jurisdictions. "Get tough" policies are popular with politicians who are responsive to continued public fears about crime. But the most immediate consequences of tougher sanctions have been overcrowded facilities and demands for increased funding for correctional agencies. There is no credible research evidence that these tougher penalties actually have reduced youth crime. Until recently, the true fiscal costs of enhancing juvenile punishments have been hidden by the enormous expenditures required by skyrocketing prison and jail populations. As we have noted, the growing problems of juvenile corrections have not successfully competed for public attention in most jurisdictions. Even more troubling, the ethos of punishment may have blunted the response of public officials to the continuing legacy of abuses within juvenile facilities. Litigation on behalf of incarcerated children has been one method of holding public officials accountable for ensuring minimum standards of decency in the care of troubled youngsters.

We believe a more promising direction for the future of U.S. juvenile justice is the rediscovery and updating of the juvenile court's historical vision. Reforms that emphasize the best interests of children must pursue the true individualization of treatments and the expansion of the range of dispositional options available to the court. Incarceration, because of its expense and its lack of positive results, should remain a last resort. Large training schools must be replaced with a continuum of placements and services. These dispositional options should include small, service-intensive, secure programs for the few violent youths and community-based options for other offenders. Correctional caseloads must be low enough to ensure that individual needs are discovered and met.

We envision the expansion of innovative correctional programs that focus on aftercare and the reentry of offenders to their communities. In fact, planning for the child's eventual return to community living should start soon after his or her admission to an out-of-home placement. Those youths placed in community programs require a great deal of structure and adult guidance. Many of these youths should attend educationally based day treatment programs and pay restitution or perform community service.

Individualized treatment and the "best interests of the child" do not necessarily mean a return to the arbitrary and often capricious decision making that has plagued the juvenile court. *It is time to recognize that the values of due process, equal protection, and proportionality are not in conflict with the best interests of children.* First and foremost, the juvenile court must become a full-fledged justice court. It is worth noting that jurisdictions possessing the widest array of treatment resources for children often are those that pay close attention to the legal rights of young people.

Although the future of juvenile justice is problematic at best, there are reasons to be optimistic that the rediscovery of justice for juveniles is possible. In Chapter 5 we reported on the Massachusetts juvenile justice revolution and its very favorable results. Below we briefly review other affirmative models for the future.

Removing Children From Jails

A central goal of juvenile justice reformers for over a century was to rescue children from adult jails. Adolescents who are held in adult facilities often are sexually and physically abused by adult inmates and staff. Suicide rates among adolescents in jails are several times higher than for youths held in juvenile facilities (Schwartz, 1988). Despite the continued verbal support for jail removal, little real progress was made on this issue for most of the 20th century. Even as late as the mid-1970s there were estimates of nearly 500,000 juveniles admitted to adult jails and police lockups (Sarri & Vinter, 1974). However, in 1980 the U.S. Congress enacted a proposal by the Justice Department to amend the Juvenile Justice and Delinquency Prevention Act (JJDPA). This legislative change has profoundly altered laws and practices. The 1980 amendment required that states receiving federal funds accomplish the complete removal of juveniles from jails within a 5-year period (Schwartz, 1989).

Although several states have been unable to achieve the congressional mandate, there has been a major decline in the number of juveniles admitted to jails and lockups. In 1986 the number had declined to approximately 60,000—a drop of 88% from the pre-amendment period. The congressional action led many states to severely restrict or abolish the jailing of children. In each of these instances the new state legislation required the support of a very broad coalition of criminal justice and child advocacy groups (Steinhart, 1988a). Further, the JJDPA has been interpreted by some federal courts as creating a private cause of action under existing civil rights laws (Swanger, 1988). This gives child advocates another tool to press for the complete removal of children from jails (Soler, 1988).

For example, in 1991 the State of Indiana legislatively abolished the jailing of children. For years, Indiana placed hundreds of children in dangerous situations in adult jails. Yet, a bipartisan coalition led by the Department of Corrections convinced state lawmakers that better alternatives existed. The jail removal movement in Indiana demonstrated again that the goals of child protection and public safety were not antithetical. Moveover, many Indiana communities have learned that sensible alternatives to jailing, such as temporary shelter care or home detention, can be created without requiring large new expenditures of public funds. Also, elected officials in Indiana and many other states learned that they could support humane policies for children without suffering the alleged political liability of appearing to be soft on crime. Successes in the jail removal area illustrate the power of legislative action to discourage harmful practices. These stories also suggest that the longstanding inferior treatment of youngsters can be quickly remedied.

Case Management: The New York City
Department of Juvenile Justice

For years, New York City's juvenile detention was notorious as one of the most brutal and inhumane places housing troubled youngsters. The Spofford Center became the target of repeated lawsuits. In 1979, Mayor Edward Koch, known for his tough law-and-order stances, created a new city agency, the Department of Juvenile Justice (DJJ), and charged it to accomplish a major overhaul of the city's juvenile detention system. A child advocate and attorney, Ellen Schall, was recruited to lead the reform process.

The first item on the reform agenda was to reduce overcrowding at Spofford. DJJ staff created nonsecure detention placements for youths not requiring secure care. They also worked with other court agencies to streamline procedures and reduced delay periods from arrest to final court hearings. Youths who were sentenced to state juvenile correctional programs were expedited to these placements. These steps alone reduced the detention population by almost half.

Next, the DJJ began reconceptualizing their approach to detention. The agency asserted that the brief period of detention should be turned into an opportunity to identify medical, educational, and social service needs and to begin meeting those needs. A sophisticated educational testing and remediation program was introduced. DJJ staff implemented one of the nation's few fully accredited juvenile corrections health programs. Detained youngsters receive 24-hour comprehensive medical, dental, and mental health services. Many previously undiagnosed health problems are diagnosed and resolved (New York Department of Juvenile Justice, 1989).

DJJ developed a complete case management system for each youth. This system organizes information about the youngster and monitors the timely provision of needed services. The case management system is fully computerized and assists staff in delivering highly individualized care. The department also has launched a voluntary aftercare program in which youths and their families may receive supportive counseling even after the youths are discharged from Spofford. This unique program is justified as a preventive service that helps very high risk youngsters. In 1989, DJJ won approval to abandon the antiquated Spofford facility. The future New York City detention system will consist of two smaller secure facilities and expanded nonsecure detention options.

The Spofford reforms demonstrate that detention need not be "dead time" while youngsters await court hearings. Detention also can be a time to respond to urgent, unmet needs of very deprived young people. In New York City detention affords the community the chance to identify and work on the severe learning problems of delinquent adolescents. The DJJ works closely with social service and educational personnel to get their clients plugged back in to school and family environments. Thus, more than just a temporary holding action, the DJJ has been transformed into a truly preventive agency working with extremely high risk youngsters. Moreover, the concern for providing improved care has not diminished the appropriate protection of the legal rights of these young people.

The DJJ has received national acclaim for excellence in public sector management from experts such as Tom Peters, the Ford Foundation, and Harvard University's Kennedy School of Government. What some have called the "Spofford miracle" demonstrates the potential for humanistic changes in juvenile justice agencies. As in the Massachusetts DYS experience, New York City found that the judicious use of secure confinement allows agency resources to be redirected to enhance the level of care for a greater number of adolescents.

Other Innovative Juvenile Justice Programs

In addition to the systemic reforms described above, several individual programs also deserve special attention. These programs share a fresh approach to managing serious offenders.

The Florida-based Associated Marine Institutes (AMI) operates a diverse, multistate network of programs for juvenile offenders. Most of the youths live at home or with foster families. Each day they are involved in AMI programs that include training in boat repair, diving, and marine biology. AMI operates an excellent education program with an exemplary record of assisting youths to complete their high school education. Each of the local AMI programs recruit local volunteers who raise money for the programs and become directly involved with the youths. There is an explicit and clear aftercare plan for every youngster. Research by Tollett (1987) indicates that AMI graduates have recidivism rates as good or better than most Florida programs. The AMI day treatment programs are less than half the cost of traditional institutional programs.

In addition to the day treatment programs, AMI also operates a small wilderness program for youngsters who otherwise would be sent to adult prisons. Called the Florida Environmental Institute

(FEI), this program engages youths in hard and productive environmental work in the Florida Everglades. The isolation of the program makes escape unfeasible and eliminates the needs for prison-like security measures. The FEI program, as with other AMI efforts, emphasizes positive activities to rebuild fragile self-images and to demonstrate the individual child's value. The AMI slogan, "One Kid at a Time," exemplifies this philosophy.

Another innovative private agency whose graduates have excellent success records is the North American Family Institute (NAFI). Founded by one of the key reformers of the Massachusetts system, Yitzhak Bakal, the NAFI incorporates self-help strategies to deal with its troubled clients. All NAFI programs use the powerful tool of positive peer influence through a sophisticated group process. Youths are taught the skills to support one another as well as to seek that support. The NAFI programs create "communities of respect and dignity" in which very strong communal norms guide everyday life. The most notable NAFI program is the Thomas O'Farrell School in Maryland (Krisberg, 1992a). Like AMI, the NAFI program starts its aftercare planning very early and helps its young clients to make a gradual return to community living. NAFI also places a very high priority on community service. Virtually all its programs are engaged in community betterment projects. Almost all NAFI youths participate in carefully structured community visits and events. The surrounding communities, in turn, have been very active in helping the NAFI programs in a variety of ways.

The Juvenile Division of the New Jersey Department of Corrections operates community-based programs for about half the youths committed to its custody. These day treatment or group home programs enroll their adolescents in local community colleges. The Juvenile Division day treatment programs emphasize vocational training and work placements. Some youths learn landscape architecture; others help operate a New Jersey state concert center.

In partnership with philanthropist Ray Chambers, the division runs a fast-food franchise called Jersey Mike's. Youthful offenders refurbished the building and have been trained in all aspects of the business. The enterprise is organized as an employee stock option plan—youths who remain crime free after a fixed period of time are given an ownership share in the franchise and all future business enterprises. They are employed, and they learn entrepreneurial skills and develop personal capital.

The Key Program, Inc., a program headquartered in Massachusetts, pioneered the concept of outreach and tracking. Young offenders live in the community; however, they are closely supervised on a 24-hour, daily basis. Youths must conform to precise and individualized plans involving schooling, work, counseling, and victim restitution. If the youngsters fail to meet these expectations, they may be securely confined for a brief period (sometimes a few days). The Key Program operates a small number of beds to temporarily house their clients who may need residential care before returning home.

The Key Program pays very careful attention to high-quality staff training and supervision. Further, Key requires that staff move to other jobs after 12 to 14 months of employment. This rule is intended to prevent staff "burnout" that is typical in intensive supervision programs. Former Key Program employees are so well trained that they are valuable candidates for other human service jobs in the New England area (Bakke, Krisberg, Neuenfeldt, & Steele, 1989).

These innovative programs are but a small sampling of possible new directions in handling serious delinquents. All of these examples involve successful collaborations between private and public agencies. These programs challenge the conventional wisdom that prison-like institutions offer the only option for serious juvenile offenders. Successful juvenile programs emphasize intensive, individualized services and strong management accountability for delivering necessary supervision and treatment.

Reinventing Juvenile Justice

Contemporary juvenile justice practices are far from the idealistic notions that motivated reformers to create a special children's court. Many child advocates question whether the juvenile justice system can ever become a full-fledged justice system or an effective part of the child welfare system (Krisberg, 1988b). It is highly problematic for juvenile justice agencies to attempt to simultaneously fulfill these distinctive goals. The philosopher George Herbert Mead (1961) noted that crime control is sought through "hostile procedures of law and . . . through comprehension of social and psychological conditions" (p. 882). Mead did not believe these two approaches could be combined. He wrote, "The social worker in court is the sentimentalist, and the legalist in the social settlement, in spite of his learned doctrine, is the ignoramus" (p. 882).

Some might argue that the fundamental dilemma of juvenile justice is the balancing of the requirements of distributive justice to produce apparently "fair" outcomes with the need to treat children in individual and flexible ways. This balancing act is complicated by chronically inadequate resources as well as by deeply ingrained prejudice against the predominantly poor families and racial and ethnic minority groups that dominate the court's clientele. Although the political rhetoric may swing back and forth from punitive themes to rehabilitative values, actual court practices are remarkably resistant to change. The current presiding juvenile court judge in Dade County, Florida, Thomas Peterson, recently has observed that juvenile court programs have remained unchanged for a generation, despite continued evidence of high failure rates.

But what if society chose to reinvent the juvenile justice system to become a more effective and just system of caring for troubled youngsters? What are the necessary components of that reinvention?

Making Delinquency a Public Health Issue

First, serious youth crime must be reconceptualized as a public health problem as well as a law enforcement problem. As with most other health issues, this perspective would immediately direct our attention to preventive strategies. By definition a juvenile justice system is reactionary. A public health perspective would allow juvenile offenders to be understood as both victims and victimizers. The linkage is undeniable among physical abuse, parental neglect, and violent youth crime. This does not mean that young people are unaccountable for their behavior. However, a public health approach offers the possibility of comprehending the origins of youthful violence and formulating rational responses.

What if the issues of teenage pregnancy and venereal disease were totally defined within the rhetoric of moral condemnation? This is the case with juvenile crime. Moral outrage provides an outlet to vent frustration, but this approach has not stopped the numbers of teenagers having babies or the spread of dangerous communicable diseases. The purely moralistic approach stifles the kinds of inquiries and experimentation that might improve the performance of the juvenile justice system.

A public health approach to delinquency inevitably would point us to the exploration of environmental factors in the promotion of delinquency. Greater attention must be placed on the harmful impact of the easy availability of guns and drugs as well as on the mass media's commercialization of violence. We must better understand how violence becomes defined as an integral part of manhood in

certain communities and how these dangerous socialization processes can be modified. Moreover, a public health perspective would
direct attention to community organizing and self-help strategies
that have proven their efficacy in many other health promotion
campaigns.

Implementing a Developmental Perspective

To support the public health paradigm, the juvenile justice system
must genuinely build knowledge about adolescent development into
its basic policies and procedures. The best research on adolescent
development must be incorporated in the professional education
and training of juvenile justice practitioners. In addition, elected
officials enacting laws and defining agency policies need more in-
depth understanding of the data on adolescent development.

If current research on child development and delinquency are
incomplete, then a very high priority must be placed on remedying
these knowledge gaps. This often entails longitudinal research de-
signs that require sizeable research investments over an extended
period of time. With few exceptions, only the federal government has
the capacity to support these inquiries. The development of new
knowledge and its dissemination to policy makers and practitioners
may well be the most important contribution to be made by the
federal government in preventing and controlling youth crime.

Protecting the Legal Rights of Adolescents

Improving the juvenile justice system also must entail better legal
protection for young people. There is little evidence that secret and
casual courtroom methods actually advance child protection. It is
worth repeating that most of the model programs described in this
chapter are very concerned about protecting the legal rights of children. The Institute for Judicial Administration (IJA) and the American Bar Association (ABA) have produced a comprehensive set of
juvenile justice standards that appropriately balance the legal rights
of children and child protection considerations (Flicker, 1982). The
IJA-ABA standards can be used as a starting point for any jurisdiction concerned about the fair treatment of young people.

Besides a framework of justice, adolescents need real access to
justice. Too often the provision of legal assistance to young people

is inferior or nonexistent (Feld, 1988a). Many adolescents and their families waive their legal right to legal counsel without full comprehension of the consequences of this decision (Grisso, 1980; Schwartz, 1989). Some have proposed that the solution to this problem is to create a nonrevocable right to counsel. Effective legal representation is the prerequisite to all other procedural safeguards (Feld, 1984).

Increasingly, child advocates are recommending that juvenile proceedings be open to the public and the media (Schwartz, 1989). Closed hearings have not been particularly successful in shielding youngsters from adverse publicity in high profile cases. Moreover, the seemingly hidden juvenile court operations have contributed to the public perception that the court is overly lenient. When open hearings have been tried there have been few negative consequences.

A corollary issue involves the quality of juvenile court judges. In many jurisdictions, assignment to the juvenile court is not a highly sought after judicial appointment. The juvenile court too often is a dead-end along the judicial career track. Even deeply committed judges may seek rotation out of juvenile court to assist their legal careers. Similar observations can be made about attorneys who practice in juvenile court. There are serious questions about the adequacy of legal training and the competence of lawyers in many juvenile courts.

The job of a juvenile court judge often is much broader than that of judges of general jurisdiction courts. Juvenile court judges often must administer detention, probation, and social service agencies. In the discharge of these administrative duties they face complex role conflicts. As legal officers they must assess the constitutionality of the state's treatment of delinquent youths; as administrators they must protect their employees and protect agency budget priorities.

In recent years, neither federal nor state agencies have funded programs to improve the legal representation of adolescents. In some states, the local bar associations have supported these activities on a very limited basis. Groups litigating on behalf of the legal rights of incarcerated minors have received minimal federal support over the past decade. As noted earlier, federally funded training efforts have focused far more on disposition and placement issues than on safeguarding the legal rights of juveniles.

Treating the Whole Child

The current organization of adolescent social and health services is characterized by rigidly drawn agency turfs and budgetary categories. This situation contributes to fragmented and often wasteful deployment of scarce public resources. It is not uncommon for the same youth and family to have a multiplicity of caseworkers assigned to them. From the vantage point of each helping professional the youth is a delinquent, an abused child, a youth in need of special educational services, or a welfare recipient. Other service providers may be working with other family members or siblings. In the typical scenario, no one possesses an overall view of the adolescent's needs. A comprehensive and integrated treatment plan rarely is created.

The categorical nature of government funding and the lack of interagency collaboration lead to difficult turf battles to include or exclude certain clients. Older adolescents, particularly those with histories of mental illness or aggressive behavior, are the most likely youngsters to be omitted by agency service criteria. These youths generally end up in juvenile correctional institutions because public corrections agencies cannot refuse to take custody of adolescents who are lawfully committed to their care. Thus, juvenile corrections agencies must manage a wide variety of youngsters that no other agencies want to serve. As the fiscal pressures mount, the juvenile corrections system becomes the ultimate, albeit not so safe, social service net.

This fragmented structure inhibits the accountability of government agencies to protect young people and to promote public safety. Further, the availability of treatment resources is highly dependent on political and media whims—homelessness last year, drug abuse this year. A more cost-effective approach would entail coordinated and integrated planning of juvenile justice and related human services. The case management approach of the New York City Department of Juvenile Justice and the regionalization of services by the Massachusetts Department of Youth Services are good examples of how service resources could be reorganized. Recently, Contra Costa County in California has formed interagency teams of youth workers to concentrate on the problems of homeless youths and runaways. Many jurisdictions currently are experimenting with the integration at school sites of a wide range of social and health services. It is premature to evaluate the successes of these efforts, but such agency boundary crossings are needed.

At the federal and state levels, serious consideration should be given to reducing the categorical approach to funding children's programs. This conventional budgetary approach contributes to a focus on symptoms rather than on underlying causes. Modest policy experiments promoting more flexible financing of prevention and intervention programs should be attempted. The basic objective of these field experiments should be treating the whole child in his or her family and community context.

Concluding Observations

Winning support for the reinvention of juvenile justice that we have advocated will be very difficult. The public is frustrated and angry about unacceptably high rates of juvenile violence. Deeply ingrained prejudices exist against impoverished families and their children. Indeed, the poor have become the new target for ambitious politicians looking to divert attention from deep problems in the economy and the continuing fiscal crisis of government. Moreover, the recent riots in Los Angeles following the jury verdict in the Rodney King case showed how racism and the isolation of racial and ethnic groups threatens to destroy the social fabric.

Jerome Miller, who initiated the Massachusetts reform movement, often asks his audiences about the kind of justice system they would like to see if their own children were in trouble. Few of us would accept the current juvenile justice as appropriate for our own children. Yet, we tolerate substandard conditions because the majority of Americans do not believe the juvenile justice system is designed to control "our children." We must urgently find ways to escape the trap of thinking about "our children" and "their children." The United States cannot possibly compete in the global economy of the 21st century if a large part of our resources are still devoted to unproductive punitive and warehousing approaches to juvenile delinquency.

It is the challenge of modern-day juvenile justice reformers to build influential and powerful support for progressive juvenile justice and child welfare policies. Although such reforms can be justified on humanitarian grounds alone, it will be crucial to demonstrate the social utility of a more enlightened social justice agenda.

Besides reforming the juvenile court, the reinvention of juvenile justice must confront the stark economic and social trends we discussed in the beginning of this chapter. Unacceptable high school dropout rates, rising teenage pregnancies, disappearing job opportunities for urban youths, and the collapsed child welfare system will virtually guarantee even higher rates of youth crime in the next decade. A new generation of "child savers" may be required to advance the cause of the urgently needed social reconstruction of our communities.

Whether an enlightened vision of juvenile justice will be limited to a few jurisdictions, or whether it will disappear altogether, is difficult to predict. In too many communities, abusive and inferior care of troubled and disadvantaged children is still the reality. Now more than ever the redemptive vision that helped create the juvenile court must be rediscovered. Although the present political milieu may not be ideal for a crusade to rescue our children, there is no choice but to continue the struggle for a humane and progressive system of juvenile justice.

Some have cynically proposed that we "write off" the current generation of underclass youths. This option is tantamount to advocating genocide—losing a generation means forfeiting the future of a whole segment of the population. Reinventing justice for children and reinvesting in children are more realistic and ennobling societal goals.

References

Alexander, F. A. (1964). *A preliminary report on the pilot investigation of some socio-psychological variables influencing the probation officer.* Paper presented at the Pacific Sociological Association Meeting.

Alinsky, S. (1946). *Reveille for radicals.* Chicago: University of Chicago Press.

Allen-Hagen, B. (1991). *Children in custody, 1989.* Washington, DC: Office of Juvenile Justice and Delinquency Prevention.

Altschuler, D., & Armstrong, T. (1984). Intervening with serious juvenile offenders. In R. Mathias, P. Demuro, & R. Allinson (Eds.), *Violent juvenile offenders* (pp. 187-206). San Francisco: National Council on Crime and Delinquency.

American Correctional Association (ACA). (1990). *The female offender: What does the future hold?* Washington, DC: St. Mary's Press.

Austin, J., Steele, P., & Krisberg, B. (1991). *Evaluating the Massachusetts Department of Youth Services: Final report.* San Francisco: National Council on Crime and Delinquency.

Austin, J., Krisberg, B., Steele, P., & Joe, K. (1990). *A court that works.* San Francisco: National Council on Crime and Delinquency.

Axelrad, S. (1952). Negro and white male institutionalized delinquents. *American Journal of Sociology, 57,* 569-574.

Bakal, Y. (1973). *Closing correctional institutions.* Lexington, MA: Lexington Books.

Bakke, A., Krisberg, B., Neuenfeldt, D., & Steele, P. A. (1989). *Demonstration of post-adjudication non-residential intensive supervision programs: A national assessment report.* San Francisco: National Council on Crime and Delinquency.

Barak, G. (1974). *In defense of the poor: The emergence of the public defender system in the United States (1900-1920).* Unpublished doctoral dissertation, University of California at Berkeley. Ann Arbor, MI: University Microfilms.

Barr, W. (1992). *Combating violent crime: 24 recommendations to strengthen criminal justice.* Washington, DC: U.S. Department of Justice.

Bartollas, C., Miller, S., & Dinitz, S. (1976). *Juvenile victimization: The institutional paradox.* Beverly Hills, CA: Sage.

Bishop, D., & Frazier, C. E. (1992). Gender bias in juvenile justice processing: Implications of the JJDP Act. *Journal of Criminal Law and Criminology, 82*(4), 1162-1186.

Blumstein, A. (1982). On the racial disproportionality of United States prison populations. *Journal of Criminology and Criminal Law, 73*(3), 1259-1281.

Blumstein, A. (1988). Prison populations: A system out of control? In M. Tonry & N. Morris (Eds.), *Crime and justice* (Vol. 10, pp. 231-266). Chicago: University of Chicago Press.

Bordua, D. S. (1967). Recent trends: Deviant behavior and social control. *Annals of the American Academy of Political and Social Sicence, 359,* 149-163.

Bortner, M. A. (1986). Traditional rhetoric, organizational realities: Remand of juveniles to adult court. *Crime and Delinquency, 32,* 54-74.

Brager, G., & Purcell, F. (1967). *Community action against poverty.* New Haven, CT: College and University Press.

Bremner, R., Barnard, J., Hareven, T. K., Mennel, R. M. (1970). *Children and youth in America: A documentary history* (Vol. 1). Cambridge, MA: Harvard University Press.

Bureau of Justice Statistics. (1987). *Children in custody, 1985.* Washington, DC: U.S. Department of Justice.

Burns, V. M., & Stein, L. W. (1967). The prevention of juvenile delinquency. In *The president's commission of law enforcement and the administration of justice task force report: Juvenile delinquency and youth crime* (pp. 353-408). Washington, DC: Government Printing Office.

California Governor's Special Study Commission on Juvenile Justice. (1960). *A study of the administration of juvenile justice in California* (from p. 191). Sacramento: Author.

California Revised Juvenile Court Law, Section 626 W & I, 1961.

Canter, R. (1982). Sex differences in self-reported delinquency. *Criminology, 20,* 373-393.

Carter, R., & Lohman, J. (1968). *Middle class delinquency: An experiment in community control.* Berkeley: School of Criminology, University of California.

Center for the Study of Youth Policy. (1990). *Juvenile arrest, detention, and incarceration trends, 1979-1989.* Ann Arbor: University of Michigan.

Chesney-Lind, M. (1988, March). Girls and status offenses: Is juvenile justice still sexist? *Criminal Justice Abstracts, 20,* 144-165.

Chesney-Lind, M., & Shelden, R. G. (1992). *Girls: Delinquency and juvenile justice.* Pacific Grove, CA: Brooks/Cole.

Chicago Police Department. (1971). *Manual of procedure: Youth division* (Sec. II, Part I). Chicago: Chicago Police Department.

Cicourel, A. (1968). *The social organization of juvenile justice.* New York: John Wiley.

Cloward, R. & Piven, F. (1971). *Regulating the poor.* New York: Pantheon.

Coates, R., Miller, A., & Ohlin, L. (1982). *Diversity in a youth correctional system.* Cambridge, MA: Ballinger.

Coben, S., & Ratner, L. (Eds.). (1970). *The development of an American culture* (from p. 192). Englewood Cliffs, NJ: Prentice Hall.

Cohen, L. E. *Delinquency dispositions: An empirical analysis of processing decisions in three juvenile courts.* Washington, DC: National Criminal Justice Information and Statistics Service.

Cohn, Y. (1963). Criteria for the probation officer's recommendation to the juvenile court. *Crime and Delinquency, 9,* 262-275.

Coles, R. *Children of crisis: A study of courage and fear.* Boston: Little, Brown.

Commonwealth v. Fisher, 213 Pennsylvania 48 (1905).

Crawford, P., Malamud, D., & Dumpson, J. R. (1970). Working with teenage gangs. In
    N. Johnson (Ed.), *The sociology of crime and delinquency*. New York: John Wiley.
Cross, S. Z. The prehearing juvenile report: Probation officer's conceptions. *Journal of
    Research in Crime and Delinquency, 4*, 212-217.
Currie, E. (1987). *Violence in the year 2000: What kind of future?* San Francisco: National
    Council on Crime and Delinquency.
Datesman, S. K. (1980). Unequal protection for males and females in the juvenile court.
    In S. K. Datesman & F. R. Carpitti (Eds.), *Women, crime, and justice* (pp. 300-319).
    New York: Oxford University Press.
Demuro, P., Demuro, A., & Lerner, S. (1988). *Reforming the CYA* (California Youth
    Authority). Bolinas, CA: Commonwealth Research Institute.
Devoe, E. (1848). *The refuge system, or prison discipline applied to delinquency*. Sprague
    Pamphlet Collection, Cambridge, MA: Harvard Divinity School.
Dineen, J. (1974). *Juvenile court organization and status offenses: A statutory profile.*
    Washington, DC: Law Enforcement Assistance Administration.
Duster, T. (1987). Crime, youth unemployment and the black underclass. *Crime and
    Delinquency, 33*, 300-316.
Duxbury, E. (1972). *Youth bureaus in California: Progress report #3*.acramento: California
    Youth Authority.
Eigen, J. D. (1981). Punishing youth homicide offenders in Philadelphia. *Journal of
    Criminology and Criminal Law, 72*, 1072-1093.
Elliott, D., & Ageton, S. (1980). Reconciling race and class differences in self-reported
    and official estimates of delinquency. *American Sociological Review, 45*, 95-110.
Elliott, D., Ageton, S., Huizinga, D., Knowles, B., & Canter, R. (1983). *The prevalence and
    incidence of delinquent behavior: 1976-1980*. Boulder, CO: Behavioral Research Institute.
Empey, L., & Lubeck, S. (1971). *The silverlake experiment*. Chicago: Aldine.
Ex parte Becknell, 51 California 692 (1897).
Ex parte Crouse, 4 Wharton (PA) 9 (1838).
Fagan, J., Forst, M., & Vivona, T. S. (1987). Racial determinants of the judicial transfer
    decision. *Crime and Delinquency, 33*, 259-286.
Fagan, J. A., Slaughter, E., & Hartstone, E. (1987). Blind justice? The impact of race on
    the juvenile justice process. *Crime and Delinquency, 33*, 224-258.
Feld, B. (1977). *Neutralizing inmate violence: Juvenile offenders in institutions*. Cambridge,
    MA: Ballinger.
Feld, B. (1984). Criminalizing juvenile justice: Rules of procedure for the juvenile court.
    Minnesota Law Review, 69, 2.
Feld, B. (1988a). *In re* Gault revisited: A cross-state comparison of the right to counsel
    in juvenile court. *Crime and Delinquency, 34*, 393-424.
Feld, B. (1988b). *In re* Gault: A cross-state comparison of the right to counsel in juvenile
    court. *Crime and Delinquency, 34*, 379-392.
Feld, B. (1988c). The juvenile court meets the principle of offense: Punishment, treat-
    ment and the difference it makes. *Boston University Law Review, 68*, 821-915.
Fenwick, C. R. (1982). Juvenile court intake decision-making: The importance of family
    affiliation. *Journal of Criminal Justice, 10*(6), 443-453.
Ferster, E., & Courtless, T. (1969). The beginning of juvenile justice, police practices,
    and the juvenile offender. *Vanderbilt Law Review, 22*, 598-601.
Figueria-McDonough, J. (1987). Discrimination or sex differences? Criteria for evalu-
    ating the juvenile justice system's handling of minor offenses. *Crime and Delin-
    quency, 33,D* 403-424.
Finkenauer, J. (1984). *Juvenile delinquency and corrections*. New York: Academic Press.

Flicker, B. (1982). *Standards for juvenile justice: A summary and analysis.* Sponsored by the Institute of Judicial Administration, American Bar Association. Cambridge, MA: Ballinger.

Foltz, C. (1897). Public defenders. *American Law Review, 31,* 393-403.

Frazier, C. E., & Cochran, J. K. (1986). Official intervention, diversion from the juvenile justice system, and dynamics of human services work: Effects of a reform goal based on labeling theory. *Crime and Delinquency, 32,* 157-176.

Gendreau, P., & Ross, R. (1987). Revivification of rehabilitation: Evidence from the 1980s. *Justice Quarterly, 4,* 349-407.

Greenwood, P., & Zimring, F. (1985).*One more chance: Promising intervention strategies for chronic juvenile offenders.* Santa Monica, CA: Rand Corporation.

Grisso, T. (1980). Juveniles' capacity to waive Miranda rights: An empirical analysis. *California Law Review, 68,* 1134-1165.

Hamparian, D. (1982). *Youth in adult courts: Between two worlds.* Columbus, OH: Academy for Contemporary Problems.

Handlin, O. (1959). *The newcomers.* New York: Doubleday.

Harari, C., & Chwast, J. (1964). Class bias in psychodiagnosis of delinquents. *Crime and Delinquency, 10,* 145-151.

Haugen, D., Costello, T., Schwartz, I., Krisberg, B., & Litsky, P. (1982). *Public attitudes toward youth crime.* Minneapolis, MN: Hubert H. Humphrey Institute of Public Affairs.

Hawes, J. (1971). *Children in urban society: Juvenile delinquency in nineteenth century America.* New York: Oxford University Press.

Healy, W. (1915). *The individual delinquent: A textbook of diagnosis and prognosis for all concerned in understanding offenders.* Boston: Little, Brown.

Healy, W. (1917). *Mental conflicts and misconduct.* Boston: Little, Brown.

Healy, W., Bronner, A., & Shimberg, M. (1935). The close of another chapter in criminology. *Mental Hygiene, 19,* 208-222.

Hindelang, M. J. (1982). Race and crime. In L. D. Savitz & H. Johnson (Eds.), *Contemporary criminology* (pp. 168-184). New York: John Wiley.

Horowitz, R., & Pottieger, A. E. (1991). Gender bias in juvenile justice handling of seriously crime-involved youths. *Journal of Research in Crime and Delinquency, 28*(1), 75-100.

Huizinga, D., & Elliott, D. S. (1987). Juvenile offenders: Prevalence, offender incidence, and arrest rates by race. *Crime and Delinquency, 33,* 206-223.

In re Gault, 387 U.S. 1 (1967).

In re Poff, 135 F. Supp. 224 (C.C.C. 1955).

In re Winship, 397 U.S. 358 (1970).

Kobetz, R. W. (1971). *The police role and juvenile delinquency.* Gaithersburg, MD: International Association of Chiefs of Police.

Kenneth, C. (1965). *Dark ghetto: Dilemmas of social power.* New York: Harper & Row.

Kent v. United States, 383 U.S. 541 (1966).

Kephart, W. (1954). Racial factors and urban law enforcement. *British Journal of Delinquency, 5,* 144-145.

Kittrie, N. (1971). *The right to be different: Deviance and enforced therapy.* Baltimore: Johns Hopkins Press.

Klein, M. (1969, July). Gang cohesiveness, delinquency, and a street-work program. *Journal of Research on Crime and Delinquency,* 143.

Kobetz, R. W., & Bosarge, B. B. (1973). *Juvenile justice administration.* Gaithersburg, MD: International Association of Chiefs of Police.

Kobrin, S. (1970). The Chicago area project: A twenty-five year assessment. In N. Johnson (Ed.), *The sociology of crime and delinquency*. New York: John Wiley.

Krisberg, B. (1975). *Crime and privilege*. Englewood Cliffs, NJ: Prentice Hall.

Krisberg, B. (1988). *Reclaiming the vision: The future of the juvenile court*. San Francisco: National Council on Crime and Delinquency.

Krisberg, B. (1992a). *Excellence in adolescent care: The Thomas O'Farrell Youth Center*. San Francisco: National Council on Crime and Delinquency.

Krisberg, B. (1992b). *Juvenile justice: Improving the quality of care*. San Francisco: National Council on Crime and Delinquency.

Krisberg, B., Austin, J., Joe, K., & Steele, P. (1988). *A court that works: The impact of juvenile court sanctions*. San Francisco: National Council on Crime and Delinquency.

Krisberg, B., Austin, J., & Steele, P. (1991). *Unlocking juvenile corrections*. San Francisco: National Council on Crime and Delinquency.

Krisberg, B., & Schwartz, I. (1986). Rethinking juvenile justice. *Crime and Delinquency, 29,* 333-364.

Krisberg, B., Schwartz, I., & Fishman, G. (1987). The incarceration of minority youth. *Crime and Delinquency, 33,* 173-205.

Krisberg, B., Schwartz, I. M., Litksy, P., & Austin, J. (1986). The watershed of juvenile justice reform. *Crime and Delinquency, 32*(1), 5-38.

Lemert, E. M. (1970). *Social action and legal change: Revolution within the juvenile court*. Chicago: Aldine.

Lemert, E., & Rosenberg, J. (1948). *The administration of justice to minority groups in Los Angeles County*. Berkeley: University of California Press.

Lerman, P. (1971). Child convicts. *Trans-Action, 8,* 35-44.

Lerner, S. (1990). *The good news about juvenile justice*. San Francisco and Bolinas, CA: Commonweal Research Institute and National Council on Crime and Delinquency.

Levin, M. M., & Sarri, R. (1974). *Juvenile delinquency*. Ann Arbor, MI: National Assessment of Juvenile Corrections.

Liazos, A. (1974). Class oppression and the juvenile justice system. *Insurgent Sociologist, 1,* 2-22.

Mathieson, T. (1965). *The defences of the weak*. London, Travistock.

Mattick, H., & Caplan, W. S. (1967). Stake animals, loud-talking and leadership in do-nothing and do something situations. In M. Klein (Ed.), *Juvenile gangs in context* (pp. 121-135). Englewood Cliffs, NJ: Prentice Hall.

McCarthy, B. R., & Smith, B. L. (1986). The conceptualization of discrimination in the juvenile justice process: The impact of administrative factors and screening decisions on juvenile court dispositions. *Criminology, 24,* 41-64.

McKelvey, B. (1972). *American prisons*. Montclair, NJ: Patterson Smith.

McKiever v. Pennsylvania, 403 U.S. 528 (1971).

Mead, G. H. (1961). The psychology of punitive justice. In T. Parsons (Ed.), *Theories of society* (pp. 878-894). Glencoe, IL: Free Press.

Mennel, R. (1973). *Thorns and thistles*. Hanover: The University of New Hampshire Press.

Miller, J. (1991). *Last one over the wall*. Columbus: Ohio State University Press.

Moynihan, D. (1969). *Maximum feasible misunderstanding.* New York: Free Press.

Murray, C., & Cox, L. (1979). *Beyond probation*. Beverly Hills, CA: Sage.

National Commission on the Causes and Prevention of Violence. (1969). *To establish justice, to ensure domestic tranquillity*. Washington, DC: Government Printing Office.

National Council of Juvenile Court Judges. (1972). *Handbook for new juvenile court judges.* Reno, NV: Author.

National Council on Crime and Delinquency. (1967). *Correction in the United States: A survey for the President's Commission on Law Enforcement and the Administration of Justice.* New York: Author.

National Institute of Drug Abuse (NIDA). (1989). *National household survey on drug abuse: 1988 population estimates.* Rockville, MD: U.S. Department of Health and Human Services.

New York Department of Juvenile Justice (1989). *Beyond custody and care.* New York: Author.

Niederhoffer, A. (1967). *Behind the shield: The police in urban society.* Garden City, NY: Doubleday.

Norman, S. (1972). *The youth service bureau: A key to delinquency prevention.* Hackensack, NJ: National Council on Crime and Delinquency.

Office of Juvenile Justice and Delinquency Prevention. (1991, May). *Juvenile court statistics, 1988.* Washington, DC: U.S. Department of Justice.

Ohlin, L., Piven, H., & Pappenfort, D. (1956). Major dilemmas of the social worker in probation and parole. *NPPA Journal, 2*(3), 211-225.

Packer, H. L. (1968). Two models of the criminal process. In H. l. Packer, *The limits of the criminal sanction* (pp. 149-173). Stanford, CA: Stanford University Press.

Pappenfont, D. M., & Young, T. M. (1980). Use of secure detention for juveniles and alternatives to its use. *Reports of the National Juvenile Justice Assessment Centers.* Washington, DC: U.S. Department of Justice.

The People v. Turner, 55 Illinois 280 (1870).

Peterson, R. D. (1988). Youthful offender designations and sentencing in the New York criminal courts. *Social Problems, 35*(2), 111-130.

Pickett, R. (1969). *House of refuge: Origins of juvenile justice reform in New York, 1815-1857.* Syracuse, NY: Syracuse University Press.

Piliavin, I., & Briar, S. (1964). Police encounters with juveniles. *American Journal of Sociology, 70*(2), 206-214.

Platt, A. (1968). *The child savers: The invention of delinquency.* Chicago: Chicago University Press.

Platt, A., Schechter, H., & Tiffany, P. (1968). In defense of youth: A case study of the public defender in juvenile court. *Indiana Law Journal, 43,* 619-640.

Pope, C. E., & Feyerherm, W. H. (1990a). Minority status and juvenile justice processing: An assessment of the research literature. *Criminal Justice Abstracts, 22*(2), 327-335.

Pope, C. E., & Feyerherm, W. H. (1990b). Minority status and juvenile justice processing: An assessment of the research literature (Part II). *Criminal Justice Abstracts, 22*(3), 527-535.

Pope, C., & McNeely, R. I. (1981). Race, crime, and criminal justice: An oveview. In R. L. McNeely & C. Pope (Eds.), *Race, crime, and criminal justice* (pp. 9-27). Beverly Hills, CA: Sage.

Pound, R. (1922). *An introduction to the philosophy of law.* New Haven, CT: Yale University Press.

Pound, R. (1928). *Outline of lectures on jurisprudence.* Cambridge, MA: Harvard University press.

Pound, R. (1942). *Social control through law.* New Haven, CT: Yale University Press.

Pound, R. (1943). A survey of social interests. *Harvard Law Review, 57,* 1-39.

Pound, R. (1957). *Guide to juvenile court judges.* New York: National Probation and Parole Association.

Pound, R. (1965). The rise of socialized criminal justice. In S. Glueck (Ed.), *Roscoe Pound and criminal justice.* Dobbs Ferry, NY: Oceana.

President's Commission on Law Enforcement and the Administration of Justice. (1967). *The challenge of crime in a free society.* Washington, DC: Government Publishing Office.

Quinney, R. (1969). *Crime and justice in society.* Boston: Little, Brown.

Reed, W. L. (1984). *Racial differentials in juvenile court decision-making: Final report.* Washington, DC: U.S. Department of Justice, National Institute for Juvenile Justice and Delinquency Prevention.

Rose Institute of State and Local Governments and the American Legislative Exchange Council. (1987). *Juvenile justice reform: A model for states.* Claremont, CA: Author.

Rothman, D. (1971). *The discovery of the asylum.* Boston: Little, Brown.

Rubin, S. (1931). Criminal justice and the poor. *Journal of the American Institute of Criminal Law and Criminology, 22,* 705-715.

Rubin, T. (1979). *Juvenile justice policy: Practice and law.* Santa Monica, CA: Goodyear.

Rusche, G., & Kirchheimer, O. (1939). *Punishment and social structure.* New York: Columbia University Press.

Ryan, W. (1971). *Blaming the victim.* New York: Random House.

Sampson, R. J. (1986). SES and official reaction to delinquency. *American Sociological Review, 51*(6), 876-885.

Sanders, W. B. (1970). *Juvenile offenders for a thousand years.* Chapel Hill: University of North Carolina.

Sarri, R. C. (1974). *Under lock and key.* Ann Arbor: University of Michigan, Institute for Social Research.

Schall v. Martin, 467 U.S. 253 (1984).

Schwartz, I. (Ed.). (1988a). Children in jails. *Crime and Delinquency, 34*(2).

Schwartz, I. (1988b). *(In)justice for juveniles.* Lexington, MA: Lexington Books.

Schwartz, I., Guo, S., & Kerbs, J. (1992). *Public attitudes toward juvenile crime and juvenile justice: Implications for public policy.* Ann Arbor: University of Michigan, Center for the Study of Youth Policy.

Sechrest, D. (1970). *The community approach.* Berkeley: University of California, School of Criminology.

Shaffer, A. (1971). The Cincinnati social unity experiment. *Social Service Review, 45,* 159-171.

Shannon, L. W. (1963). Types and patterns of delinquency referral in a middle-sized city. *British Journal of Criminology, 4*(1), 24-36.

Shaw, C. (1930). *The jack-roller: A delinquent boy's own story.* Chicago: University of Chicago Press.

Shaw, C. (1942). *Juvenile delinquency and urban areas.* Chicago: University of Chicago Press.

Shaw, C., with the assistance of McKay, H.D., & McDonald, J. F. with special chapters by Hanson, H. B., & Burgess, A. W. (1938). *Brothers in crime.* Chicago: University of Chicago Press.

Shaw, R., & McKay, L. (Eds.). (1942). *Juvenile delinquency and urban areas.* Chicago: Chicago University Press.

Sheridan, W. H. (1966). *Standards for juvenile and family courts.* Prepared in cooperation with the National Council on Crime and Delinquency and the National Council of Juvenile Court Judges. Washinton, DC: U.S. Children's Bureau.

Skolnick, J. (1975). *Justice without trail: Law enforcement in democratic society* (2nd ed.). New York: John Wiley.

Smith, D. A., Visher, C. A., & Davidson, L. A. (1984). Equity and discretionary justice: The influence of race on police arrest decisions. *The Journal of Criminal Law and Criminology, 75*(1), 234-249.

Snyder, H. (1985). *Juvenile court statistics, 1985.* Pittsburgh, PA: National Center for Juvenile Justice.

Snyder, H. N. (1988). *Court careers of juvenile offenders.* Pittsburgh, PA: National Center for Juvenile Justice.

Snyder, H., Finnegan, T. A., Nimick, E. H., Sickmund, M. H., Sullivan, D. D., Tierney, N. J. (1987). *Juvenile court statistics, 1984* (from p. 188). Pittsburgh, PA: National Center for Juvenile Justice.

Snyder, H., Finnegan, T. A., Nimick, E. H., Sickmund, M. H., Sullivan, D. D., & Tierney, N. J. (1990). *Juvenile court statistics, 1988.* Washington, DC: U.S. Department of Justice, Office of Juvenile Justice and Delinquency Prevention.

Soler, M. (1988). Litigation on behalf of children in adult jails. *Crime and Delinquency, 34,* 190-208.

Stamp, K. M. (1956). *The peculiar institution.* New York: Random House.

Standard Juvenile Court Act—Text and commentary. (1959). *Journal of National Probation and Parole Association, 5,* 324-391.

State v. Ray, 63 New Hampshire 405 (1886).

Steinhart, D. (1988a). California legislature ends the jailing of children: The story of a policy reversal. *Crime and Delinquency, 34,* 150-168.

Steinhart, D. (1988b). *California public opinion poll: Public attitudes towards youth crime.* San Francisco: National Council on Crime and Delinquency.

Sumner, H. (1968). *Locking them up: A study of initial juvenile detention decisions in selected California counties.* San Francisco: National Council on Crime and Delinquency.

Sussman, F. (1959). *Law of juvenile delinquency.* New York: Oceans.

Swanger, H. (1988). Hendrickson v. Griggs: A review of legal and policy implications for juvenile justice policy makers. *Crime and Delinquency, 34,* 209-227.

Teilmann, K. S., & Landry, P. H. (1981). Gender bias in juvenile justice. *Journal of Research in Crime and Delinquency, 18*(1), 47-80.

Terry, R. (1967). Discrimination in the handling of juvenile offenders by social control agencies. *Journal of Research in Crime and Delinquency, 4,* 218-230.

Thomas, C. W., & Sieverdes, C. M. (1975). *Juvenile court intake: An analysis of discretionary decision-making. Criminology, 12,* 413-432.

Thornberry, T. P. (1979). Sentencing disparities in the juvenile justice system. *Journal of Criminal Law and Criminology, 70,* 164-171.

Tollett, T. (1987). *A comparative study of Florida delinquency commitment programs.* Tallahassee, FL: Department of Health and Rehabilitative Services.

Unwin, E. A. (1974). *California correctional system intake study.* Sacramento: California Office of Criminal Justice Planning.

U.S. Department of Health, Education, and Welfare. (1973). *National study of youth service bureaus—Final report.* Washington, DC: California Youth Authority.

U.S. Department of Justice. (1989). *1989 census of public and private juvenile detention, correctional and shelter facilities.* Washington, DC: Office of Justice Programs, Office of Juvenile Justice and Delinquency Prevention.

U.S. Department of Justice. (1990). *Juvenile court statistics.* Washington, DC: Office of Justice Programs, Office of Juvenile Justice and Delinquency Prevention.

U.S. Department of Justice. (1991). *The 1990 annual jail census.* Washington, DC: Bureau of Justice Statistics.

U.S. Department of Justice, Federal Bureau of Investigation. (August 11, 1991). *Crime in the United States, 1990.* (Uniform Crime Reports). Washington, DC: Author.

U.S. Department of Justice. National Criminal Justice Information and Statistics Service. (1974). *Children in custody: A report on the juvenile detention and correctional facility census of 1971.* Washington, DC: Government Printing Office.

U.S. House of Representatives, Committee on Education and Labor. (1980). *Juvenile justice amendments of 1980.* Washington, DC: Government Printing Office.

Van Vleet, R., Rutherford, A., & Schwartz, I. (1987). Reinvesting youth corrections resources in Utah. In I. Schwartz (Ed.), *Reinvesting youth corrections resources: A tale of three states* (pp. 19-32). Minneapolis: University of Minnesota, Hubert H. Humphrey Institute of Public Affairs.

Velde, R. (1981). Blacks and criminal justice today. In C. Owens & J. Bell (Eds.), *Blacks and criminal justice* (pp. 17-23). Lexington, MA: Lexington Books.

Weinstein, J. (1968). *The corporate ideal in the liberal state.* Boston: Beacon Press.

Weissman, H. (1969). *Community development in the mobilization for youth.* New York: Association Press.

Wichita Police Department. (n.d.) *Duty manual* (Sec. 61). Wichita Police Department.

Wilhelm, S. (1970). *Who needs the negro?* Cambridge, MA: Schenkman.

Williams, J. R., & Gold, M. (1972). From delinquent behavior to official delinquency. *Social Problems, 20,* 209-221.

Williams, W. A. (1973). *The contours of American history.* New York: New Viewpoints.

Wilson, W. (1987). *The truly disadvantaged.* Chicago: University of Chicago Press.

Witmer, H., & Tufts, E. (1954). *The effectiveness of delinquency prevention programs.* Washington, DC: Government Printing Office.

Wolfgang, M. (1982). Abolish the juvenile court. *California Lawyer, 2*(10), 12-13.

Wolfgang, M., Figlio, R., & Sellin, T. (1972). *Delinquency in a birth cohort.* Chicago: University of Chicago Press.

Yetman, N. R. (1970). *Voices from slavery.* New York: Holt, Rinehart and Winston.

Younghusband, E. (1959). Dilemma of the juvenile court. *Social Service Review, 33,* 10-20.

Zimring, F. (1977). Privilege, maturity and responsibility: Notes on the evolving jurisprudence of adolescence. In L. Empey (Ed.), *The future of childhood* (pp. 312-335). Charlottesville: University of Virginia Press.

Author Index

Subject Index

About the Authors

James F. Austin, Ph.D., is Executive Vice President for the National Council on Crime and Delinquency (NCCD). He received his master's degree in sociology from DePaul University in Chicago and his doctorate, also in sociology, from the University of California, Davis. He serves as a director for several programs, most notably the National Prison Capacity Program, Technical Assistance; Coordinator for the Bureau of Justice Assistance; Experimental Tests of Electronic Monitoring Program, Oklahoma Department of Corrections for the National Institute of Justice; and the Assessment of Minority Over-Representation in California for the  Office of Criminal Justice Planning. He has authored numerous publications including *The Impact of the War on Drugs: The NCCD Prison Population Forecast* (with Aaron McVey) and *America's Growing*

Correctional-Industrial Complex. In 1991 he was awarded the Peter P. Lejins Research Award by the American Correctional Association.

Barry Krisberg, Ph.D., is President of the National Council on Crime and Delinquency (NCCD). He received his master's degree in criminology and a doctorate in sociology, both from the University of Pennsylvania. He was appointed by the legislature to serve on the California Blue Ribbon Commission on Inmate Population Management. His memberships include the American Correctional Association, the National Association of Juvenile Correctional Administrators, and the Association of Criminal Justice Researchers. He is the former president and fellow of the Western Society of Criminology and is a former member of the California Attorney General's Policy Advisory Committee. He has several books and articles to his credit, including: *Crime and Priviledge, The Children of Ishmael, Excellence in Adolescent Care: The Thomas O'Farrell Youth Center*, and *Juvenile Justice: Improving the Quality of Care*.